Windows into Science Classrooms: Problems Associated with Higher-Level Cognitive Learning

Windows into Science Classrooms: Problems Associated with Higher-Level Cognitive Learning

Edited by

Kenneth Tobin
Jane Butler Kahle
Barry J. Fraser

 The Falmer Press
(A member of the Taylor & Francis Group)
London · New York · Philadelphia

UK The Falmer Press, Rankine Road, Basingstoke, Hampshire, RG24 0PR

USA The Falmer Press, Taylor & Francis Inc., 1900 Frost Road, Suite 101, Bristol, PA 19007

First published 1990

British Library Cataloguing in Publication Data
Windows into science classrooms.
    1. Secondary schools. Curriculum subjects: Science. Teaching.
    I. Tobin, Kenneth. II. Kahle, Jane Butler. III. Fraser, Barry, J.
    ISBN 1-85000-542-7
    ISBN 1-85000-543-5 (pbk.)

Library of Congress Cataloging-in-Publication Data
Windows into science classrooms: problems associated with
    higher-level cognitive learning / edited by Kenneth Tobin, Jane Butler Kahle, Barry J. Fraser.
        ISBN 1-85000-542-7 ISBN 1-85000-543-5 (pbk.)
        1. Science—Study and teaching. 2. Cognitive learning.
    I. Tobin, Kenneth George, 1944– . II. Kahle, Jane Butler.
    III. Fraser, Barry J.
    Q181.W75 1990
    507'.1—dc20   90-32248
                                                                 CIP

Jacket design by Caroline Archer

Typeset in 10½/12 pt Bembo by
Graficraft Typesetters Ltd, Hong Kong

Printed in Great Britain by Burgess Science Press, Basingstoke on paper which has a specified pH value on final paper manufacture of not less than 7.5 and is therefore 'acid free'.

Contents

Contents

Editors' Preface

The ideas and perspectives discussed and analysed in this book reflect the accumulated experiences of five researchers from two continents. The opportunity for two American researchers to spend a sabbatical leave at a university in Coastal Australia* provided the impetus for the reported work. Initially, our work was defined as a short, specific study of classroom interaction patterns. As our team grew to the five authors in this book (together with a sixth person who was involved in some classroom observation), other interests and perspectives came into play and these necessitated a longer and broader project. After our work was completed, we realized that we had gone far beyond the usual research papers; indeed, we had a book-length manuscript. At that point, we had the good fortune to meet with Malcolm Clarkson of Falmer Press, who was both encouraging and patient with us. Although we all were together in the classrooms of Dalton, we were separated when we returned to our home institutions to reflect and to write.

The book you are about to read is the result of a year or two of writing, critiquing and synthesizing information. These activities occurred in four locations on two continents. Therefore, if anyone or anything should be thanked or acknowledged by us, it is the marvel of electronic communication!

A qualitative study records, interprets and analyzes actual occurrences. In addition, the researchers try to place their syntheses in a theoretical framework. Our work includes both aspects: individually, we recorded and interpreted observations; and, collectively, we validated assertions and interpretations in order to build a theoretical base. Separate chapters, therefore, look through windows into science classrooms using different colours of glass. That is, different aspects of the total classroom are reported and interpreted in most chapters. Only Chapters 1, 2 and 8 involve a wholistic view of the classroom or the teaching and learning experience.

---

* To preserve the anonymity of the teachers and school involved, fictitious names are used for the teachers, the school, the city and the State.

Last, we must thank the two most important and most harassed members of our team — Sandra and Peter, the two teachers who invited us into their classrooms. Without their patience, understanding and cooperation, we would not have had the very special and rare opportunity to learn about barriers to higher-level cognitive learning in science.

One of the authors, Kenneth Tobin, taught high school science in Perth, Western Australia for ten years before commencing a sixteen-year career in teacher education. Tobin completed undergraduate and graduate degrees in physics at the Western Australian Institute of Technology (now renamed Curtin University of Technology) and a doctorate in science education at the University of Georgia. For his first ten years as a science educator, he pursued studies of teaching and learning science from a process-product perspective. In the past five years, he has undertaken programmatic research in science and mathematics classrooms using interpretive methods. His work has been recognized with fourteen awards from several professional associations, including the Raymond B. Cattell award from the American Educational Research Association. Tobin has published more than 100 papers, monographs and books in refereed sources. Tobin's current research interests are focused on studies of teacher enhancement and include investigations of the knowledge, beliefs and metaphors which teachers use to make sense of teaching and learning. Presently he is Head of Curriculum and Instruction at Florida State University, a Board member of the National Association for Research in Science Teaching and North American Editor of the *International Journal of Science Education*.

Jane Butler Kahle, an international scholar in the area of gender issues, began her career teaching high school biology in rural Indiana. Purdue University's inservice summer institutes allowed her to complete a Master's degree and a PhD in biology education. She is the author or editor of five books, as well as twelve chapters and numerous papers. In the past, Dr Kahle's work with preservice and inservice teachers has been recognized by the National Science Teachers Association (STAR award recipient), and she has served as president of the National Association of Biology Teachers. Currently, she is chair of the Board of Directors of the Biological Sciences Curriculum Study and Section Q of the American Association for the Advancement of Science, and is president of the National Association for Research in Science Teaching (NARST). She is a member of the National Research Council's Committee on High School Biology and of the Association of American Colleges' Advisory Committee on the Undergraduate Curriculum. Kahle's research is focused on factors affecting the entrance, retention and achievement of girls and women in science courses and careers. She has won several national and international awards for her research. Her role within the research team was to analyze the teaching and learning patterns for possible gender differences.

Barry J. Fraser taught high school science in Melbourne and completed his PhD in education at Monash University, also in Melbourne. His first two university positions in education were at Monash University and Macquarie University in Sydney. Currently he is at Curtin University of Technology in Perth, where he is Director of a centre offering postgraduate education opportunities for science and mathematics teachers. As well, he is Director of a federally funded centre which aims to improve the teaching and learning of science and mathematics, especially for girls. He is author of hundreds of books, book chapters, journal articles and conference papers and has won various awards for his research. One of his major research interests is classroom environment, and this provided a focus during his involvement in the research reported in this book.

Floyd H. Nordland taught high school biology in both rural and suburban Minnesota. A coach and an award-winning teacher, Dr Nordland also worked as one of the State coordinators for the Biological Sciences Curriculum Study (BSCS). In 1962, he took advantage of the National Science Foundation's inservice summer institutes to complete his Master's degree at Purdue University, where he also finished a PhD degree in plant physiology. Since 1969, he has taught methods of teaching biology to prospective secondary teachers, and has developed and taught an experimentally designed biology course for elementary teachers. Both courses, taught at Purdue, emphasize the integration of content and pedagogy. He has won an Ohaus award from the National Science Teachers Association as well as the Alumni Teaching Award at Purdue University for his teaching excellence. Dr Nordland has served as a consultant in science training projects in the Philippines and Nigeria. His research interests are based on Piagetian theory, and his role in the team was one of content expert.

Leonie J. Rennie taught high school science in Perth and played an advisory role to science teachers in rural Western Australia. She has been a cowriter in several science curriculum projects. Prior to taking up her present position in science education at Curtin University of Technology, Dr Rennie taught and supervised programs for preservice teachers at the University of Western Australia. Her prize-winning doctoral thesis at this University focused on the structure of attitudes in science education, and much of her research continues to be in this area. In the research reported in this volume, she was particularly concerned with the affective aspects of the students' and teachers' behaviours in their classrooms.

Kenneth Tobin
Florida State University, Tallahassee, Florida, USA
Jane Butler Kahle
Miami University, Oxford, Ohio, USA
Barry J. Fraser
Curtin University, Perth, Australia

Participating Teacher's Foreword

'You won't mind a couple of people observing a class or two?' was the casual request from a colleague. As a senior teacher in our science department, it had become commonplace for practising teachers or young graduate teachers to visit our school, spend time in a variety of our classes, and examine the programs and materials developed by our hard-working staff. We tended to enjoy discussing our curricula and methodology with these visitors, and we often picked up some new ideas in the process.

Imagine my 'horror' and then apprehension, when the 'couple' expected was actually five or six, the people were not younger, developing teachers, but older 'wise people' — peers from tertiary institutions — and the 'class or two' was to be one class, every day, for almost three months!

In retrospect, the 'horror' was more like total amazement, but the apprehension was real! How would I react to continuous observation of the same class of students, without an opportunity to 'word them up' with respect to behaviour, responsibilities, etc. More to the point, how would the students in the class react? On the other hand, a group of 'totally' objective people, not involved with the day-to-day routine of a secondary school might come up with some interesting observations and interpretations of the class which could be quite different from mine. I was aware of how involved one tended to become with school, teaching and carrying out the administrative responsibilities of a senior teacher. Very easily, there could be activities, interactions or curriculum possibilities that I was missing out on, usually because of a lack of time.

I felt misgivings. All teachers like to receive praise, but how would I react to the probable questioning of my classroom behaviours, my understanding of the class and my interpretation of the objectives, teaching and assessment? Certainly, this experience would be a challenge, perhaps even to my perceptions of myself as a teacher. Yet, at the same time, I was intensely curious. What do I do that is 'right' and, of course, what do I do that is 'wrong'? (Perhaps I was a little less curious about the latter, although it might be through that discussion that I learn to improve or modify my own teaching behaviours.) Eventually, curiosity won out. I was keen to become involved, although unsure of the probable outcome.

The manner of the five or six observers became most important once the process had begun. All were determined to approach Peter and me positively, ensuring that we were informed fully of where we all were going. We quickly learned that we were not going to be told of 'rights' or 'wrongs'. We participated in a discussion with at least three observers each week, which was often tape recorded so that all observers could discuss our replies at their own weekly meeting. In addition, Peter and I received copious 'field notes' from each class contact; these were photocopied from each of the observer's notes. Sometimes I wondered if it would have been easier not to have seen these! To find out that a group of girls had spent ten minutes discussing the school social of the previous night, or the mathematics quiz during the last lesson, caused an awful sinking feeling in the pit of my stomach. How did I miss those interactions? On occasions, of course, some observations were reassuring: 'X and Y argued over how the half life of a radioisotope affects degeneration of tissues' or 'Sally re-explained the concept of half like to Natalie'. But, somehow, those observations made less impact on me than those concerning 'off-task' behaviours. Fortunately, when we discussed the previous week's observations of classes, our inquirers were gentle on us, essentially searching for the reasons why we behaved as we did, rather than making judgements as to how effective the observed behaviours might have been (which, of course, we already had assessed for ourselves).

As time went by, Peter and I became more accustomed to the research procedure, and our students become quite blasé about the continuous presence of the researchers. The students enjoyed my discomfort when wearing a microphone, as well as the importance attached to the additional attention that they were receiving. In some cases, students took the opportunity to question our observers while, in a few instances, individual students became very attached to members of the observation team and began to elicit specific advice and information relevant to their futures.

Meanwhile, I found the experience rewarding as well as frustrating. I thoroughly enjoyed the challenge of our discussions centred on educational philosophy, curriculum directions and ideals. For many years, I had resisted suggestions by colleagues to undertake further study, perhaps in science education, believing that reducing the many hours of preparation and marking at home meant that I would become less effective in my teaching. My interviews with the observers, however, were stimulating and challenging and I found myself wanting to read more about current educational theories and research.

At the same time, however, I was consistently defensive in relation to my classroom management. In organizing the students into group-based activities, I was using a teaching model which I very much wanted to 'work', but with which I'd had little previous experience. In earlier years, I had tried out this teaching technique, in short two-three week bursts, and had found that the classes responded very positively. In most of our schools, however, science benches are bolted to the floor so that any group experiences, out of necessity, are of short duration. This time, at last, I had a room with movable benches! After five months with my class, I realized that I also was fortunate to be teaching a group of students who were generally interested in science and communicative. This was an ideal situation for group work! The gradual move to group participation occurred just prior to the arrival of the research team.

Having spoken to most of my students in casual out-of-class situations, I was aware of some of their out-of-class problems and felt quite possessive of them. Perhaps this awareness became my greatest dilemma because, when I recognized that a few were 'off-task' in their classroom behaviour, I found it almost impossible to sanction them in a public manner in front of 'strangers'. All too often, it was a quiet word in their ears while other students were undertaking group work. For a few individuals, this was ineffective as a long-term answer. In looking back, I was fortunate that this problem applied to only a few students in the group and that, to an extent, the classroom peer group applied their own pressure in my support.

I found that, towards the end of our ten weeks together, I was regretting the end of the study. While the consistent tension of accommodating the non-teaching observational team in the classroom would be removed, I certainly would miss the friendship, honesty and stimulation that the researchers had provided through our weekly interviews. Also, I had re-evaluated some of my teaching practices and had become more sensitive to the achievement of girls in science classrooms. These aspects always had been pet concerns of mine, but now I had read and discussed research work providing a foundation for my 'feelings'.

The next step was clear. I now am enrolled in further part-time, postgraduate study. I am thoroughly enjoying the process of keeping abreast of recent studies in the field of science education — both in classroom behaviour and in curriculum development and administration. While I can maintain and extend the friendships made in those weeks, I feel that I am now more aware and well informed as a teacher with philosophies better founded on evidence gleaned from a wide variety of experiences. For this new-found understanding, interest and realization, the research team has earned my profound gratitude.

Sandra
Southside High, Dalton, Coastal Australia

Chapter 1: Learning Science with Understanding: In Search of the Holy Grail?

Kenneth Tobin, Jane Butler Kahle and Barry J. Fraser

Research Perspectives: Windows with Different Coloured Glass

When members of our research group got together in Coastal Australia, each of us had specific reasons for dedicating ten weeks to observing and thinking about secondary science teaching. Each of us had experience in teaching secondary science, albeit a decade ago for most of us, and each of us had active research agendas. As we talked, however, we all voiced concerns about science teaching and learning today. We recounted incidents of lessons taught and learned by rote memorization. We discussed a study which indicated that science teaching was failing to help minority youngsters develop cognitively. We analyzed the message behind the reports that teachers frequently direct higher-order questions only to a few selected students in the classroom. We argued about whether boys and girls receive equal challenges in most science classrooms. Eventually, we realized that, although individually we would investigate different aspects of teaching and learning in our study, collectively we would try to identify barriers to higher-level learning in secondary school science.

Our task, once clarified and identified, clearly was one of international focus and concern. Recent reports and research findings have identified serious shortcomings in elementary and secondary education and have proposed major reforms in education (IEA, 1988; Office of Technology Assessment, 1988a, 1988b; Raizen and Jones, 1985; Weiss, 1987). In an age of technological application and advancement, where business and industry have difficulty recruiting employees with the necessary knowledge of science, the evidence suggests that there is something of a crisis in science education. For example, Weiss (1987), Tobin and Gallagher (1987b), Gallagher (1989) and Humrich (1988) report that most science curricula emphasize learning of basic facts and definitions from science textbooks and relatively little emphasis is placed on applications of knowledge in daily life or on the development of higher-order thinking skills. Even though many programs purport to be inquiry-based, most show little evidence of inquiry on the part of students and teachers (National Research Council, 1989). According to the National Science Board, 'the age of technology is failing to provide its own children with the intellectual tools for the 21st century' (National Science Board, 1983, p. v).

Tobin and Gallagher (1987b) and the National Research Council (1989) report that the activity types which are most prevalent in high school science classes involve the teacher working with the class as a whole group. Seatwork activities also are common. Such activities allow students to work from the textbook and to undertake tasks from worksheets, the chalkboard and the textbook. Small-group activities frequently do not occur and usually are confined to the data collecting components of laboratory activities. Despite bold rhetoric in school brochures and textbook forewords, science programs typically are not inquiry oriented, do not have a laboratory emphasis and do not excite the majority of students. Students learn science from textbooks and lectures and the curriculum is focused by tests which emphasize rote learning of facts and procedures.

Teachers use textbooks as a source of student activities (see, for example, Tobin and Gallagher, 1987b). In some instances, the activities emphasize higher-level cognitive learning, but in most cases the activities stress learning facts and algorithms. Teachers often ask students to make summaries from the textbook and to answer end-of-chapter questions. However, the cognitive demand of such activities is low and they usually involve students in a brief search through the text for relevant information and transcription of the information into their notebooks.

A considerable amount of research in education has focused on gender differences and school learning. There is concern in science education that, compared to boys, girls have lower levels of interest and achievement and enrol less often in science (Erickson and Erickson, 1984; Kahle, 1985; Kelly, 1978; Welch, 1985). The differences are most pronounced in physical sciences but also are evident in biological sciences. Because learning in classrooms involves internal cognitive processing for learners, it is possible that gender differences in science achievement could originate partly from differential opportunities to engage in academic tasks. For example, Kahle's (1985) study of high school biology teachers, which successfully encouraged girls to enrol in elective chemistry and physics courses, identifies specific teaching behaviours and instructional practices which ameliorate gender differences in attitudes, achievement levels and enrolment patterns. Those teachers, compared to a national American sample, use more laboratory activities, discussions and quizzes. In addition, approximately two-thirds of their students (both girls and boys) note that the teachers encourage creativity, stress basic skills (mathematics, graphing, laboratory techniques) and discuss future courses and careers. Her study suggests specific strategies which might improve the learning environment for all students.

On the other hand, Kelly (1985) describes the social-cultural effect of schools on girls' interest in science. Kelly discusses school science as a masculine endeavour in which males ask and answer more questions and work with laboratory equipment to a greater extent than females do. Many studies have documented that teachers interact differently with girls and boys in science classes (Kahle, 1988; Whyte, 1986). For example, when teachers interact with students in question-answer sessions, they do so with an expectation that certain students will provide appropriate answers (Tobin and Gallagher, 1987a). Sadker and Sadker (1985) report substantial differences in the engagement patterns of males and females in science classes. Compared to females, males receive more praise, more criticism, more remediation and more acceptance responses from teachers. In addition, boys are almost eight times as likely as girls to call out in class. When girls do call out, they are more likely than boys who call out to be told to raise their hands before responding.

Tobin (1988) reported gender differences in whole-class interactive activities. Teachers tend to involve males and females to an equal extent in lower-level cognitive interactions, but to involve males to a greater extent than females in higher-level cognitive interactions. Males also participate in a more overt manner than females by volunteering to respond to teacher questions by raising their hands when teachers ask questions in a whole-class setting. The major consequence of this engagement pattern is that 'target' males are involved in responding to questions intended to stimulate thinking or to elicit responses that provide a bridge to a new area of content. Although some females also are involved in this manner, most females are not. Because teachers use whole-class interactive settings to introduce new content and to pose key questions, students who are not target students can engage predominantly only in a covert manner on important parts of the curriculum. This pattern of male students being more involved than females in whole-class interactions is apparent in classes taught by male and female teachers.

There is little evidence that the majority of science teachers are concerned with the extent to which students understand what they are to learn or with implementing the curriculum to emphasize student understanding of science. Rather, the findings of research suggest that most teachers feel constrained to prepare students for tests and examinations and cover science content from textbooks. This practice deprives many students of opportunities to learn with understanding. Furthermore, gender differences in the way in which students engage in learning tasks are widespread.

Fortunately, not all teachers implement the curriculum in this manner. Tobin and Fraser (1987) report that science teachers, identified by their colleagues as exemplary, focus on students' learning with understanding, use strategies to encourage students to engage in higher-level cognitive tasks and maintain a classroom environment conducive to learning. Tobin and Fraser's studies of exemplary practice illustrate that intensive investigations of teaching and learning environments can produce knowledge to guide practice, policy formulation and research. However, it is not sufficient to know that higher-level learning is possible in classes taught by exemplary teachers. In order to influence the quality of science learning in all classes, it is desirable to develop a theory of teaching and learning science that addresses questions concerning what teachers and students do, why they do what they do, whether they would like to change what they do and, if so, how best they would facilitate changes in science classrooms. The development of such a theory is a goal of the research described in this book.

One distinctive methodological feature of our research was the way that quantitative information obtained by structured observation and by administering classroom environment questionnaires was combined with qualitative information from the use of interpretive methods. This combination of qualitative and quantitative methods is consistent with recommendations made for educational research in general (Firestone, 1987; Fry, Chantavanich and Chantavanich, 1981; Howe, 1988), although the use of qualitative and quantitative methods together in learning environment studies is still the exception rather than the rule (Fraser and Tobin, 1989). The present research builds upon the success of combining these methods in other recent science education research involving target students (Tobin and Gallagher, 1987a) and exemplary teaching (Tobin and Fraser, 1987). Not only did the use of classroom environment questionnaires provide an important source of students' views of their classrooms, but a triangulation of qualitative and quantitative data enabled greater confidence to be placed in the findings and richer insights to be gained into classroom life.

Past research on classroom environment has produced a rich yield in just twenty years (Fraser, 1986, 1989). Consistent and strong associations have been established between the nature of the classroom environment and student cognitive and attitudinal outcomes (Fraser and Fisher, 1982; Haertel, Walberg and Haertel, 1981), and those findings have practical implications about how to improve student learning by creating classroom environments which emphasize dimensions found to be empirically linked with learning. Classroom environment instruments have proved to be a useful source of process criteria in the evaluation of educational innovations and curricula (Fraser, 1981a). Student achievement and satisfaction have been found to be greater in classrooms in which there is a close match between the actual classroom environment and the one preferred by students (Fraser and Fisher, 1983a, 1983b). Comparisons of students' and teachers' perceptions of actual and preferred environments suggest that teachers commonly hold more favourable views than do students of the same classrooms, and that the actual environment of most classes falls short of the one preferred by students and teachers (Fraser, 1982; Fisher and Fraser, 1983). In addition to these and other research applications, it is important to note that teachers have successfully used student perceptions of actual and preferred classroom environments as a practical basis for improving their classrooms (Fraser, 1981b; Fraser and Fisher, 1986).

Participating Schools and Teachers

The selection of participants in interpretive research is an important decision that needs to take account of what is known at the time and what should be done next. Participating schools and teachers can be wisely selected so that the potential exists for identifying promising problems and seeking solutions from which grounded theory can emerge or be enhanced. In this study of higher-level cognitive learning, we were anxious to avoid schools of the type involved in earlier studies (for example, Tobin and Gallagher, 1987b). What we needed was a school with a tradition of focusing on student learning, a school that had tried different organizational arrangements to enhance learning, and a school in which teachers worked together to build and maintain an environment conducive to learning with understanding. Southside High was such a school. Set in a fashionable suburb of Dalton in Coastal Australia, the school had a reputation for using innovative practices to provide a curriculum that catered for the needs of individuals. A study of teaching and learning at Southside High provided a rare opportunity to investigate what happens in a science program in which students do laboratory activities and learn in an independent manner at their own pace. In contrast to other government high schools in Coastal Australia, where teachers are appointed according to the needs of the statewide school system, teachers at Southside High in its early days had been appointed on the basis of the compatibility of their philosophies of education with the policies and goals of the school. Furthermore, the school's open area design facilitated team teaching and self-paced learning.

In the first five years of the school's existence, recognition of the diverse nature of student abilities and interests led to the implementation of a curriculum which enabled students to learn in a self-paced manner and to study science topics in which they were interested. Workbooks were prepared and used to provide students with independence, and teachers focused on enhancing students' self esteem and motivation levels so that they might learn content in a meaningful and integrated manner. Students were given considerable autonomy in selecting when and for how long to study particular topics. Some of the practices at Southside High were somewhat unique in Coastal Australia. For example, students were on first name terms with teachers, homework was not mandatory, public address messages did not interrupt teaching and learning, and bells did not signal the end of class periods.

Ten years after its foundation year the legend of Southside High lived on. Even though the practice of hand-selecting teachers was discontinued after five years, many practices associated with open education continued. Tales about Southside High provided a stark contrast to gloomy portraits of science teaching sketched by Stake and Easley (1978) in the USA and replicated by Tobin and Gallagher (1987b) in Australia.

A research team of six people was assembled to undertake data collection for this investigation of higher-level cognitive learning of science at Southside High. However, only five of the six people in the team contributed chapters to this book. From the outset, we knew that the study would consist of intensive observations of teaching and learning, interviews with teachers and students, and extensive interpretation of data by the research team. Multiple perspectives were required for the formulation of problems and for the collection, analysis and interpretation of data. We began with an assumption that an interpretive study was most appropriate because of the enduring nature of the problems associated with teaching and learning science. A phenomenological approach, based on extensive experience in science classrooms, a variety of data sources and varied perspectives on what was happening and why it was happening, was likely to reveal new problems or at least frame familiar problems in different ways that would enable fresh interpretations to be obtained. Because of the power of using qualitative and quantitative data in the same study for the purpose of providing convincing evidence for assertions, an early decision was made to incorporate a range of qualitative and quantitative data sources into the design of the study.

For each member of the research team, the study represented part of his or her ongoing research into some aspect of teaching and learning science. Yet, for each of us, prior experiences were unique. When viewed as a collection of scholars, the research team had diverse experiences in terms of the questions investigated in earlier studies and the methods utilized. Despite these differences in background, there were philosophical consistencies in terms of beliefs about what constitutes science, how students learn science and what teachers' roles would be in an ideal science classroom.

Theoretical Framework: Constructivism

The research team shared a constructivist epistemology and interpreted data from that perspective. Within the constructivist view, learning is defined as the acquisition of knowledge by individuals through a process of construction that occurs as sensory data are given meaning in terms of prior knowledge. Learning is always an interpretive process and always involves individuals' constructions (Novak, 1988; von Glasersfeld, 1988). Constructivism is not an option to be invoked by teachers and students on specific occasions or during selected activities. Whether the teacher and students believe that they learn by constructivist processes influences what happens in classrooms and how activities are planned and implemented, but does not influence the mechanisms involved in learning. Von Glasersfeld (1988) predicts a dramatic change of teachers' roles in classrooms when a constructivist epistemology is adopted:

> The teacher's role will no longer be to dispense 'truth' but rather to help and guide the student in the conceptual organization of certain areas of experience.

From a constructivist perspective, the major curriculum challenge for teachers is to focus on student learning with understanding rather than to stress content coverage only. Such an approach is at odds with common practice. The traditional role of teacher as curriculum designer has been to adapt materials from textbooks or teachers' guides for specific classes of students. In most instances, this role involves partitioning the content and activities into manageable 'chunks' so that students could cover all or most of the work in the time available.

Tobin and Gallagher (1987b) and Gallagher (1989) suggest that beliefs about the nature of science and student learning are at the heart of traditional approaches to science curriculum design and implementation. For example, science teachers who perceive science as a representation of the truth about the physical and natural universe are likely to have that type of emphasis in their science curriculum. Similarly, if knowledge is regarded as a fluid entity to be siphoned from the teacher to students, activities might be framed to facilitate transfer and distribution of science knowledge. Salient beliefs about the nature of science include whether science is perceived as: 'truth seeking or the construction of explanatory models that encompass increasingly wider ranges of phenomena' (Novak, 1988, p. 77); a process of generating knowledge or a set of knowledge products which explain the natural and physical universe; and tentative and changing or true and unchanging. These three pairs of perceptions can be thought of as forming continua on which teachers' beliefs can be mapped, with the planned science curriculum being dependent in part on teachers' beliefs pertaining to each of the continua. What type of science is appropriate for students in high, middle and elementary schools? How do teachers make conscious acts to represent science knowledge as constructions which change with time? To learn science from a constructivist philosophy implies direct experience with science as a process of knowledge generation in which prior knowledge is elaborated and changed on the basis of fresh meanings negotiated with peers and the teacher.

If the main goal of a science course is to educate students so that their knowledge resembles that of scientifically literate adults, teachers have a responsibility to provide an environment which focuses experiences and discussions. If students are to learn content from a specific domain, teachers will structure the learning environment to ensure that each student has appropriate direct experiences with specific phenomena and is engaged in discussions that facilitate learning.

A learning model based on constructivism has been developed and tried with success in mathematics by Wheatley and his associates (for example, Yackel, Cobb, Wood, Wheatley & Merkel, 1988). The model incorporates cooperative learning and social collaboration. Initially students are arranged in small groups of two or three to solve problems. Their role is to cooperate and negotiate a satisfactory solution to the problem. Each child has the responsibility to understand what others in the group are doing and the answers which they obtain. If a student has an alternative answer, he or she is expected to disagree, to seek clarifications and justifications from others, and to provide explanations of his/her own procedures and solutions. The teacher's role is to monitor student engagement and manage the learning environment without providing hints and cues that will lead students to learn procedures and solutions by rote. Following small-group work, students share what they have done and learned with the rest of the class. Once again, the focus is on communicating findings and explaining why the findings are plausible. Students are given the task of understanding why certain solutions are identified as appropriate by their class mates. The model assumes that speakers have reasons for what they say and that listeners should seek to understand the rationale underlying what is proposed. The communication process should result in agreement about what has been learned and what are accepted as plausible solutions to problems. This negotiated consensus represents a viable knowledge domain which is understood and accepted by the participants. The process involves all participants in a cognitively active manner and highlights the necessity for teacher and students to have clearly defined roles in class activities. The curriculum must be such that students can engage in meaningful problem solving activities that enable them to learn with understanding rather than by rote, students must understand what they are to do in small-group and whole-class activities, and the teacher must adopt a facilitative role in maintaining an environment conducive to learning.

Research in science classrooms has not described activities or student engagement of the type that occurs in the elementary mathematics classes involved in Wheatley's studies. What are the obstacles that teachers face that deter them from organizing science activities in such a way that students learn with understanding? If students are to benefit from a science program, it is essential that learning tasks are potentially interesting and challenging. For many years, science educators have been concerned about whether the science curriculum is inappropriate because the concepts are too abstract and formal for learners, most of whom are at the concrete stage of cognitive development. However, that was not the scenario in the high school science classes described by Gallagher (1989), Tobin and Gallagher (1987b) and Stake and Easley (1978). Learning tasks were at a low cognitive level and appeared to promote rote, rather than meaningful, learning. Are the activities in which students engage in high school science classes lacking in challenge and interest? Does that lack contribute to the problems faced in science education?

Doyle (1983) argues that the reward structure operating within classes is an important force that needs attention before the effects of other instructional variables can be fully understood. Teachers constantly motivate students by referring to tests and examinations. This teaching style focuses student attention on the content to be tested. If the teacher emphasizes specific knowledge or tasks as having relevance for the test, students tend to concentrate to a greater extent. Classroom processes reflect test questions which emphasize recall of facts and application of algorithms to solve 'formula-type' questions. In the study described in this book, we wanted to examine the types of assessment used in classes in which higher-level cognitive learning was valued. In such circumstances, we wondered whether learning activities would reflect teachers' goals for students to learn with understanding at their own pace. Also, would assessment tasks encompass what students know and to what extent they understand science phenomena?

In addition, we wanted to assess the opportunities which children had to engage in higher-level cognitive activities. We were interested in how teacher-student interaction patterns affected cognitive outcomes. We hoped to elucidate why boys dominate interactions in science classes. Why are target students more likely to be male than female? Why do boys get involved in laboratory activities to a greater extent than girls? Why do more boys than girls enrol in the physical sciences? These are just a few of the persistent questions that we hoped to address in this intensive investigation of interactions in science classes. We knew that the answers would not be obvious because the problems had been present for some time. Perhaps we would find that the teachers involved in the study used teaching behaviours and instructional strategies which minimized gender differences. In addition, by selecting teachers regarded as better than average, we might find patterns of behaviour and beliefs that allow teachers to transform, rather than to reproduce, the masculine image of science.

Why do teachers do what they do? In the first place, teaching involves change on an incremental and daily basis. If something does not work out well, the teacher often can put things right by making slight adjustments to the manner in which the curriculum is implemented. Those adjustments are both possible and successful if a teacher has a high degree of pedagogical content knowledge (Shulman, 1987). We had

9

reason to believe that the experienced teachers in our study possessed such knowledge and such skills.

Reconstructing the Classroom: The Remainder of the Book

Our study began. We had agreed upon a philosophy of teaching and learning science (constructivism), had identified equitable teaching as important and had decided to focus on higher-level cognitive learning. Furthermore, experienced teachers in a unique school had volunteered to cooperate with us. We anticipated a hectic, but productive, ten weeks.

Each chapter describes those ten weeks from a different perspective. For example, Chapter 2 contains a description of the methods used in the study and presents background information about Southside High. In the third chapter, Tobin examines characteristics of the two participating teachers (whom we refer to as Sandra and Peter throughout this book) and of the implemented curriculum. Specifically, teachers' beliefs associated with specific roles, their conceptualization of certain teaching roles and their understanding of the content taught are described. Those characteristics, then, are related to what happens in each classroom. Chapter 3 also identifies teaching metaphors which are used to understand teaching roles as a means of changing teacher beliefs and actions in the classroom.

Chapter 4 discusses the two classrooms from the perspective of gender differences. Kahle explores the manner in which each teacher interacts with male and female students. In addition, she discusses the effect of different teaching techniques and the unconscious acts of teachers which reinforce society's sex role stereotypes.

In Chapter 5, Nordland discusses the cognitive demands of the tasks, materials and tests in relation to the cognitive aptitudes of students. His analyses involve the cognitive level of the learning tasks as well as the cognitive level of the science content in the textbooks and references used by Sandra and Peter. Nordland describes the cognitive demands of the activities implemented in both classes, the cognitive requirements of tests used to examine student learning, and the aptitudes of students in each class, as measured by a standard Piagetian task and in terms of a task developed from an activity implemented in Peter's class.

In Chapter 6, Rennie utilizes qualitative and quantitative data to investigate both classrooms and compare the manner in which different students engaged in the learning process. The chapter focuses on the attitudes of students and the way in which they interacted with one another, the teacher and other resources during learning tasks. Rennie examines student motivation to learn and the extent to which different activities facilitated overt student engagement in learning tasks in each class.

Fraser provides a view of classrooms through the students' eyes by reporting student perceptions of the classroom environment in Chapter 7. He relates quantitative data about student perceptions with qualitative data about teachers' beliefs and metaphors and the views of individual students. The final chapter contains a synthesis of the findings and presents implications for further research, for teaching and learning in classrooms and for teacher preparation and enhancement.

In summary, our book describes ten weeks in Sandra's and Peter's classrooms from five different perspectives. As we analyzed interaction patterns, texts and materials and as we collected teacher interviews, classroom anecdotes and student comments, we looked for patterns across our field notes. Each of us focused on a specific aspect (for example, teaching metaphors, gender differences, engagement patterns, classroom environment or cognitive demands), yet our analyses went beyond individual research questions. For example, our observations and data were tested against a constructivist philosophy as well as analyzed for evidences of pedagogical content knowledge. Last, we synthesized our findings and hypothesized implications for future research. For ten weeks, we were part of two high school science classrooms; as time wore on, both teachers and students were able to ignore (or casually accept) our presence. The daily and accumulative record of the teaching, learning and socializing that went on in these classrooms provided windows into science classrooms.

References

DOYLE, W. (1983) 'Academic work', *Review of Educational Research*, 53, pp. 159–99.
ERICKSON, G.L. and ERICKSON, L.J. (1984) 'Females and science achievement: Existence, explanations and implications', *Science Education*, 68, pp. 63–89.
FIRESTONE, W. (1987) 'Meaning in method: The rhetoric of quantitative and qualitative research', *Educational Researcher*, 16(7), pp. 16–21.
FISHER, D.L. and FRASER, B.J. (1983) 'A comparison of actual and preferred classroom environment as perceived by science teachers and students', *Journal of Research in Science Teaching*, 20, pp. 55–61.
FRASER, B.J. (1981a) 'Australian research on classroom environments: State of the art', *Australian Journal of Education*, 25, pp. 238–68.
FRASER, B.J. (1981b) 'Using environmental assessments to make better classrooms', *Journal of Curriculum Studies*, 13, pp. 131–44.
FRASER, B.J. (1982) 'Differences between student and teacher perceptions of actual and preferred classroom learning environment', *Educational Evaluation and Policy Analysis*, 4, pp. 511–9.
FRASER, B.J. (1986) *Classroom Environment*, London, Croom Helm.
FRASER, B.J. (1989) 'Twenty years of classroom environment research: Progress and prospect', *Journal of Curriculum Studies*, 21, pp. 307–27.
FRASER, B.J. and FISHER, D.L. (1982) 'Predicting students' outcomes from their perceptions of classroom psychosocial environment', *American Educational Research Journal*, 19, pp. 498–518.

FRASER, B.J. and FISHER, D.L. (1983a) 'Use of actual and preferred classroom environment scales in person-environment fit research', *Journal of Educational Psychology*, 75, pp. 303–13.

FRASER, B.J. and FISHER, D.L. (1983b) 'Student achievement as a function of person-environment fit: A regression surface analysis', *British Journal of Educational Psychology*, 53, pp. 89–99.

FRASER, B.J. and FISHER, D.L. (1986) 'Using short forms of classroom climate instruments to assess and improve classroom psychosocial environment', *Journal of Research in Science Teaching*, 5, pp. 387–413.

FRASER, B.J. and TOBIN, K. (1989) 'Combining qualitative and quantitative methods in the study of classroom learning environments', paper presented at annual meeting of American Educational Research Association, San Francisco.

FRY, G., CHANTAVANICH, S. and CHANTAVANICH, A. (1981) 'Merging quantitative and qualitative research techniques: Toward a new research paradigm,' *Anthropology and Education Quarterly*, 12, pp. 145–58.

GALLAGHER, J.J. (1989) 'Research on secondary school science teachers' practices, knowledge and beliefs: A basis for restructuring', paper presented at annual meeting of American Association for the Advancement of Science, San Francisco.

HAERTEL, G.D., WALBERG, H.J. and HAERTEL, E.H. (1981) 'Socio-psychological environments and learning: A quantitative synthesis', *British Educational Research Journal*, 7, pp. 27–36.

HOWE, K.R. (1988) 'Against the quantitative and qualitative incompatibility thesis: Or dogmas die hard', *Educational Researcher*, 17(11), pp. 10–16.

HUMRICH, E. (April 1988) 'Sex differences in the Second IEA Science Study: US results in an international context', paper presented at annual meeting of National Association for Research in Science Teaching, Lake Ozark, Missouri.

IEA (INTERNATIONAL ASSOCIATION FOR THE EVALUATION OF EDUCATIONAL ACHIEVEMENT). (1988) *Science Achievement in Seventeen Countries: A Preliminary Report*, New York, Pergamon Press.

KAHLE, J.B. (1985) 'Retention of girls in science: Case studies of secondary teachers', in Kahle, J.B. (Ed.) *Women in Science: A Report from the Field*, Philadelphia, PA, Falmer Press.

KAHLE, J.B. (1988) 'Gender and science education II', in FENSHAM, P. (Ed.) *Developments and Dilemmas in Science Education*, Philadelphia, PA, Falmer Press.

KELLY, A. (1978) *Girls and Science: An International Study of Sex Differences in School Science Achievement*, Stockholm, Almqvist and Wiksell.

KELLY, A. (1985) 'The construction of masculine science', *British Journal of Sociology of Education*, 6(2), pp. 133–54.

NATIONAL RESEARCH COUNCIL (NRC) (1989) *Everyone Counts: A Report to the Nation on the Future of Mathematics Education*, Washington, DC, National Academy Press.

NATIONAL SCIENCE BOARD COMMISSION ON PRECOLLEGE EDUCATION IN MATHEMATICS, SCIENCE AND TECHNOLOGY (1983) *Educating Americans for the 21st Century*, Washington DC, National Science Foundation.

NOVAK, J.D. (1988) 'Learning science and the science of learning', *Studies in Science Education*, 15, pp. 77–101.

OFFICE OF TECHNOLOGY ASSESSMENT (OTA) (June 1988a) *Educating Scientists and Engineers: Grade School to Grad School* (OTA-SET-377), Washington, DC, US Government Printing Office.

OFFICE OF TECHNOLOGY ASSESSMENT (OTA) (December 1988b) *Elementary and Secondary Education for Science and Engineering* (OTA-TM-SET-41), Washington, DC, US Government Printing Office.

RAIZEN, S.A. and JONES, L.V. (1985) *Indicators of Precollege Education in Science and Mathematics*, Washington, DC, National Academy Press.

SADKER, D. and SADKER, M. (1985) 'Is the O.K. classroom O.K.?' *Phi Delta Kappan*, 55, pp. 358–61.

SHULMAN, L.S. (1987) 'Knowledge and teaching: Foundations of the new reform', *Harvard Educational Review*, 57, 1, pp. 1–22.

STAKE, R.E. and EASLEY, J.A., JR. (1978) *Case Studies in Science Education* (Vols 1 and 2), Urbana, Illinois, Center for Instructional Research and Curriculum Evaluation and Committee on Culture and Cognition, University of Illinois at Urbana-Champagne.

TOBIN, K. (1988) 'Differential engagement of males and females in high school science', *International Journal of Science Education*, 10, pp. 239–52.

TOBIN, K. and FRASER, B.J. (Eds) (1987) *Exemplary Practice in Science and Mathematics Education*, Perth, Curtin University of Technology.

TOBIN, K. and GALLAGHER, J.J. (1987a) 'The role of target students in the science classroom', *Journal of Research in Science Teaching*, 24, pp. 61–75.

TOBIN, K. and GALLAGHER, J.J. (1987b) 'What happens in high school science classrooms?', *Journal of Curriculum Studies*, 19, pp. 549–60.

VON GLASERSFELD, E. (1988) 'Environment and communication', paper presented at sixth International Congress on Mathematics Education, Budapest.

WEISS, I.R. (November 1987) *Report of the 1983–86 National Survey of Science and Mathematics Education*, Research Triangle Park, NC, Research Triangle Institute.

WELCH, W.W. (1985) 'Sugar and spice and all things nice?', *Australian Educational Researcher*, 12, pp. 5–23.

WHYTE, J. (1986) *Girls Into Science and Technology*, London, Routledge and Kegan Paul.

YACKEL, E., COBB, P., WOOD, T., WHEATLEY, G. and MERKEL, G. (1988) 'The importance of social interaction in children's construction of mathematical knowledge', Unpublished paper, West Lafayette, Indiana, Purdue University.

Chapter 2: Methods and Background

Kenneth Tobin

Methods Used in the Study

The Classes Involved

Two science teachers, Sandra and Peter, from an urban high school in the city of Dalton, Coastal Australia participated in the study. The school was selected because of its tradition of emphasizing student-centred, self-paced learning. The head of department for physical science, Dennis, was asked to nominate two teachers, an 'above average' male and female teacher. When approached by one of the research team, both of the nominated teachers agreed to participate in the study.

Peter's class contained eleven boys and twenty girls. According to Peter, his class consisted of approximately ten top students, with the remainder being intermediate in ability. He explained that students elect to be in this class by choosing to study more chemistry in grade 10. Peter nominated eight students whom he regarded as the most able in the class and also named the bottom five students. Each group contained approximately equal numbers of males and females.

Sandra's grade 10 class consisted of fourteen boys and eighteen girls. In spite of the fact that all of the class members had been placed in this 'advanced' class, it was clear that they varied considerably in ability and attitude. Sandra explained that most of the students in her class were above average. She described the class as a 'great bunch of kids', of whom about six were very able and the rest were less able and less motivated. When Sandra was asked to nominate the most able students in her class, she readily nominated four females and two males. She went on to select two females and two males as being among the low achievers in her class. While some students were contemplating leaving school at the end of the school year, others were planning which subjects they would study in grade 11. Many students also had responsibilities outside school. For example, one female student regularly was called upon to be absent from school to care for her younger brothers and sisters while her parents travelled. (She was absent for seventeen of approximately forty-four days during the study.) Other students had part-time employment including working in a fast food restaurant, assisting in a pet shop and pumping petrol at a service station. These part-time jobs sometimes meant that students kept late hours and came to school tired. Factors such as these probably were present in Peter's class as well. During interviews, Peter did not mention them as being particularly significant. The fact that Sandra mentioned factors associated with the personal lives of students and Peter did not is a significant difference between the two teachers which is highlighted in later chapters.

Design of the Study

The observation component of the study took place over a ten-week period from August to November of 1986. During the first five-week period, both teachers taught the topic of Vertebrates and, during the second five-week session, the topic of Nuclear Energy was taught. An interval of two weeks, during which students were on vacation, separated the two topics.

A team of six researchers visited the classes at various times throughout the study (although only five of the researchers contributed chapters to this book). The schedule for the first topic was arranged so that each researcher observed each teacher for a minimum of six lessons in the five-week period. Eighteen lessons were observed by at least one of the research team and two observers were in each classroom. One lesson for each teacher was not observed.

During the second topic, the data collecting schedule was modified to allow the various members of the research team to gather data which were appropriate for their specific foci. All lessons were observed by at least one member of the research team. Jane Butler Kahle pursued the question of gender-related differences, both at Southside High and in the broader educational community in the city of Dalton. Floyd Nordland concentrated on the cognitive developmental level of the students in both classes, explored the extent to which students understood the content of several of the activities in which they engaged in class, and gathered interview data concerning gender differences in science classrooms. Barry Fraser examined student perceptions of the learning environment during both topics and obtained a measure of the environment that students preferred during the Vertebrates topic. Leonie Rennie and Kenneth Tobin focused on both classes and observed Sandra and Peter for a minimum of eight lessons each. Rennie quantified students' attitudes to science during each topic and the extent to which students engaged in learning tasks. She then related the quantitative data to intensive qualitative observations which focused on student interactions in each class. In contrast, Tobin focused on the teacher and the manner in which the program was implemented.

The research team continued to interact with the teachers for a year after the classroom observations. Each teacher was provided with written reports of the study and the findings were discussed with them in depth. Feedback from the teachers about the written reports of the study was used as another data source.

Data Sources and Data Collection

Participant observer data collecting strategies were employed. These involved observing classrooms, interviewing teachers and students on a daily basis, working with students during class time, obtaining written responses to specific questions, examining student notebooks and test papers and analyzing teacher assessments of student performance.

The presence of members of the research team in the classroom for such a long time undoubtedly influenced teacher and student behaviour. However, we tried to minimize disruptions due to our presence. Field notes were given to Peter and Sandra on a regular basis so that they would not be concerned by our note-taking and interviewing of students. Although we interviewed students on an informal basis during class time, we did not disrupt individuals for prolonged periods of time (that is, for more than three minutes). In any event, the familiar pattern of engagement in both classes was for students to be involved in learning tasks and attend to their social agendas throughout the lesson. Thus, our brief interviews with students fitted with a pattern of intermittent engagement which appeared to be well established in both classes.

When the field notes were written, we gave them to the teachers so that they would not feel anxious about what we were writing and so that they could give us feedback on their accuracy. The following notes from an interview of August 19 provide an indication of the manner in which the field notes were initially received:

> I handed Peter the field notes and he eagerly read through them. He was impressed with the detail. 'Did I do all of that?' he exclaimed. As he read the field notes he explained that Britta likes to call out answers and that he was on the look out for that.... After he had read the field notes he explained that he was pleased to have the opportunity to discuss them with students. This would probably happen when he had a few more. He would then photocopy them and have a class discussion on what happens in class.... Peter also commented that he did not think my presence in the classroom had made any difference to the way that the class behaved after the first few minutes.

Sandra's reactions to the presence of the research team and to receiving the field notes were described clearly in an interview at the conclusion of the Vertebrates topic. She was pleased to receive the field notes and the feedback on her teaching. However, she felt self-critical and guilty that she had not observed all of the things described in the field notes. In her years as a teacher, she had only had observers in her classroom on two occasions, when she was training to be a teacher and when she applied for a permanent teaching position. She did not think that the presence of the research team changed her approach a great deal. However, she worried about our presence during the Vertebrates topic and was reluctant to discipline students while we were there.

As the study progressed, the research team made decisions about the aspects of teaching and learning on which they would focus, the data to be collected and procedures to be adopted in collecting and validating data. For example, at team meetings, decisions were made about the content of interviews, who would conduct interviews, who was to be interviewed, which learning environment scales were likely to be most salient in the two classes, and which items to incorporate in the student attitude inventory. In addition, decisions were taken to assess the cognitive developmental level of all students, determine the extent to which students were able to understand difficult problems and concepts encountered in the course, and assess the reading difficulty of the texts. Care was taken to ensure that data were obtained from a variety of sources and that multiple perspectives were represented in the data obtained from researchers, teachers and students.

Interviews usually were non-structured. Before each interview, the team decided what information it would like to have but, during the interview, the goal was to allow Peter and Sandra to speak without interruption and to avoid leading questions and comments. When questions were pre-planned, it was not unusual for most of them to be replaced by other questions because of the direction in which the interview ultimately headed. For example, in one of the early interviews with Sandra, only half of the following planned questions were asked:

What science studies have you done in the past?

What is your typical preparation for a lesson on Vertebrates?

How did you acquire the knowledge you have to teach Vertebrates?

Why do you teach the way you do?

Describe the circumstances in which students best learn in your class?

What would you like the students to achieve from the Vertebrates topic?

What are you looking for when you move about the classroom?

Describe what typically happens when you arrive at a group?

How has your teaching style evolved over the years?

Why is Steve sitting at group one?

Why does Hayley move about the room so much?

What irritates you most about teaching this class?

How is the final grade arrived at?

Who sets the final test on Vertebrates?

What would you change in the content if restructuring were possible?

The following extract of Sandra's earlier interview, in which specific key questions were not pre-planned, is provided as an example of the kinds of questions raised and the manner in which they were posed:

From your own learning experiences, do you think that this describes what you actually did?

Did you actually dissect a heart during your university courses?

When students are working on a dissection, suppose a student at Table 1 asks a question which you answer. Presumably the question will come up again?

Then one might ask, why not call the class to attention and go over this point with all of them?

What I'm really trying to get at, of course, is why you handle things as you do.

Is there something about chemistry that is different from when you were doing the Vertebrates unit?

Another thing that we talked about is the way that these students are good on a one-to-one basis, but they have a tendency to socialize. Some people watching your class might think there is an excessive amount of off-task time. Would you just like to talk about that in general?

How would you describe the support system at Southside High? If you wanted to do experimentally based laboratory instruction in biology, you might require glassware, solutions, cultures ...

Data Analysis and Interpretation

As soon as possible after each lesson, all data were compiled into written field notes which were circulated among members of the research team. Team meetings were scheduled three times a week and occurred prior to visits to the school. Team meetings were used mainly to discuss the data and its interpretations. On the basis of the results, data collecting strategies were formulated with the intention of gathering additional information to support or refute assertions. Throughout the study, assertions were formulated, modified or rejected. The findings were organized as a set of assertions together with supporting evidence, exceptions and illustrative vignettes.

Assertions about gender differences in Peter's class are provided as an example of the changes which occurred in assertions as the study progressed. When we began the study, we felt that gender differences might occur in the manner described by Tobin and Gallagher (1987), who found differential involvement of males and females in whole-class settings and in laboratory activities. However, after the first observation, the following assertion was postulated on the basis of the evidence: 'There are no gender differences in Peter's class in interactions or work patterns'. By the end of the second week, however, evidence from observations and interviews led to the following assertions about gender-related differences in participation in Peter's class:

- During individualized activities the teacher interacts with some students more than others.
- There are no gender differences in public interactions.
- Girls participate in individualized activities to a greater extent than boys do.

After three weeks, a pattern of gender-related differences in interactions with the teacher had been established to support a hypothesis of the following form: 'There are gender differences in Peter's class in whole-class interactions and in seatwork interactions with the teacher'. Thus, in a period of three weeks, an assertion of no discernible gender-related differences in engagement patterns was reversed and differentiated in the form of three assertions which were supported throughout the remainder of the study.

A similar evolution occurred in assertions formulated about gender differences in Sandra's class. In the first week, there was no evidence of gender differences of the type observed in other studies. Hence the following assertion appeared in the interpretive notes: 'There is no evidence of gender differences in Sandra's class'. In the second week of the study, two assertions indicated that gender-related differences were apparent during the Vertebrates topic:

- Females are more involved in social discourse.
- More females move around the room and visit other tables.

Finally, by the end of the Vertebrates topic, a third assertion became evident to the research team:

- Sandra's management style enabled three to five female students to monopolize her time when it suited them.

Background Information About Peter

Peter was an enthusiastic teacher who was keen to establish himself when he arrived at Southside High. As a result of his experiences at two other schools in Coastal Australia and one in Canada, Peter had honed a teaching style with which he was satisfied and he had the confident manner of a professional who knew his job. Yet, his move to Southside High imposed some constraints on the manner in which Peter was able to teach. Southside High had a tradition of being an open school which respected the role of the student in learning. Students were given a degree of independence in many aspects of the program and most treated staff as coworkers rather than as authority figures (for example, students usually used a teacher's first name during interactions). Although the science curriculum was based on the lower secondary science syllabus prescribed by the Education Department, the school adopted a self-paced style of presentation based on student use of workbooks. The workbooks, which were designed by staff over a number of years, allowed students to progress at their own pace and to utilize a range of resources to answer questions about specific science topics. Students learned science by answering the questions and discussing them with their peers and the teacher. However, the workbooks constrained the curriculum in a manner which frustrated many of the current staff at Southside High, including Peter. In Peter's case, existing teaching strategies had to be modified so as to utilize the workbooks and provide students with a program that was in some degree self-paced.

Peter also felt constrained by the policy of assigning teachers to teach in a number of rooms at Southside High. Because of that policy, he was reluctant to change the arrangement of desks in the room in which we observed him teach. He noted that:

> One of the things that really gets me here is that I'm seldom in the same classroom. This year I'm in seven classrooms. I love to work in the one classroom where I can set up aquariums and all sorts of things. Here that's impossible.

Like most science teachers in Coastal Australia, Peter regarded the more specialist courses offered to students in grades 11 and 12 as more interesting, demanding and important. During 1986, Peter was teaching biology and human biology to grade 11 students. These teaching assignments were demanding in terms of the time required to prepare for five different classes and assess students in courses based on a philosophy of continuous assessment. Peter noted that he worked back at school until 5 p.m. on most afternoons. However, Peter could not complete the essential work in school hours and found it necessary to work at home on most nights of the week. Thus, his role as teacher conflicted with his other roles, particularly as a family man. Peter stated that:

I go home at night and the demands of the family are un-
believable.... About one hour of marking at home per night.
I don't get a lot of time for other things. Even on the weekends
I'm locked away in a room marking and I resent that sometimes.
Marking is horrendous; every night we are constantly assessing.

The demands of teaching five classes necessitated compromises in
terms of Peter's ideal for the teaching and learning of science. Because the
workbooks were expected to be used and because they defined the content of science topics in grade 10 general science, Peter was able to get
students started each day by referring them to their workbooks. In
addition, because the workbooks were written so as to utilize a wide
range of resources, the teacher could implement the curriculum without
taking an active role in presenting and sequencing science content. In
other words, if time demands were such that compromises had to be
made, the grade 10 science program was packaged to such an extent that
teachers could minimize planning and rely instead on the workbooks and
their experience in having taught grade 10 science previously. Any planning that was necessary could be done during class time as students
worked through the workbook activities in a self-paced manner.

Peter was an outdoors type of person who had commenced his
teacher education in physical education. Even though he had changed his
career goal to science teaching, his interests in the outdoors and physical
education were ever present. Peter was an enthusiastic teacher who
emphasized field trips and encouraged his students to be involved in a
variety of excursions. When talking with Peter about science, his strong
interest in field work was evident. Obviously he valued learning in a field
environment and he took steps to ensure that students had every opportunity to learn in that way. Peter adopted an energetic role in other
components of the school program as well. For example, he often volunteered to drive the school bus and he organized a lunchtime science
competition in conjunction with Science in Schools Week. These additional activities were a further burden on the time available to plan and
implement the science programs in his five classes.

Peter's efforts as a science teacher had not gone unnoticed. He had a
reputation as an above average teacher among his science teaching colleagues and the school administration rewarded his interest and competence in administration by making him responsible for grade 10 students
in 1987. In addition, he was elected by his colleagues to the School
Board.

Peter was not a particularly popular member of the staff at Southside
High. One of his colleagues noted that Peter 'has a few problems and
hang-ups. His fitting in with the staff is a very difficult question. He has
had problems with other staff in every school at which he taught.' Peter
regarded himself as different from other teachers and questioned his own

capacity to relate well with other staff at Southside High. However, he noted that he and other staff generally felt that he had good rapport with students. In describing his differences with other staff, he noted:

> ... I am different. I tend to wear a collar and tie a fair bit and stuff like that and that's definitely a no-no in this place and in most schools. Actually very few teachers wear the old collar and tie. And I tend to be conservative and probably authoritarian in some ways.... I'm a very different sort of individual I suppose. My interests are very different from the average teacher. I enjoy the opera and stuff like that. I'm committed to classical music and stuff like that. Next weekend I'm taking 30 kids away on a weekend camp.

Background Information About Sandra

Sandra had a background of employment which included periods of working as a scientist and teaching in three states of Australia. Despite the fact that her father and mother were successful teachers, Sandra did not consider teaching as an initial career. She completed a science degree with majors in chemistry and biochemistry and subjects in mathematics, science, physics, chemistry and biology. Sandra felt that her success in science had to do with a high interest in science subjects when she was at school. After completing her degree, she worked for a year as a bacteriologist when she participated in a research program. At the time, Sandra was one of few women involved in research of this type.

After a move to another city, Sandra commenced a teacher education program when it became apparent that she could not pursue a career in science. She noted that one of the strong points about her program was that she spent about two days a week for the entire year in schools. During this period of induction into teaching, she was assigned to a senior science teacher who allowed her to 'do her own thing'. During this program, Sandra observed a range of teaching styles and concluded that there is not just one optimal style of teaching, but that there are many styles that might be suitable in a given set of circumstances. When she did her training, discovery teaching was in vogue, but Sandra found that it did not work well for her. However, she was not really in favour of a teacher-directed approach either. Sandra noted that, if students could move through the activities efficiently and achieve the objectives and be accurate in their work, then she could arrange time to have small group discussions and to go over the work to make sure that the students understood it.

When asked if she felt that part of her role as a science teacher was to encourage young women who were capable and interested in taking science, Sandra agreed that it was. She remarked that, in a recent exercise in which students had to indicate the careers in which they were interested, she found that two of her most capable girls were intending to pursue a career in preschool education. Sandra gave some non-verbal signals that she disapproved of their choice and indicated that some boys, who were less capable, had opted for career paths in science. Although Sandra had given encouragement where she could, she was cautious because she felt that it was important to be enthusiastic and supportive of student choices.

Sandra indicated that the parent community at Southside High was strongly oriented towards the sciences. Southside High had a good retention rate in science classes from the lower school (grades 8 to 10) to the upper school (grades 11 and 12). Sandra noted that one of the arguments in favour of using student workbooks was that students in the lower school enjoyed their science so much that they gained the necessary confidence to continue in upper school. Students and parents seemed secure with the workbooks. They could see what students had to do and, as they worked through the activities, they could keep track of their progress.

Sandra taught in two separate school systems before coming to teach in Coastal Australia. As a consequence, she had diverse experience with different curricula. In one State, she had little freedom to deviate from the syllabus but, in the other, she had considerable autonomy and was free to cater for student needs to the extent that she wanted. In other States, she saw the folly of allowing teachers to follow their own paths because, in many instances, students did not have a chance to obtain the prerequisites for further study in science. Before moving to Southside High as a head of department, Sandra taught at another metropolitan high school in Dalton for six years. Although she was qualified to teach chemistry and biology, she taught biology and human biology because there was a shortage of teachers in those subjects. At the time of the study, Sandra had been teaching high school science for ten years. She was a head of department with responsibility for lower secondary science (grades 8 to 10) and biological sciences, and taught biology to grade 12 students, human biology to students in grades 11 and 12, and general science to students in grade 10. During the study, Sandra also taught an electronics elective to grade 10 students.

An aspect of Sandra's background which appeared to influence her science teaching was her experience as a scientist. Sandra viewed science as a process and was less concerned than were many other teachers with helping students to learn facts in order to succeed in end-of-topic tests. She valued student participation in optional parts of the courses and in laboratory investigations. On numerous occasions, she expressed the belief that students learned best when they did the work for themselves.

This belief, which was reflected in the way in which Sandra organized learning activities in her classes, is dealt with in detail in the next chapter.

Sandra indicated that the knowledge acquired during her formal degree work was sufficient for her to teach biology and chemistry. When asked how she learned the content to teach Vertebrates, she laughed and said that it was learned through her high school biology course and by teaching the topic in other schools. Each time that she taught the topic, she retained a little more in her head, although she tended to rely on books to look things up. She noted that she was not sure that she wanted to memorize all of the material anyway as 'information changes with time' and she learned new things as the years went by. She felt that the *Web of Life* biology course also had influenced her teaching of Vertebrates particularly and of science generally.

Southside High School

Background information about Southside High was obtained by examining a collection of historical documents such as memoranda, school bulletins and personal diary entries which had been retained by John, the first head of the science department at Southside High, and by interviewing former and present school staff. The three staff who provided the information used in this chapter are: John; Gerry, a staff member who taught at the school for its first ten years; and Dennis, the head of physical sciences.

Philosophy and Curriculum Organization

Southside High commenced in 1977 as a school with numerous differences from traditional high schools in Coastal Australia. The foundation staff of the school were selected on the basis of their philosophy of education and willingness to teach at the school. In contrast, staff at most other government high schools in Coastal Australia were appointed to schools according to the needs of the statewide school system. The foundation staff also were given considerable autonomy with regard to the school curriculum, which was formulated in accordance with a philosophy written by the school principal in collaboration with senior teachers. The philosophy, which was to 'unite all components of the school's programs in the accomplishment of its goals and objectives', consisted of ten statements which are summarized below:

· Children are active participants in their own learning.
· Each student has different interests, propensities and abilities; each will respond differently and will express different needs. It

is the function of the school to determine for each student how he/she learns best.

- It is the function of the school to exploit the natural curiosity of children, to encourage them to seek, explore and discover through their learning programs.
- Learning is something that students do: it is the role of the teacher to observe and diagnose individual needs, to be a consultant, a guide and a facilitator.
- The relationship between student and teacher should be based on mutual respect, sympathy and understanding.
- The school should foster affective as well as cognitive growth.
- Teachers should be involved in decision making in all matters of policy and curriculum relating to the functioning of the school.
- The school should be seen to be a part of and indeed to function as a part of the wider community. The community, rather than the school, is the learning environment and community involvement should be accepted as an automatic condition to the functioning of the school.
- The curriculum should be the tangible expression of the total school philosophy.
- Knowledge is seen as a composite of inter-related components, formally referred to as subjects. The school accepts the holistic concept of knowledge and organizes courses and programs using integrated approaches, relating the separate disciplines to broad themes or ideas.

The teachers at Southside High were encouraged to be innovative and were prepared to try new approaches and evaluate their effects on student learning. John, the first head of the science department, noted that:

> We did some incredible things. For example, because we had student centred work, therefore the teacher shouldn't really do any teaching from the blackboard. So, Gerry and I went to see how long we could go without using a blackboard. I think that we went eight months without writing one word on a blackboard.... It probably isn't good. We never said it was the best thing to do, but the interesting thing was to try it.... We also tried background music because it was supposed to be student centred ... It didn't work but it was interesting to try ...

The staff of the school translated the school philosophy into organizational and operational procedures. Initially it was decided to follow the development of themes across subject areas. As a consequence, new

Table 2.1: Themes and related science topics for Grade 8 in the initial five years at Southside High

Theme	Science Topic
Who am I?	Tuning in with the senses
	Mice and men
Exploring the near environment	Science of music
	The chemistry of food
	Skin and clothes
	Electric circuits
Exploration	Plants
	Minerals and crystals
	Places and people

curricula were developed and existing curricula were adapted to teach the themes selected for particular grade levels. Examples of the themes and related science topics for grade 8 are shown in Table 2.1.

A particular consequence of the school philosophy was that the development of student independence and individual decision making was valued highly. One of the general aims of the school was:

> Southside High ... will ultimately distinguish itself by the stress it places on the concepts of staff professionalism and the recognition of the individuality of students with the consequent need to adapt learning programs accordingly. The open or flexible spaces are a convenient device or aid to the implementation of programs which allow for the individual potential of students to be realized.

Students at Southside High had responsibility for their own progress. John noted that students have to be educated to accept this responsibility. He said that '... this can only be done by gradually placing students in positions of self discipline and providing supportive guidance. We must accept some failure as part of the learning process. The result of this is that the vast majority of grade 10 students show a degree of self discipline in this area that far exceeds that which I have seen in any other school'. In addition, recognition of the diverse nature of student abilities and interests led to a system which enabled students to learn at their own rates and study science topics in which they were interested. Thus, students were given considerable autonomy in selecting when to study particular topics, for how long to study specific topics and which topics to study. In order to provide students with this degree of independence, workbooks were prepared to enable them to work independently of one another and the teacher and to facilitate self-paced learning. The science course was student-centred, with teacher-centred aspects occupying no more than five per cent of the allocated time.

Students in grades 8, 9 and 10 were not streamed into ability groups. Individual differences were catered for within the printed materials by allowing students to progress at their own rates and permitting them to select topics suited to their ability. According to John, the advantages of not streaming were seen in high motivation of students and positive social attitudes. More able students could progress further than in conventional schools because of the self-paced nature of the program and the availability of additional topics to study. Students were timetabled for science in 100-minute blocks, which enabled a variety of activities to be undertaken in a flexible manner. Students were responsible for their own time keeping and there were no sirens or bells to signal the end of class time.

Another consequence of adhering to the school philosophy of education was that there was no compulsory homework. John explained the policy in the following manner:

> If we are going to stick with these aims, then we will set them the work to be done and they will decide when to do it. If they decide to do some work at home, they will get better results, but that is their decision. We insisted on marking everything which they did so that they would feel that it was important and that we were pleased with what they had done. If students wanted to do extra work to get ahead, well and good. But, if they did everything in class, that was all right as well. They saw homework in a very positive light. They didn't do it because the teacher wanted them to do it, but they saw that doing homework was a way of achieving something for themselves not for the teacher.

The staff set out to establish a relationship in which teachers and students were partners in learning and the image of teachers being 'aloof professionals' was avoided. A feature of the relationship was the first name basis on which staff and students addressed one another.

An innovative open-area design was incorporated into the school buildings. Classrooms were separated by a movable wall which could be opened to provide a large flexible space to accommodate more than sixty students. In the first five years of the school's operation, a block of approximately sixty students was timetabled for science with two or three teachers. This enabled innovative approaches to teaching to be utilized. In the first few years, team teaching was used extensively. However, after five years, John noted that:

> Team teaching in science has virtually been abandoned. It was an exciting technique with many advantages but was abandoned partly because of the difficulties that some staff had in adapting,

but mainly because of the difficulties which some students had in coping with the open area situation.

The discipline policy of the school was based on the philosophy that relationships between students and the teacher should be based on mutual respect, sympathy and understanding. Students were recognized as possessing dignity, integrity and rights, as well as obligations. As a consequence, there were no rules. Rather, a code of conduct evolved to guide student behaviour. Teachers adopted the policy of being positive about students' work and behaviour. If students transgressed, they were never disciplined in front of the class, and public sanctions of all types were avoided. Instead, teachers adopted a positive approach to problem students by providing encouragement and counselling. Based on the same philosophical point, teachers avoided making public comparisons of student performance and achievement.

School-based curriculum development worked on a model in which objectives were prescribed and a 'best activity' was written to enable students to accomplish each objective. The activities were incorporated into student workbooks. John said that the approach underlying the workbooks was not related to discovery learning which, in his view, is an inefficient learning process when science content is to be learned. He described the approach as individualized and expository, because either the content to be learned usually was in the workbooks or students were told where to locate relevant information. Students were provided with workbooks and sets of textbooks were available as resources to be used in class. John described the philosophy of the workbooks in the following terms:

> The ultimate philosophy in some of these books is that, if you've got something boring to do, the students like doing it better if they do it themselves than if you tell them to do it. So, in a lot of these, there will be sections which ask students to read a paragraph and then copy it into their notes. The students, in general, like that. If you ask a class to copy this paragraph down off the board, ... they hate it. They'll be bored. So they've made this decision themselves and the teacher hasn't told them; they've decided to copy this paragraph down, and there's no real pressure as to whether they do it in one minute or two minutes; they can make that decision and they respond very positively.

The thematic approach was tried out for approximately two years until it became evident that it was not working. Content areas were compromised in order to meet the needs of themes, which were somewhat arbitrary. As a consequence, the themes were modified in such a manner that integration occurred between subjects, but on a smaller scale. However, the topics which evolved in grades 8 and 9 were the remnants of the thematic approach. For example, the chemistry of food and the science of sound were continued for several years even though the thematic approach was dropped. When the thematic approach was discontinued, the new units which were written were closely aligned with traditional science. Vertebrates and Nuclear Energy were included in the curriculum on this basis. However, the way in which science was to be taught was already in place, and the workbooks and teaching methods were well and truly established and were utilized throughout the school.

In that first year, the original staff worked closely together to formulate a curriculum that was consistent with the school philosophy. Not surprisingly, the teachers identified strongly with the approach that was adopted in the school. They understood the rationale for what was being attempted and they worked hard to ensure that the curriculum was implemented as intended. However, the influence of new staff became a problem immediately after the first year of operation. In many cases, new staff, who had not been involved in the initial decisions, wanted to teach differently. This lack of cohesion was seen by John to be a problem. In a written report in 1979, John noted that:

> The school philosophy should not be a static set of rules; rather it should evolve where necessary. However, new staff members must be fully inducted into the system as it stands and they must initially accept the views of the majority. It is too easy for an individual teacher to reject what has been established over many years by many people involved in hours of discussions.

The Second Five Years

Dennis was asked to describe the factors associated with the last ten years at Southside High which influenced the science program at the school. Dennis explained that, following the departure of John, there was a two-year period when strong academic leadership was not evident in science. This lack of leadership influenced the quality of the workbooks and resulted in a run-down of laboratories and equipment. Dennis commented that the quality of the workbooks had declined to the extent that he rarely used them. Even so, at the time of the study, there still was an emphasis on the production of materials based on a self-paced philosophy.

After three or four years, the school ceased to become experimental and the procedure of 'hand-selecting' staff was discontinued. This change in procedure was a catalyst for further change. New staff tended to be more diverse and had ideas of how the curriculum should be implemented. Gerry noted that:

> ... very few people were actually committed to a self-paced, student-centred, student-choice, student-responsibility type of learning. Very few people had that type of philosophy.

The incoming teachers had different backgrounds and philosophies and, in the case of senior staff, they had the power to influence policy. Even though the actual policy statements did not appear to change much over a ten-year period, what actually was taught and the way in which it was taught tended to be left to individual teachers to decide. Gerry noted that there was a decreasing amount of teamwork in the second five-year period. The department size of fifteen was large and there was a lack of leadership in the direction of student-centred learning. The approach to teaching became a matter for the professional judgement of the teacher and the team approach, which had characterized Southside High in the past, diminished rapidly.

Some aspects of the student-centred approach to teaching and learning were retained. The most notable of these was use of the workbooks, which in the past had facilitated a self-paced, independent approach to learning. According to Gerry, virtually all of the staff were involved in revising the workbooks. The 'old hands' prepared new materials and less experienced teachers 'modified workbooks superficially'. Very few topics ran for more than one or two years without revision. However, the relatively large number of teachers involved in revisions, together with the wide range of perspectives on what students should learn and how science should be taught and learned, resulted in differences in the extent to which various topics were student-centred and materials-centred. Gerry noted that several topics ended up 'being quite mediocre'. As a consequence, the workbooks evolved from being very materials-centred towards being text-centred. Gerry explained that Vertebrates was introduced as a topic because, in the thematic approach to teaching, some teachers felt that biology as a discipline had a low profile. Because of this perception, topics of a traditional nature (for example, Flowering Plants, Vertebrates, Invertebrates) were prepared and introduced into the curriculum. In a parallel manner, physical science topics, such as Nuclear Energy, were produced. Gerry described Nuclear Energy as a real 'hotch potch'. Several teachers had attempted revisions, but the topic was never written to the satisfaction of most science teachers. Dennis also commented on a 'marked decline' in the quality of workbook materials over the years:

> You could tell the early ones because they were very much more student-oriented. The kids were doing activities pretty much all of the time when using the old workbooks. But in the last three or four years of writing workbooks, what has happened is that staff came with neither the expertise nor the desire to write

workbooks. So, you get some workbooks that are absolutely diabolical.

The Tenth Year

Policy statements regarding the science program indicated that the student-centred approach to learning was retained at the time of the study, at least at the policy level. In fact, the 1986 policy statements communicated to parents in the school bulletin resembled those of ten years earlier. The inquiry orientation of the policy is well illustrated in the following extract from the school bulletin:

> Science at Southside High is a student-oriented, laboratory-centred course aimed at helping the students understand their biological and physical environment. The materials used in science are drawn from many curriculum materials produced by the school. The approach to each topic relies heavily on student enquiry and student experimentation. A multi-media approach is adopted where possible with use being made of tape recordings, slides, work cards and reference books. Students are encouraged to carry out independent research in the many areas and to work at rates commensurate with their abilities. A component of the course is also directed towards preparing students for grades 11 and 12 where this is appropriate. (p. 38)

The science program also allows for greater flexibility than the usual curriculum in its attempts to accommodate students at both ends of the academic spectrum. In describing the provisions made in the curriculum for students of varying aptitudes, the bulletin noted:

> In Science, the school based curriculum materials are constructed to appeal to students of all abilities. Because the materials are designed to allow students to proceed at their own rates, the teacher is released to assist individuals, particularly low-ability students. (p. 15)

An integral part of the science program was the workbooks which were developed for every topic of study in lower school science (that is, grades 8 to 10). The workbooks facilitated the kind of individualized learning valued and practised in the school in its formative years. However, as the initial group of foundation teachers left the school and were replaced by others, the approaches to teaching varied from the policy which was adopted uniformly in the initial years of Southside High. In the case of both grade 10 classes involved in this study, three workbooks had been used for science topics earlier in the year and workbooks were used for both Vertebrates and Nuclear Energy. Dennis asserted that staff should not have felt an obligation to use the workbooks in their teaching. He indicated that: 'At the beginning of the year, it was emphasized that the workbooks were a resource for staff to use in the way in which they wanted'.

Although science at Southside High had changed substantially over a period of ten years, several features continued. Perhaps the most obvious feature was the school buildings. The flexible area design remained, despite the fact that the philosophy of student-centred learning (which was shared by the twelve original staff at Southside High) was advocated by few current staff during the year of the study. Thus, the concertina walls which separated Sandra's and Peter's science rooms were shut. Whereas John and Gerry earlier had taught as a team with their sixty students, Sandra and Peter taught their separate classes independently. The separate rooms were bounded by their own four walls. Yet, they shared a wall through which sound easily penetrated. The sounds of students at work in the separate classrooms often was a source of distraction.

Because of the initial focus on student-centred learning, self-paced learning and student choice, the science rooms were designed for these purposes. A small chalkboard at the side of each room was available for teachers to use, but it was not easy to use it with the whole class. Similarly, use of an overhead projector with a whole class was difficult because the accompanying screens were too small. The rooms were designed primarily for individualized and small-group activities. Teachers who did not teach in that way were bound to encounter some difficulties, frustrations and constraints when they used the rooms.

Other factors which persisted at Southside High were the use of science workbooks, a policy of not setting too much homework for students in grades 8–10, the option for students to refer to teachers by first name and concern for maintaining a caring environment in which students could learn. These factors probably were evident because the first school principal and deputy principal were still at the school, and because Gerry, an influential science teacher, was also one of the foundation staff.

Reference

Tobin, K. and Gallagher, J.J. (1987) 'The role of target students in the science classroom', *Journal of Research in Science Teaching*, 24, pp. 61–75.

Chapter 3: Teacher Mind Frames and Science Learning

Kenneth Tobin

Although the acquisition of higher-level cognitive outcomes has been an intended outcome of high school science programs for many years, the goal appears to have been elusive. Tobin and Gallagher (1987b) reported that Australian high school teachers emphasized activities which focused on rote learning of science facts and algorithms to solve quantitative problems. Teachers were concerned mainly with covering the course content in the time that was allocated. Students also were concerned with getting the work done, obtaining correct answers and receiving satisfactory grades. Little concern was shown for teaching or learning with understanding and the principal driving forces exerted on the implemented curriculum were external examinations and teacher tests, both of which emphasized recall of science facts and the solving of quantitative problems. These tests and examinations were predictable and teachers and students worked hard to be successful on them.

Tobin and Gallagher reported that the activity types which were most prevalent in high school science classes involved the teacher working with the class as a whole group. Whole-class non-interactive and whole-class interactive activities were used as a means of maintaining effective management and covering content. Seatwork activities also were common. These allowed students to work from the textbook and to solve problems from mimeographed sheets, the chalkboard and the textbook. Small-group activities occurred infrequently and usually were confined to the data-collecting components of laboratory activities.

The types of activities prescribed by the teacher constrained the opportunities that students had to learn during class time. Students were placed most often in a situation in which they listened to the teacher or a peer, copied down notes or worked from the textbook. Opportunities to clarify and test understandings were limited, as were opportunities to elaborate, evaluate, synthesize, resolve conflict and reflect on what was being learned. Similarly, laboratory activities usually were not intended to generate new knowledge. Rather, they were designed to confirm knowledge and, in most cases, students followed a recipe to collect data which confirmed content covered earlier in the course.

Tobin and Gallagher (1987b) suggested that most science teachers have a *cultural transmission view* (Pope and Keen, 1981) of teaching in which the teacher is mainly a transmitter of information, rules or values. According to this view, the learner acquires 'absolute truth' by a process of iterative accumulation or absorption. Pope and Gilbert (1983) noted that the epistemological underpinning of this approach is realism. Metaphorically, knowledge is regarded as a fluid entity which can be transferred from the teacher to students.

In contrast, in a *progressivist view* (or *constructivist view*) of teaching, the acquisition of knowledge is an act of change in the pattern of thinking brought about by experiential problem-solving situations. Pope and Gilbert noted that: 'Reality is the interaction of human beings with their environment — by engaging in the reconstruction and interpretation of experiences' (p. 250). This view assumes that meaningful learning occurs as a result of personal actions on data derived from active engagement in activities in which students discuss ideas and problems with their peers, manipulate equipment, work independently, listen to the teacher in whole-class settings and respond to teacher questions. Because knowledge is personalized, active teaching is required to monitor student understandings and to facilitate learning through the use of cues, prompts and clarifications.

The constructivist classroom has the potential to provide an environment in which higher-level cognitive learning is enhanced in science. Although classrooms based on a cultural transmission (or an absorption) model of learning probably would be suitable for learning facts and algorithms which could be used to obtain correct solutions to problems, there would be little scope for students to relate knowledge to prior learning, to clarify understandings and to learn in a meaningful way.

Although students have responsibility for what is learned, teachers have a direct influence on the context in which classroom learning occurs. Consequently, factors likely to influence teacher plans for implementing the curriculum include the beliefs of teachers, metaphors used to conceptualize teaching roles, knowledge of the science content to be taught and knowledge of how to teach specific science content. These cognitive factors that have a direct influence on the manner in which the teacher structures the learning environment are referred to as *teacher mind frames*. Thus, the main purpose of this chapter is to consider teacher mind frames and interpret them from the perspective of, first, what was observed to happen in the two science classrooms involved in this study and, second, what opportunities were provided to facilitate student learning.

According to Schon (1983), teachers have knowledge which enables them to undertake complex tasks in the day-to-day events of their professional lives. Much of this knowledge drives routines which are put into action in an almost unthinking way. In many cases, this knowledge is used in a subconscious way and teachers are unable to explain what they have done during a lesson or why they have done it. Teachers obviously have a great amount of tacit or intuitive knowledge which influences what they and their students do in classrooms.

Studies by Tobin and his colleagues (for example, Tobin and Espinet, 1989) suggest that teachers' beliefs about teaching and learning influence the implemented curriculum in science. The highest level of cognition is represented in a cognitive belief structure which exerts a strong influence on various perceptual and memory operations by processing and retrieving information in ways that are consistent with an individual's existing world view and self-concept. As a consequence, individuals almost always perceive new information in a manner that conforms to their present world view. One explanation of why individuals are so steadfast in maintaining present orientations, conceptions and perspectives in the face of contrary evidence is provided by considering cognitive beliefs. Goodenough (1971) noted that belief systems take on appealing, compelling and emotionally-laden dimensions, and that individuals are reluctant to give them up because of the cognitive disorder that would seem to follow from disbelief. An example of this is Tisher and Power's (1973, 1975) finding that teachers implement the curriculum in a manner which is congruent with their beliefs about teaching. For example, classes taught by teachers who value an inquiry approach to science exhibited both teacher and student behaviours which reflected the process of inquiry. Power (1977) also emphasized the relationship between teachers' beliefs and the implemented curriculum:

> Teacher's beliefs about what constitute the most effective classroom procedures are one of the most potent factors which influence their behaviour and which can influence the degree to which a new curriculum is implemented. (p. 11)

An assumption underlying this study was that many of the teachers' beliefs and knowledge about teaching and learning are metaphorical. The assumption is consistent with the theoretical perspectives of Black (1979), Schon (1979) and Lakoff and Johnson (1980). It is proposed that, as teachers reflect on teaching and consider the various roles that they might adopt, they make sense of their roles by the use of metaphors (Black, 1979; Lakoff and Johnson, 1980). Thus, metaphors underlie the understandings ascribed to important concepts about teaching and learning. When a teacher considers whether or not a particular role is appropriate for use in science teaching, one of the considerations which is brought to bear on the decision is the teacher's personal epistemology (that is, beliefs about the nature of knowledge and how it develops). If the role is consistent with the teacher's personal perspective (Pope and Keen, 1981), the decision might be to adopt the role. However, if the role and the perspective are incompatible, the role might be considered inappropriate. Thus, beliefs about how students learn can have a direct influence on the roles utilized by teachers.

This chapter is devoted to the manner in which Sandra and Peter endeavoured to facilitate meaningful learning of higher-level cognitive goals in a high school science program. The chapter consists of seven sections which describe: the beliefs about teaching and learning held by the two teachers involthed in the study; the metaphors which appeared to underlie the way in which the teachers conceptualized teaching; the images which the teachers projected during instruction; the constraints under which the two teachers operated; planning of the two science topics; the implemented curriculum in each classroom from the perspective of facilitating learning; and conclusions.

Beliefs About Teaching and Learning

Philosophers (for example, Fenstermacher, 1986) and anthropologists (for example, Stefflre, 1965) define a belief as a proposition, or statement of relation among things, accepted as true. To accept a proposition as true is to value it in some way, for logical, empirical, social or emotional reasons. Thus, a belief is a way to describe a relationship between a task, an action, an event or another person, and an attitude of a person towards it (Eisenhart, Shrum, Harding and Cuthbert, in press). For example, the belief that students learn science by listening to the teacher and reading books could link positive attitudes (such as rewarding and gratifying feelings) to activities such as lecturing to students or directing students to read a textbook.

Two procedures were used to infer teacher beliefs and values during this study. First, specific aspects of the classroom observations were discussed with teachers during regular interviews throughout the study. As the teacher explained and justified his/her behaviour in specific situations, beliefs and values were inferred. Second, the repertory grid technique (Munby, 1984) was used to obtain an alternative view of the structure of each teacher's beliefs. The possible meanings and impact of these beliefs on instruction were discussed with each teacher after the repertory grid results were available.

The Repertory Grid Technique

Peter and Sandra were asked to list the events which would occur in a series of general science lessons taught under favourable circumstances to a grade 10 class at Southside High. An event was defined as an activity in which students or the teacher were involved, such as writing, listening and working with equipment. As each teacher described the events which would occur, the researcher recorded each one separately on a card. Care was taken to use the teacher's words in describing each task.

When Peter completed listing the events, he was given the set of cards and asked to arrange the activities using any grouping criteria. In this instance, twenty-one events were sorted into nine groups. Peter then was instructed to explain why the events in each group were classified together. The reasons for classifying the events into the nine groups were noted carefully in the teacher's own words. As one group was being described, Peter thought of another event that would occur in his lessons. This event was added to the list of events and was categorized in the appropriate group. The twenty-two events described by Peter are presented in Table 3.1 and the nine grouping criteria are listed in Table 3.2.

The twenty-two events were listed as the rows of a matrix and the nine grouping criteria comprised the columns. Peter then was asked to enter data into the matrix by indicating the relevance of each grouping criterion to each event using a scale of: 3 = strongly related; 2 = somewhat related; and 1 = not at all related.

Peter's 22 × 9 matrix was factor analyzed using a principal factor analysis with PROMAX rotation to obtain two-, three-, four- and five-factor solutions (see Table 3.3 for the four-factor solution). These solutions were used as a basis for further discussion with Peter. During the discussion of the factor analysis results, Peter was asked to explain which solution was most pleasing to him and why the grouping criteria had clustered in the manner shown by the analyses.

Similar procedures were adopted when Sandra completed the repertory grid activity. She listed twenty-four events which would occur in an ideal sequence of lessons with her grade 10 general science class (see Table 3.4). Twenty-two of the events were listed initially, and two were added during the grouping process when it became apparent to Sandra that she inadvertently had missed them.

When Sandra grouped the twenty-four events, she used four criteria which she described as what students come in with, resources which are needed, management of the program, and student involvement (Table 3.5). As Sandra spoke about the events and the criteria for grouping them, it was evident that she was very concerned that students should learn as a result of their own active engagement in a student-centred environment. Because of the relatively small number of grouping criteria, and because student involvement was rated as highly relevant to each event, Sandra's ratings were not factor analyzed. Visual inspection of the ratings assigned to the three grouping criteria which varied (that is, what students come in with, resources which are needed and management of the program) indicated that what students come in with and management of the program are similar to one another and to student involvement (which had a constant rating of 3).

Table 3.1:   Events which Peter identified using repertory grid technique

Event No.	Event
1	Rapport with students
2	Questions from students
3	Teacher-student interactions
4	Students on-task and involved
5	Teach in same classroom
6	Go off on tangents
7	Lessons are sequenced
8	Rounding off lessons
9	Interact with groups
10	Interact with individuals
11	Challenge students
12	Use different techniques
13	Challenge students to think
14	Get students out of classroom
15	Student-student interactions
16	Write with pens
17	Pages ruled up
18	Work done on time
19	Challenge more-able students
20	Expository approach
21	Hands-on activities
22	Students produce a paper

Table 3.2:   Criteria used to group the twenty-two events identified by Peter

Group Identification	Criterion for Grouping	Event Numbers
A	Interactions	2, 3, 9, 10, 15
B	Standards	16, 17, 18
C	Motivation	4, 11
D	Creating a stimulating learning environment	6, 12, 13, 19
E	Teaching techniques	20, 21, 22
F	Classroom management	7, 8
G	Convenience for teacher	5
H	Total change of learning environment	14
I	Relating to students	1

Table 3.3: Rotated factor pattern coefficients for a four-factor forced solution for Peter's data

Grouping Criterion		**Factor Pattern Coefficients**			
		Factor 1	*Factor 2*	*Factor 3*	*Factor 4*
A	(Interactions)	0.83	0.01	0.24	−0.24
B	(Standards)	−0.06	−0.06	0.67	0.07
C	(Motivation)	0.77	0.24	−0.10	−0.10
D	(Stimulating environment)	−0.05	0.88	−0.10	−0.10
E	(Teaching technique)	0.20	0.75	−0.00	0.01
F	(Classroom management)	0.37	0.45	0.16	0.31
G	(Convenience)	−0.05	−0.01	0.06	0.39
H	(Total change)	0.96	−0.11	−0.21	0.13
I	(Relating to students)	0.89	0.10	0.02	0.01

Table 3.4: Events listed by Sandra during the repertory grid technique

Event No.	Event
1	Students seated in groups
2	Discussing how to solve a problem as a group
3	From a given problem generate a hypothesis for testing
4	Each student would have some input
5	Set up a controlled experiment to test hypothesis
6	Have equipment available
7	Use equipment to solve a problem
8	Collect and record results in a reasonable form
9	Generate further questions to investigate
10	Use additional resources to investigate the problem further
11	Students report to the rest of the class
12	Students question to require justification of result
13	Teacher centred activity to set up the initial problem
14	Write up a report on the investigation
15	Prepare summary version of report to share with others
16	Synthesis activity in which teacher helps students to pull strings together
17	Assess what students have done
18	Different groups take different objectives
19	Investigations in one area lead to investigations in another
20	Students are motivated and keen
21	Problems are interesting
22	Students achieve all objectives through this process
23	Students have prerequisite knowledge
24	Teacher monitors student progress

Table 3.5: Criteria used to group events identified by Sandra

Group Identification	Criterion for Grouping	Event Numbers
A	What students come in with	1, 4, 20, 23
B	Resources which are needed	6, 7, 10
C	Management of the program	13, 16, 17, 18, 21, 24
D	Student involvement	2, 3, 5, 8, 9, 11, 12, 14, 15 19, 22

Peter's Beliefs

The results of the factor analyses for Peter's data (see Table 3.3) indicated that a four-factor solution was interpretable. In actual fact, the two-, three- and five-factor solutions differed only slightly from the preferred four-factor solution in terms of loadings on factors and the way that the criteria clustered. On the basis of the grouping criteria which loaded most heavily, the factors were named *learning*, *teaching*, *standards* and *convenience for the teacher*. The factor pattern loadings contained in Table 3.3 indicate that interactions, motivation, total change of learning environment and relating to students were the criteria most strongly associated with the learning factor (that is, factor 1). The second factor (teaching) was most strongly associated with changing the learning environment to be stimulating, with teaching techniques and with classroom management. Standards was the only criterion associated with the third factor. The fourth factor was defined by convenience for the teacher and classroom management. Classroom management did not load strongly on any of the factors. This probably occurred because the sense in which Peter used the term classroom management related to the way in which the curriculum was implemented. In this sense, the criterion was pervasive and it is little wonder that it loaded on three of the four factors, as management of the implemented curriculum is clearly related to learning, teaching and the convenience of the teacher.

The factor structure is used below as a basis for discussing Peter's beliefs as inferred from the repertory grid analyses, interviews and observations of teaching.

Learning
Peter emphasized the importance of striking up immediate rapport with students. He noted that this usually happened in the first sixty seconds of a lesson and might involve something totally unrelated to the lesson (for example, a joke). Usually the basis for establishing rapport was common ground between the teacher and students, and this might have taken the form of a comment directed to a number of students.

Emphasis also was given to the need to interact with students and to encourage them to interact with one another. In this sense, Peter said that he badgered students to interact and to ask questions. He stated that he 'did not like students who are passive and just want to write. I don't see writing as a very productive exercise'. Later, Peter mentioned that he liked to interact with students in small groups or on a one-to-one basis. He specifically referred to an out-of-school situation in which he had been coaching several students to improve their science:

> If there are just three of you sitting in a room, there are no barriers and you can really get through to them and find out where the problems are and where they need help and really work with them. But you can't in a classroom situation because of the peer group pressure and what have you.

Peter noted that he liked to see students on-task and involved in an intense way. He stated that 'I get a real euphoric surge when kids really get involved in the activity and work to such an extent that your presence in the classroom is no longer required — as if you put the plane on automatic pilot'.

Peter also was critical of the approach used at Southside High whereby students were required to do an enormous amount of writing and 'were not given much time to sit and think about what they're doing'. Peter hoped that there were opportunities for students to interact with one another and the teacher in his classes, but acknowledged that his students were forced into a situation in which they had to learn by rote for tests. In addition, Peter was not enthusiastic about the workbook approach which restricted students to reading and writing and provided them with a 'crutch' which was not available in grades 11 and 12. The requirement to use the workbooks was a constraint which reduced the amount of time which Peter had for interacting with students.

Peter was enthusiastic about the importance of interactions in promoting student learning. He noted that he rarely sat behind the front bench, and that he preferred to be among the students and feel that they could relate to him. He talked disparagingly about the tendency of some teachers to walk into the class, pile their books on the front bench and teach from behind the teacher's demonstration bench. 'The more interaction the better', he noted. During an interview during the Vertebrates topic, Peter commented that:

> I guess a lot of my teaching reflects that I want to interact with the kids. A lot of people would condemn me because I try and interact with them too much. I don't leave them alone to get on with their work. Mind you I have a perception of kids being left alone not doing a lot of work anyway.... I just have this uncontrollable urge to interact with them ... get them away from

those workbooks because I'm not really sold on the workbook approach.

I just have this almost uncontrollable urge always to want to interact with them. And usually, to a large extent, it's me wanting to interact with the entire class. . . . I enjoy that immensely. I like very much their input and I guess as an observer from the outside you'd find that I tend towards those kids who interact with me the most . . . They will respond and they always provide some sort of an answer. But I always make an attempt to drag other kids into it too. But there are obviously kids who feel very threatened by that and I think it's unfair to dwell on them.

Peter liked to focus interactions on students' personal interests and he perceived an immediate increase in student attention when he referred to an out-of-school incident which was relevant to the topic being discussed:

They get a lot from the explanation that the teacher provides as long as it's aimed at a level that they can understand and it's altered so that it is meaningful to them. A lot of teachers just go on with a lot of jargon that's quite irrelevant but, when you can specifically relate things to them and to people in their class, I think it's a much more meaningful learning experience. That's why I like the question and answer session and establishing rapport and firing questions at them. I'm getting questions back from them and engaging them in that. I think that's probably one of the things I'm quite good at in a classroom situation with a class of kids I like working with.

Peter's beliefs also were influenced by his own experience as a high school student when he discovered that learning was meaningful when it was related to personal life experiences. Peter stated:

From my educational experiences as a kid in the classroom, the things that I remember the most were the comments the teacher made that made a lot of it relevant. . . . So you find in my teaching that there are a lot of comments about that . . . Really the intimate detail about whether the fish has got a three-chambered heart or whatever and stuff like that just goes by and by. Some of it would appear again if they go on to do biology in upper school but I think most of it is lost and it's just the little comments along the way that are particularly relevant to them.

Teaching

Peter believed that there was some need for the expository approach in science lessons, although he was quite clear about the futility of too much time being allocated to lectures. He noted that lectures were a way of 'impressing kids with your ability as a teacher and your knowledge of content'. He also noted that 'It's good in a laboratory situation to be able to impress students by displaying your skills by the use of a microscope or something like that'. This quotation provides evidence of Peter's need to gain the respect of students by impressing them with his science-related knowledge and skills.

Some additional insights into Peter's beliefs about teaching and learning were gleaned from several interview comments which alluded to teachers that he did or did not admire. For example, he greatly respected the teaching of Martin, his first head of department, who was a strong 'traditional' teacher who was able to assist grade 12 students to perform at the highest level on external examinations. In contrast, Peter was not impressed with the head of department of the school at which he taught in Canada. He stated that she did not have the necessary experience for the job, that she spoke in a high-pitched voice which was ridiculed by students, and that her mode of teaching was to go into the classroom and cover a part of the textbook. According to Peter, she lectured from beginning to end of the lesson and there were no discussions, no laboratory activities, no slides, no library work and no films. The pace of learning was lockstep and, at the end of the work in a chapter, the students learned by rote for the test.

The above viewpoints were consistent with values which Peter demonstrated in his teaching and in interviews conducted throughout the study. Peter thought that the teaching of biology and human biology to grades 11 and 12 students was more important than teaching general science to grade 10 students, and he valued external examinations and the high standards which were implied in such a system. Also, he did not value lecturing as an effective means of facilitating student learning. Instead, he advocated interactions between students and the teacher, use of audiovisual aids and use of the library.

Much of what Peter said during interviews suggested that his own teaching style was shaped by his experiences as a high school student. Peter noted that, while at school, he was not regarded as one of the brightest students and that he found many aspects of learning quite difficult. He was critical of expository methods of teaching and learning and noted that he could not maintain concentration beyond thirty minutes. Peter's beliefs are encapsulated in the comments provided below:

> How I think that a lot of kids learn is simply from the interaction that occurs between fellow students. When I was in school, I relied to a large extent on a very bright kid with whom I was good friends ... So that's why in just about every lesson I allow large portions of interaction between kids ... I know my mouth runs away with me at times.... But even then I'll stop and allow them twenty minutes, particularly for interaction in small groups.

For example, in the interaction between Rachel and Nicola, Rachel is the bright student and Nicola is not so bright. Nicola is very dependent on Rachel and I see that as a good thing. It's not hindering Rachel and it's helping Nicola immensely. That's why I favour them sitting where they want to sit and organizing themselves ... and allowing a tremendous amount of interaction between individuals who obviously enjoy working with one another.

Despite Peter's belief that students learn best as a result of interacting with peers, he regarded 'lock-step', whole-class teaching as providing a means of monitoring student understanding. Peter noted that:

I must confess that I find it difficult to have a class that's working at its own pace. ... I do like to keep the kids together as much as possible ... because then, as a teacher, I have a far better understanding of where everyone is at in the class.

Standards

Peter believed that he differed from most other teachers at Southside High in terms of the standards to which he adhered. During the interview associated with the repertory grid, he stated:

I'm very much an advocate of standards, I suppose. I could quite easily see myself embracing reintroduction of the old junior examinations at the end of grade 10.

In terms of standards of student work, Peter insisted that students write in pen, as distinct from pencil. He maintained that part of the teacher's role was to convince students that they had the ability to be successful with their work. He believed that using a pen was important because it was an indication that students had the confidence that their work would not have to be erased. Peter also insisted that students rule margins on the left-hand side of their pages to make their work appear neater. The final event which Peter associated with standards was the need to submit work on time. On one occasion, he related this need to his personal inconvenience of having to assess work that was not submitted on time.

Convenience for the teacher

Peter commented that fewer laboratory activities were being conducted because of the distance of some of his teaching rooms from the central equipment store. Because of the time constraints under which he worked and the relatively long distance over which equipment had to be transported, his inclination was to adopt other methods of covering the work. Scheduling his program into more than one room also influenced the manner in which the curriculum was implemented in other ways as well.

For example, he noted that he did not set up aquaria and displays and that reorganizing furniture for alternative grouping arrangements was inconvenient because of the probable impact on others using the same classroom.

When the classroom management criterion was formulated, Peter referred to the sequencing and completion of lessons, not to the disciplining of students. However, when Peter completed the grid, he appeared to broaden the definition of management to include management of students. Thus, events such as keeping students on-task and involved, teaching in the same classroom, interacting with individuals, using different strategies and challenging students to think were all rated as being strongly associated with classroom management. The use of the broader definition probably explains why the criterion was moderately associated with three of the four factors.

Sandra's Beliefs

During the repertory grid activity, Sandra began by describing how students would be grouped for science. From that moment on, she focused on student involvement in activities related to designing and implementing solutions to given problems. The essence of Sandra's beliefs about learning is contained in the following comment:

> If kids do something for themselves they remember it better. The way to learn best is by doing it, writing it in their words, discussing it with the person next to them, asking a question or explaining it to someone else.

Sandra advocated problem-solving activities in which students had access to resources such as textbooks, reference books, equipment and the teacher. She perceived the purpose of the resources to be the facilitation of learning, which clearly was conceived of in terms of student involvement. In Sandra's ideal class, students would identify problems, design controlled investigations, use equipment to collect data, record the findings of the investigation, report the findings to peers and justify the conclusions. When describing her ideal class, Sandra said that, if students could move through the activities efficiently, achieve the objectives and be accurate in their work, she would arrange for them to have small-group discussions in which they could go over the work and ensure that they really understood it. She emphasized the importance of students working out things for themselves and helping others to learn. Sandra noted that 'by finding out the information for themselves, they work through the material once but, if they explain it to someone else, they must really understand it'. Students would not have to undertake every investigation because Sandra believed that they would learn from one another as they shared their findings in an environment characterized by debate and questions requiring explicit evidence to support findings. In this manner, all students learned as a result of their own investigations and those of their peers. Although this type of learning was seen as being better than rote learning, Sandra acknowledged that rote learning was necessary to pass the end-of-topic examinations.

Sandra recognized the constraints of having to prepare students for end-of-topic examinations which emphasized recall of science facts. During an interview, Sandra commented that:

> The optional activities are excellent. The activities such as the one that Peter did yesterday, that I gave him the other day, that my kids will be doing as a next assignment, etc. are very important. But you've also got to give them content. And you don't want to disadvantage the kids at the end of the year. They need to know that they're going to get sufficient content for that test at the end because that is one of the things used to compare them with other students activities and yet, on the other hand, you'd like to do a lot more of the optional activities. And every now and then I think it would be better to take three weeks and 'chalk and talk' them through the content and give yourself two weeks to do the options. I haven't quite got to that point yet, but I'm working towards it.

Even though the tests assessed facts about science, Sandra recognized that the way in which she organized the class during Vertebrates and Nuclear Energy was not efficient for learning facts. With specific reference to Nuclear Energy, she noted that she looked for different types of outcomes in her science classes:

> It's a difficult topic because there is just so much factual information that was outlined in their objectives. And the really good kids can learn that all off by heart and the less able kids are going to learn the factual information, but they might not be able to use it and might just give it back to you. So I look for different things. I accept that they will learn a certain amount of factual things but, given five weeks and given that mode of working in groups, it's not as efficient in terms of learning lots of little facts. In the long run, [I expect them to learn] that there are naturally occurring atoms and isotopes which produce radiation, and that either using naturally occurring isotopes or making our own can lead to beneficial use of radioisotopes. The dominant view about nuclear energy is that it's wrong and its dangerous. If nothing else, I would like them to come out of it recognizing that there can be neutral purposes and there can be beneficial purposes of our knowledge of nuclear energy.

Sandra was critical of the time which students spent writing during science lessons. In an evaluation of the Nuclear Energy topic, she said: 'They did all that written work, but you wonder how much they really learned. It's a fundamental flaw in our organization of grade 10.' She felt that at least half of the students would not understand the concepts taught in the topic because there was too much to learn in a five-week period. She would like to see changes in the approach taken so that students could be more active in their learning by engaging in more research (that is, using references, magazines and newspapers), more hands-on activities and more enrichment work for the more able students.

Sandra perceived science knowledge as a product of scientific thought and endeavour and emphasized the fact that science knowledge changed with time. She felt that this type of awareness should be an outcome of a science program:

> If you learn it by heart, in fifteen years or twenty-five years your kids might learn something else by heart. Things will change as a result of the way that scientists work. It's not something that's static. Kids at grade 12 need to be reminded constantly that this is where it is at, at the moment. They need to do experiments, even though they're not really doing it as a scientist; at least they can see that it's not a static subject ... Ideally it should happen all the time, but it's something that has to happen over a year's time. Kids would feel uncomfortable with too much. They would come and say 'What do I have to know? What's the real answer?' And they want a definite one-liner that they can write down as right.

In accordance with a belief that students should have opportunities to develop understandings about science, Sandra frequently provided students with direct experiences in the form of teacher demonstrations and laboratory activities. Sandra perceived her role in terms of monitoring student progress, assessing learning, providing resources when they were requested and assisting students to synthesize findings from a set of investigations. During an interview, Sandra was asked why she had utilized a joint, a lung and a heart in consecutive lessons in the one week. Sandra responded:

> The reason is to get the kids more involved in handling and less involved in copying down. And I really think that in the long run it should mean that students remember difficult information if they have actually gone through it themselves rather than writing it and memorizing it ... When I was a student, when I actually did it myself, I found out more than I would have found out by just hearing it.

Sandra's teaching and her responses to interview questions indicated that she firmly believed that students should progress at their own rates in their science activities. Thus, students were organized into groups so that they could collaborate on their work and help one another learn. Sandra perceived her role in terms of monitoring student progress and helping each student to learn by answering questions and providing information as each student recognized the need. Even though this procedure resulted in Sandra answering most questions many times, she was prepared to defend her approach to teaching and learning and she intended to use this style of teaching again when she next taught Vertebrates and Nuclear Energy. During an interview she was asked why she didn't answer questions just once for the whole class. Sandra replied:

> The students who were ready would have asked the question. Other students would be asked to stop when it's not really relevant to them. The students who aren't up to that point won't absorb the information as they aren't able to relate to it. You find that, twenty minutes later or the next day, it will come up again. Or you will find that they have put down a slightly disjointed version because they've heard it but, because they haven't covered the preceding information, they will have a hard time following it. So that's why I wouldn't do it all together.

During her teacher education program, Sandra had opportunities to observe a range of teaching styles. 'There is no one style of teaching; ... there are many styles', remarked Sandra. She expressed the view that one style of teaching should not be judged as better than another. A particular style might suit a specific teacher and class but not be at all suited to other teachers and classes. Sandra had a strong aversion to whole-class activities. Although she used whole-class activities for short periods of time in both topics, and had used whole-class activities predominantly in topics such as Chemistry, she did not believe that students learned effectively with them. In an evaluation of her teaching of Nuclear Energy, Sandra commented on the extent to which a few students were able to monopolize her time in individualized activities as they endeavoured to understand concepts such as half life. She went on to say:

> You can do it as a whole-class thing, but I think the same kids are going to get the same out of it ... By doing the whole-class thing you're not really helping because they've got a slightly different misconception and a slightly different way of looking at it. ... Then you go around and still find that kids have other misconceptions that I hadn't covered until I talked to them.

Thus, Sandra's preference to avoid whole-class activities was based on the value that she attached to students' understanding of their work. She realized that each person constructed his/her own personal understandings of science concepts and, because of this fact, the best way to deal with misconceptions was to work with students on an individual basis. In her discussions of whole-class activities, Sandra did not advocate their use. On the contrary, she indicated that learning in whole-class activities was often a passive affair. In a discussion with a member of the research team, Sandra commented on the extent to which students had grasped the concept of half-life. She noted that:

> I'm not sure that I got enough of that through. I don't think that there was much of it in the book. When I mention it orally half the class listen sufficiently and the other half sort of listen, but I'm not really sure how much they're listening really. You can have them quiet but I'm not really sure whether they really take it in and keep it. You sort of hope that, if it keeps happening often enough, eventually it'll soak in.

In her final comment, Sandra describes learning in a whole-class activity metaphorically in terms of a physical entity, a fluid. Her somewhat frustrated comment seems to suggest that whole-class teaching is an approach which she has tried with little success. The comment reflects the value that Sandra attaches to students being overtly involved in problem-solving activities and progressing at their own pace.

Sandra's beliefs about teaching and learning were of a constructivist nature. She valued students being involved in activities from which they would learn and perceived her teaching role in terms of facilitating the process of learning. Her beliefs about what students ought to learn were consistent with her perceptions of what she believed that they would need when they left school. She did not perceive science as a body of knowledge which was immutable; rather, she wanted students to be involved in the processes of science, develop the intellectual skills associated with doing science and create science content as a result of doing activities. Her belief was that science with a problem-solving orientation was preferable for students in grade 10. However, other beliefs about her role as a teacher and head of department also influenced what and how she taught.

As a head of department, Sandra recognized that she had opportunities to modify the curriculum to accord better with her beliefs about what ought to be in the science curriculum. However, Sandra also recognized a need for the school to have a consistent policy about the curriculum and she valued democratic decision-making within the science department. As a consequence, she recognized that the majority of the science staff wanted to teach in the manner which had become the tradition at Southside High. This tradition involved the use of workbooks and a style of teaching and learning that was essentially self-paced. Clearly these beliefs took precedence over her beliefs about teaching and learning and what students ought to learn. As a consequence, compromises were made to the implemented curriculum to accord with the views of other science staff, the traditional approach at Southside High and other forces which act to influence the implemented curriculum.

A Comparison of the Beliefs of Peter and Sandra

Peter and Sandra both appeared to have constructivist beliefs about student learning which emphasized the importance of interactions between students and with the teacher. Both teachers referred to the importance of students constructing their own understanding of science knowledge. However, beliefs about the teacher's role in facilitating learning provided an area in which the two teachers appeared to differ.

When Peter discussed his teaching role, he projected himself as the educational leader whose actions made it possible for students to learn. Emphasis was given to the needs of the *teacher* in terms of presenting content, interacting with students and being inconvenienced by a variety of factors. Sandra explained her role as a facilitator of student learning. At all times, she stressed the involvement and potential difficulties of the *students* and the procedures that she should adopt to facilitate learning for individuals.

Sandra's beliefs about the transitory nature of scientific knowledge were explained on several occasions during interviews. Sandra viewed science as a process and her beliefs about the roles of the teacher and learner in science classes were consistent with this view. In her ideal curriculum, Sandra envisaged students being involved in a self-paced manner and solving problems which had personal relevance to them. Under these ideal circumstances, Sandra's role would be to assist students to understand the science underlying the problems which they were attempting to solve and to utilize process skills.

Peter's ideal curriculum also would have involved students working with materials to solve problems which had relevance to the world outside of the classroom. Concrete evidence of Peter's ideal curriculum was the Science of Sailing topic which he designed and implemented as an option to follow Nuclear Energy. However, Peter did not attach the same importance as Sandra to the view that science was a process and that science knowledge changed over time. Although Peter stated that science content was emphasized to the detriment of science processes, he did not use this viewpoint to justify the level of emphasis in his ideal or implemented curriculum. He appeared resigned to allowing his science lessons to remain the way that they were. Observations of Peter's lessons during Vertebrates and Nuclear Energy indicated that the implemented curriculum concerned learning of science content and that little emphasis was given to acquiring or applying process skills.

Both teachers used metaphors to describe the way in which they managed the science classroom. These metaphors were evident in discussions with teachers and in actions when they taught.

The Metaphorical Nature of Teaching

Lakoff and Johnson (1980) emphasized the importance of metaphor in providing partial understanding of one kind of experience in terms of another kind of experience. Lakoff and Johnson regard metaphor as essential to human understanding and as a mechanism for creating new realities. Metaphor pervades the conceptual system and is the primary mechanism for understanding. Lakoff and Johnson stated that:

> Metaphors may create realities for us, especially social realities. A metaphor may thus be a guide for future action. Such actions will, of course, fit the metaphor. This will, in turn, reinforce the power of the metaphor to make experience coherent. In this sense metaphors can be self-fulfilling prophesies. (p. 156)

Metaphors Underlying Peter's Teaching

Peter's teaching behaviour was influenced by metaphors that he used to conceptualize teaching. Peter described his teaching role in terms of two metaphors: the teacher as *Entertainer* (in that 'teaching is like acting; you're like an actor on a stage and you've got to sell your performance'); and the teacher as *Captain of the Ship*. During an interview with two of the research team during the Vertebrates topic, Peter described the way in which he used both metaphors to justify his approach in a particular activity:

> I think of teaching pretty much as performing. . . . I do love interacting with students. It was my way of stopping the class and pulling about eight kids out of the class, to do an activity which involved these students and also the entire class, that had me, I guess, as the sort of captain of the ship out the front and directing. . . . I get a lot of the adrenalin surge out of teaching. I am the kind of teacher who does love to direct and dominate.

The observations and interviews suggest that these metaphors influenced the way in which Peter perceived his role and the way in which he taught. In a particular activity, Peter appeared to teach according to the metaphor that he used to conceptualize teaching at that particular time. For example, when he was entertaining the class, he was humorous, interactive and amenable to student noise and risque behaviour. On such occasions, he often sang, or threatened to sing, and once he sang and played a guitar. For example, during a discussion on uranyl nitrate, Peter said that he was reminded of a Diana Ross song which he would sing except that he had forgotten the lyrics. On another occasion, Peter said 'Be quiet or I'll commit you to a fate worse than death'. Immediately the students began to chant: 'Peter, Peter, Peter'. Peter said 'No, I only know love songs and I'm not going to do that here'. Peter as Entertainer quipped his way through whole-class activities and socialized with students during seatwork activities. The teacher and the students were relaxed, but little work was accomplished.

As the Captain of the Ship, Peter was assertive and business-like. He was in charge of the class and emphasized whole-class activities in order to maintain control of a teacher-centred and teacher-paced learning environment. While Peter was Captain of the Ship, he was particularly severe on students who stepped out of line and often scolded them in a strong voice. In this mode, he tended to call on non-volunteers and ensured that all students listened and participated in an appropriate manner. When Peter was Captain of the Ship, most content was covered and the class resembled a traditional classroom with students mainly listening to the teacher perform in an expository manner. Peter said that:

> The teacher has to be in charge, in control. Different teachers have different abilities to be able to let things go and then bring them back. And some people can do that all the way through a lesson and other people can't even do it once. So it's all tied up with the magnetism, the rapport and the respect which I guess that those kids have for you as a person, as an individual, as a teacher. Some of the things that I did in the classroom, I wouldn't dream of doing on a Friday afternoon because it's Friday afternoon. You let them go and you're gone. You've got to sense how well they're responding to you. I mean that, if they respond and you let them go and they don't respond, you haul in the reins and you hang on for the rest of the session. A lot of it is your perceptions of what they're like on that particular day. That's part of good teaching I suppose.

This study suggests that Peter's teaching behaviour was driven by the metaphors which he used to conceptualize teaching. Considerable research needs to be done in order to identify other metaphors that science teachers use regarding teaching and learning and the science concepts that they endeavour to teach. In this study, we observed that Peter taught in quite different ways which were in accord with a change in metaphor. An assertion which needs to be investigated is that a change of metaphor could result in sustained changes in teaching behaviour. If this were the case, approaches to science teacher education could be improved substantially by focusing on a variety of metaphors for teaching.

A Metaphor Underlying Sandra's Teaching

Sandra's teaching was influenced by the metaphor of *Teacher as Resource* in both topics. Sandra made herself available to students and assisted them to complete the work and understand science. The metaphor appeared to define her role and constrain her from behaving in certain ways. For example, few whole-class activities were conducted in the ten weeks of instruction and, when they did occur, they were designed to clarify the schedule or provide details related to the administration of the program. Of particular note was Sandra's non-initiating role as she moved from one individual to another throughout each lesson. Her role usually was responsive and reactive rather than initiating. In particular, extension and elaboration were left to other resources such as the text-book, the workbook or reference books. In addition, unless students specifically requested help, Sandra was unlikely to diagnose partial under-standings or misunderstandings. Her monitoring style appeared to be related to whether students were on-task or off-task and not to whether students understood the science underlying the activities in which they engaged.

Sandra endeavoured to provide all students with equal access to her attention during activities. This tendency to check on all students, even if they were working, deprived Sandra of time to reflect and to assist those who needed additional assistance. In a discussion of her strategy of moving continuously around the classroom, Sandra noted that:

> I always feel bad because I haven't been far enough. You count up mentally the number of times that you've been to each student ... and whether you've seen each person. For example, Mike, Digby and the two girls seem to organize themselves so well that you'll get ten minutes into the lesson and you'll realize you haven't seen them yet. They stay on-task, bar the occasional lesson, and consequently they're the ones you feel you're leaving out. And yet, when you go over and ask, or just look over their shoulder, they say that they are OK and they keep going.

Sandra was untiring in her efforts to share the teacher resource among the student consumers. To the extent that she was free to do so, Sandra responded to student needs by asking questions, providing explanations and generally assisting students to remain cognitively active. Her Teacher as Resource role is illustrated in the pattern of movement during the Nuclear Energy topic (see Table 3.6). Sandra visited each group on at least one occasion and visited three of the groups on seven

Table 3.6: Sandra's pattern of movement between groups

Group	Purpose	Group	Purpose
7	Management	4	Understanding
5	Management	2	Social
7	Management	6	Understanding
3	Understanding	7	Understanding
2	Understanding	8	Understanding
1	Understanding	3	Understanding
2	Management	5	Understanding
7	Management	2	Understanding
8	Management	1	Understanding
7	Understanding	7	Understanding
4	Understanding	5	Management
3	Understanding	6	Understanding
2	Understanding	5	Understanding
7	Understanding	5	Management
8	Understanding	3	Understanding
5	Management	2	Management
8	Management	1	Understanding
3	Understanding	2	Management
5	Management	4	Management

separate occasions. The pattern represents one of constant movement around the class. Even when Sandra visited a group, she usually interacted with two or three of the students at the table on an individual basis. Few visits to groups exceeded thirty seconds in duration.

Sandra's assertive and resourceful role in the classroom is well illustrated in the following transcript of several minutes from a lesson on Nuclear Energy. After a brief three-minute introduction in which she reminded students of their working schedule, Sandra began moving about the classroom, assisting students who had their hands raised and moving close to students who appeared to be restless or off-task.

> *Male student:* How come there are no smoke stacks?
> *Sandra:* Why do you have smoke stacks in these?
> *Male student:* Because you're doing it by heat, coal or whatever you call it.
> *Sandra:* So you're burning a fuel.
> *Male student:* Yeh. And this one? That's heating isn't it?
> *Sandra:* ... and it's heating, but is there any burning?
> *Male student:* Uh uh [shakes his head].
> *Sandra:* Any carbon dioxide produced?
> *Male student:* So doing it by a reactor instead of a ...
> *Sandra:* Yeh. Yeh.

Sandra then dealt with a management matter relating to the choice of reference books and moved to answer the next question:

Female student: The mechanism of an atom bomb starts with an atom which is unstabilized and shoots out a neutron which starts a chain reaction.

Sandra: Good.

Female student: This lets out energy.

Sandra: Good.

Female student: Which starts it again.

Sandra: Good!

Female student: Is that right?

Sandra: Yes. So that tells you how you get a chain reaction. OK. In an atom bomb you want a big enough chain reaction that is uncontrolled.

Female student: Right.

Sandra: So to make it a big enough one you need enough uranium nuclei.

Female student: Yeh.

Sandra: So that wherever the neutrons go ...

Female student: Yep.

Sandra: ... they're going to hit something.

Female student: Right.

Sandra: So if you make sure it's a big enough mass ... you have a mass larger than what they call a critical mass. Critical mass is that borderline value. Below the critical mass you'll get your chain reaction but it fizzles out.

Female student: Yep.

Sandra: Above the critical mass it keeps going in an uncontrolled way. So with your bomb you start with two masses separate ...

Female student: Yep.

Sandra: ... both less than the critical mass.

Female student: Uh uh.

Sandra: When the bomb detonates you put them together. At that stage it becomes started off and it will become uncontrolled.

Female student: When it's over the critical mass?

Sandra: Yes. Over the critical mass. That critical mass is the critical word.

At that Sandra walked off with a laugh. She dealt with two management matters and then moved to Wayne who had his hand raised:

Wayne: When do you find out all of this information?

Sandra: It's really just asking you to think about what you already know.

Wayne: Nothing.

Sandra: In which case you have a nice essay to do for me by Friday. That little essay topic which asks you to research or find out more about nuclear testing and ...

Wayne: If I knew about this I wouldn't be here learning about it.

Sandra: You what?

Wayne: If I knew about this I wouldn't be here learning about it now.

Sandra: If you knew about the science of providing nuclear energy you wouldn't be learning about it. But this isn't just the science. This is general knowledge, current affairs, isn't it?

Wayne: Not for me ...

Sandra: This is relating to argument ...

Wayne: I've done that then ...

Sandra: Your ideas.

Wayne: That's all I know.

Sandra: Then you put down ...

Wayne: That's all my ideas ...

Sandra: No it's not ... You do have ideas, like it or not. You think. You make some ideas between now and when you finish this topic. So you've got some ideas of how things work

She then left Wayne, dealt with two further management related matters and spoke with another male student who had his hand raised:

Male student: What could be ...?

Sandra: What can start moving?

Male student: Yeh. I don't know.

Sandra: Think about anything that moves in the kitchen. That moves then you use it or whatever.

Male student: Ah! A beater.

Sandra: A beater. And what energy creates the moving energy?

Male student: Electrical.

Sandra: Good. Francesco. What are you doing?

During the above five-minute segment of the lesson, Sandra dealt with four questions related to the Nuclear Energy topic. In each case, she avoided a temptation to give the students an answer that they could remember and write directly into their notebooks. Instead, she endeavoured to get them to speak and think about the question. Her own questions and explanations were designed to channel student thinking along productive lines. In the case of the female student asking about the atom bomb, Sandra ascertained that she knew about a chain reaction, but probably had not grasped the concept of critical mass. Having allowed the student to explain how the chain reaction was involved in the bomb, Sandra elaborated on the answer in a manner that was understood by the student, who was then able to write the answer to the question in her own words. The discussion involving the source of movement energy provided an example of a student who had a mental block. He didn't know how to start to answer the question. In this instance, Sandra simply posed another question to get him started. The tactic worked and he was able to proceed to answer the question.

The discussion with Wayne took quite a different form. In a sense, Wayne was challenging Sandra's role as a stimulator of thinking. Essentially Wayne was requesting Sandra to adopt a different teaching role. He regarded himself as an 'empty vessel in need of topping up with knowledge'. Sandra did not succumb to his requests for the correct answers, but restated the task for him and indicated in firm terms how he should make a start.

Discussion of Metaphors for Teaching

Peter and Sandra both used metaphors to conceptualize their teaching roles, and these conceptualizations had a strong bearing on the way in which the curriculum was implemented. However, other cognitive factors also influenced how Peter and Sandra taught. Routines associated with roles associated with life outside of the classroom also appeared to be influential.

Images Projected by Teachers During Instruction

Teachers have lives outside of the classroom and, as well as assuming the role of teacher, they also assume roles in business, social, sporting, family and political facets of their lives. Images projected in these various roles evolve over the years and become a part of a person's 'self'. As a teacher moves from one activity to another throughout the day, images which are projected consciously during one activity might be suppressed in another or might be evident but less prominent. In other instances, a teacher consciously might project an image from another role in order to gain the respect of colleagues, students or individuals.

During an interview, Peter said that he hoped that students perceived him as a person not just as a teacher, and that they saw him as approachable and someone with whom they could talk. He wanted them to see him in different roles, such as a father and as a person interested in photography. As he taught, Peter projected these and a multitude of other images such as: an outdoors type of person; someone appealing to women; a family man; a scientist with expertise in biology/anatomy; an entertainer; a leader; one of the boys; an important teacher in the school; an anti-nuclear advocate; a person in control; and a person who is 'with it' and can bridge the generation gap. In contrast, Sandra projected images which were more consistent with nurturing learning.

Images Projected by Peter While Teaching

The way that Peter taught was influenced by images which he attempted to project to students. As a validity check on the extent to which the above images were projected in class, the researcher arranged for Peter to ask his grade 10 class to verify whether or not the images were apparent to them. The reaction of the class was a surprise to Peter. He stated that:

> I was surprised at how unanimous the kids were at agreeing with them. I left the appealing to women until last — there was a very mixed reaction to that.

Peter was concerned with his image within the school and often presented himself to the class as a tough, outdoors person who was very masculine. For example, during the Nuclear Energy topic, he sat between Mike and Jeffrey. The seat wobbled as he sat on it. Immediately he sprang to his feet, grasped the chair by the legs, wrenched one leg from it and placed the stool on the front bench for all to see. 'There', he exclaimed 'that is the best way to get rid of broken furniture. Otherwise it stays around for a long time'. This incident was typical of the 'macho' image that Peter projected in a number of science lessons.

Peter often referred to his family life and his appearance during lessons. He mentioned his wife and young children and told students of incidents associated with his previous teaching appointments, particularly his teaching appointment in Canada. The effects of these tales were generally positive and added a human dimension to Peter as far as the students were concerned. However, the tales about life in Canada were regarded as tedious by many students.

Peter worked hard to project and promote himself as a scientist with expertise in biology. During the Vertebrates topic, he constantly referred to his work at university and his major in anatomy. Such references seemed to be designed to enhance his credibility and gain the respect of students. Peter associated knowledge of science facts with being a scientist and, during the Vertebrates topic, he appeared to try to impress students with his presentation of complex terminology which he remembered from his anatomy courses. He often wore a laboratory coat during science classes and, in the context of promoting himself as a scientist, he referred on several occasions to his experiences with 'human cadavres'. During the Nuclear Energy topic, Peter often referred to the course which he had designed related to the science of sailing. On this occasion, he projected himself as a capable scientist who had designed his own science curriculum.

Peter's principal mode of knowledge transmission was in whole-class interactive activities. He systematically called on students with their hands down, but also allowed students such as Jeffrey and Diane (who almost always volunteered to be involved) to be very active in whole-class interactions. However, Peter frequently was sarcastic and some of his remarks, which sometimes were belittling and sexist, could have discouraged some students from volunteering to contribute.

When Peter moved around the classroom during seatwork activities, he interacted with female students to a greater extent than he did with male students. He regularly took time to speak with eight girls whom he described as being vivacious. At times, Peter seemed to project himself in a manner that was slightly risque and suggestive. Some of his comments (for example, 'Here's the chalk for your hot little hand') were greeted with giggling and sniggering on the part of students. Several of the girls in the class appeared to anticipate such comments and they looked for opportunities to misinterpret what Peter said, as was the case in the interaction below:

Peter: Have you paid up yet?
Nicola: That's disgusting. [She laughs loudly along with her friends.]
Peter: ... for the excursion.

For some time after the incident, Nicola continued to laugh and reiterate that his comment was disgusting. Although Nicola's behaviour in this instance was immature, having misinterpreted Peter's initial question, Peter 'played along' in his follow-up response and did nothing to discourage her continued remarks about the comment. Nicola's behaviour became increasingly disruptive, not only to her own work, but to the work of other students as well.

On other occasions, Nicola was the target for belittling remarks from Peter. As she endeavoured to answer a question in a whole-class mode on one occasion, Peter interrupted to ask 'What exactly are you talking about? What are two advantages of fusion? What do you mean by that?' Not surprisingly, Nicola did not provide any further response to Peter's questions and she could have felt put down by his public treatment of her.

Some of Peter's remarks seemed to draw attention to himself. For example, when commencing a review lesson on Nuclear Energy, he remarked: 'Don't start clapping slowly will you. You'll have to throw money before I start taking my clothes off.' Later in the lesson, Peter started to sing ('I wanna bop with you baby all night long ...') as he approached Diane. He then retorted 'It's all right Diane, don't get excited'. Other students, such as Britta, Rachel, Danielle and Christine were also the targets for some risque interactions involving Peter during a number of lessons.

In his interactions with the research team, Peter projected himself as a person who is attracted to females. The following segment of an

interview typifies his attitudes to some of the female students whom he
taught:

> *Interviewer:* How do you usually deal with the situation when male
> students socialize with females in the class?
>
> *Peter:* Ah, little Greg who sits at the front likes to wander down
> and talk to Nicola ...
>
> *Interviewer:* Nicola, yeh.
>
> *Peter:* ... and Nicola's a rather gorgeous kid. If I was Greg I'd be
> down there every second five minutes too.
>
> *Interviewer:* Uh huh ... that's right. I remember that one too.
>
> *Peter:* I mean I'm not that old and sort of over the hill ... In the
> past I probably would've jumped on the kid for something like
> that, but now it's more a light-hearted approach.... [I'd say to
> Greg] that, if I was your age I wouldn't want to be drifting down
> there. I'd want to sit beside my doll and just gaze into her eyes
> right through the entire session.... And that embarrasses the kid
> like hell.... But really I'm trying to say to him that I don't think
> it's on. I really don't think you can afford to do that and still get
> through your work.

Peter's projected images could represent attempts to gain the respect
of students. Other teachers in the school occupied senior positions in
science education and had authored science textbooks, State Education
Department curriculum materials and the workbooks which were used.
Peter's attempts to present himself as a scientist might have been associated with a desire to be recognized by students as an important and
competent teacher in the school. His other projected images also might
have been associated with attempts to be regarded by students as a 'good
fellow'. His physical aggression with the chair might appeal to fifteen
year-olds as the type of thing that a male student would do to impress his
peer group. Similarly, the suggestive comments that he made in class,
particularly to female students, could represent attempts at bridging the
generation gap.

Images Projected by Sandra while Teaching

Sandra was sincere, caring, interested, scientific and authoritative as she
moved about the classroom and provided assistance to students. She
listened in a courteous and patient manner to each student who requested
her presence or assistance. Sandra noted that the more she came to know
students the more she empathized with their personal situations and
became hesitant to demand too much of them. At the same time she
realized that she should not lower her expectations because it was better
to have high expectations so that students could rise to the challenge and

achieve at a higher level. Sandra always appeared to know what she was doing and exhibited an array of attitudes such as an inquiring and open mind.

Constraints to the Implemented Curriculum

A thread which permeated the interviews with teachers was a belief that teaching in schools is a matter of making the most of constraints (that is, the cognitive constructions of teachers which prevent them from doing what they believe they ought to be doing). Factors which constrained Peter and Sandra from doing what they believed they should be doing are discussed in this section.

Despite Peter's desire to make science content relevant, to allow students to learn from their interactions with others and to allow them to work at their own pace from the workbooks, his lessons were characterized by teacher controlled instruction and an emphasis on rote learning of facts. Apparently, the constraints of teaching at Southside High School, particularly the need to use workbooks, resulted in a curriculum which differed from his ideal. Peter was not keen to use the workbooks, but was required to because the science staff had made a commitment to use them and had paid for new workbooks to be produced at the time of the study. In addition, because a common examination was set for all grade 10 students, Peter believed that his students would be disadvantaged relative to students in other classes if they did not cover all of the content likely to be examined.

In both topics, Peter's class did not complete all of the core and option activities intended by him. From the outset of each topic, Peter indicated to students what work had to be done, what would receive less emphasis and what would be omitted. However, as each topic progressed, the class lagged behind the schedule and content previously identified as important was covered in a relatively short period of time. For example, during the Vertebrates topic, Peter noted that the class probably would not have time to do an activity involving testing for food types. He said that he might bring in one tray and allow students to do one test. In that case, he said, the class could do the topic of excretion on Friday and the topic of reproduction on Monday. During an interview, Peter made the following remarks in relation to the pacing of the Vertebrates topic:

> The problem with this topic is that the time has just fallen away on us. And I didn't realize. I'm in my first year in the school and I'm teaching these topics for the first time, because the workbooks are all specific to a particular school and I maintain that a teacher really doesn't know what's in the workbooks until he

has taught with them. It's fine to pick up a workbook and flip through it, but you have to go through the physical exercise of teaching it before you really know what's in that workbook. Time has run away from us and I guess that what should be placed first and foremost is the completion of the workbook, because that is practically what the test is based on.

In an interview, Peter indicated that the food testing laboratory activity was something that he 'just wanted to get through quickly' and he said that he did not expect students to benefit from the activity to a great extent. He noted that:

[I expect them to remember] ... very little — just the fact that we use indicators to test for certain foods, and that there are different food types. I can't see the value of having them spend a lot of time fiddling with those activities. The activities need to be controlled closely by the teacher, otherwise the kids lose sight of where they are going.

Peter was constrained in the way in which he taught because of the design of the classrooms at Southside High School. Because the original design did not incorporate chalkboards as a prominent feature of the science classroom, Peter attempted to use the overhead projector to replace the missing chalkboards. Interestingly, the lack of chalkboards did not prompt Peter to change his approach to teaching in fundamental ways as had been the case when Southside High was established. Probably his beliefs about teaching would have resulted in self-paced learning not being considered as a realistic alternative. Peter noted that:

I must confess that I find it difficult to have a class that's working at its own pace. I do like to keep the kids together as much as possible because then, as a teacher, I have a far better understanding of where everyone is at in the class.

On numerous occasions, Peter indicated that he was not implementing the curriculum in the manner that he considered ideal. The constraints that Peter felt are well illustrated in the following quotation from an interview:

It would be my dream, if I ever got away from the shackles of a big science department like I'm in here at the moment and if I got into a small district high school, probably to write my own course on getting kids to immerse themselves in experimental design and setting up experiments.

There was evidence to suggest that Sandra also was constrained from implementing the curriculum in a way that she considered ideal. Throughout the repertory grid activity, Sandra focused on describing her ideal grade 10 curriculum at Southside High. At a glance, Sandra's implemented curriculum appeared to have many of the characteristics advocated for the ideal curriculum. Students worked in groups, assisted one another to complete the work and worked at their own pace. Sandra adopted the monitoring role which she perceived as most appropriate and moved continuously about the classroom. However, students did not engage in the manner envisaged in Sandra's ideal classroom. The activities in the workbooks were not challenging enough for the majority of the students as most activities involved recalling factual information and copying information from a textbook or reference book. In addition, several students were not motivated to learn science, others did not possess prerequisite knowledge and skills, most did not have input into a group problem-solving process and nearly all students had a social agenda to which they attended in a disruptive manner.

The decision to assess all students with a common examination at the conclusion of each topic also shaped the implemented curriculum. Because the examination emphasized recall of factual information, the curriculum provided opportunities for students to learn the content needed to be successful on the examination. Sandra felt that the workbooks contained too much content for the time available, and that the need to cover it in order to prepare students for tests resulted in too little time being available for optional activities which emphasized problem-solving to a greater extent. According to Sandra and a number of students who were interviewed, most activities in the workbook were not interesting and involved the use of equipment only occasionally. Thus, the emphasis on preparing students for end-of-topic tests and the reliance on workbooks produced a curriculum in which students were not free to pursue problems which they perceived to be interesting or particularly demanding.

Although Sandra answered many questions each lesson, most were at a low level of cognitive demand. Almost all of the questions were initiated by students and were related specifically to completing activities in the workbooks. Because of the demands of maintaining an environment conducive to learning, it would have been difficult for Sandra to have engaged students with higher-level cognitive questions. Her time was occupied completely with answering questions raised by students who were attempting to complete workbook activities and with circulating around the room so as to minimize disruptive behaviour.

Sandra noted that peer pressure was one reason for using the workbooks. However, when it was suggested that Sandra could have used her position as head of the department to change the emphasis in the workbooks, she felt that such changes couldn't be made because of the attitudes of her colleagues who believed that the use of the workbooks was most desirable. She stated that Southside High was identified with self-paced learning and most of the experienced teachers used workbooks and advocated their use. Furthermore, because of uncertainties concerning the future structure of the general science course, there was no interest among staff in revising the workbooks.

Sandra was at odds with several of her colleagues in relation to homework policy as well: 'I tend to like the kids to do something at home during the week. Not so much as in upper school where they do three to four hours per week, but an hour or two.' Sandra indicated that one of the reasons why she liked to emphasize homework in grade 10 was to build good study habits for grades 11 and 12. She felt that homework should not simply mirror what was done at school, but should elaborate or involve different content. Traditionally, Southside High had not pre-scribed homework for students. The remnants of this policy were still in evidence at Southside High during the study, mainly because one of the foundation staff members still taught at the school. According to Sandra, he vigorously defended the policy of not assigning homework to stu-dents. Because of the resistance of a number of the science staff, Sandra was constrained from implementing the science curriculum in the manner that she regarded as ideal. In this instance, her implemented curriculum did not contain as much homework as she would prescribe in other circumstances.

Substantively the science program at Southside High had changed a great deal in the ten-year period. However, some of the surface features of the previous self-paced approach to learning remained in place and became obstacles which could not be surmounted by Sandra and Peter as they endeavoured to implement their ideal curricula. The major con-straints faced by Sandra and Peter were associated with some of the traditions of Southside High. Despite a turnover of most of the original science staff in the school, several aspects of the original philosophy were still evident after ten years. In particular, although self-paced learning was not stipulated, the workbooks utilized in the original self-paced science program were still used by all staff. In addition, students called teachers by their first names, class periods were not commenced or ended by sirens or bells, and homework was not prescribed on a regular basis as a matter of policy. Of course, the open architecture of the school, which had facilitated team teaching and student-centred learning, was still in existence. However, the partitions between Peter's and Sandra's class-rooms were always closed and team teaching was not used. Further-more, Peter would have preferred more chalkboards.

Planning

McCutcheon (1980) reported that the richest source of planning was the mental planning that teachers did. Few teachers developed written unit plans. Indeed planning in the teacher's 'planbook' was described as a routine which teachers used to 'jog' their memories about the substantive mental planning which had occurred at an earlier time. The notes in the planbook consisted of lists of activities, page numbers in the textbook or teacher's guide and, in some cases, some notes about the concepts to be covered. Teachers tended to glance at their plans before a lesson as a reminder of what to do and then as a checklist to ascertain whether they had completed what they had planned. The reflection in which teachers engaged before writing the entries in their planbook was judged by teachers to be the essence of planning. On some occasions, the products of their thoughts appeared on paper; however, in most cases the products were never written. Planning appeared to take the form of a mental rehearsal of the lesson. This mental dialogue often encapsulated reflection on what had happened in similar lessons in the past.

The value of this approach to planning is supported in the writings of Schon (1983) and Dewey (1922). The teachers in McCutcheon's study did not only reflect or deliberate prior to constructing their written plans, but they also reflected at almost any time during the day. These deliberations continued throughout the entire year when teachers were at work, on holidays and engaged in recreational activities. McCutcheon noted that mental planning of teachers allows them to relate theoretical knowledge to particular cases and to allow for the forces which tend to shape the implemented curriculum. However, McCutcheon noted that, despite the potential for incorporating theory into the planning of teachers, most teachers did not do so. Instead they tended to reflect on practical problems associated with getting through the day, maintaining order, obtaining the needed materials and resources and allocating time to activities.

Peter's Planning

Peter noted in an interview that he did not plan for teaching the content of grade 10 general science at this stage of his career. His priority was to plan for the grades 11 and 12 subjects of biology and human biology and to mark student work. He emphasized that in grade 10 the work to be done was set out in the workbooks and that tests and examinations were focused on that work. Peter stated that:

> I do not plan content at this stage of my career.... Again with this workbook approach much of it is fixed for you anyway in that the kids are working from those books and working through those books. When you are locked into a system in which students are supposed to do their examinations in the fifth week, you can't afford to go off on tangents too frequently; otherwise the bulk of the kids just don't get through it. And again they rise and fall on how well they do on that content examination.

During an interview, Peter explained that he had not taught Nuclear Energy for about five years. With respect to the content, he explained that:

> I've just got completely away from it and I'm not prepared to do a lot of preparation to bring myself back to the peak ... You have time constraints all the time. I could go off and make myself a nuclear physics expert, I suppose, or just read a couple of paper backs. But in terms of my teaching career I've gone beyond that now and I'm more into reading things that are of personal interest to me.... I was going to other teachers to make sure that I was up to answering the questions that were in the workbook.

Although Peter acknowledged that he was not as relaxed when he taught Nuclear Energy compared to other topics and that he was less effective for the students who tended to ask the better questions, he did not regard his lack of content knowledge as particularly problematic. In fact, he rationalized his lack of knowledge and disinclination to prepare before each lesson with the following comment:

> I sometimes wonder whether people worry too much about the content. Science is a content dominated subject area and we seem to spend hours and hours pushing kids through topics but very rarely worry about how we're teaching or whether they're really understanding what we're teaching or whether they're really enjoying what we're teaching. There's so much in science that we push off to one side and put in the too-hard basket (for example, getting kids involved in the experimental method and experimental design). How do you teach kids to be involved in something like that? Because it's difficult to do, we pay lip service to it.

Frequently, Peter had not planned in sufficient depth to teach the science content and laboratory activities. In terms of content planning (especially in Nuclear Energy), Peter typically used seatwork activities as opportunities to pour over a reference or student text immediately prior to introducing specific content in a lecture. In addition, during both topics, he regularly left the room during class time to collect texts, equipment and other teaching aids. In fact, during a typical hour, Peter would leave the classroom on five occasions.

There was some evidence that Peter commenced lessons with a plan of what to cover, but he exercised flexibility in implementing the plan. The flexible approach was most evident in the Vertebrates topic. During an interview during the Vertebrates topic Peter noted:

> ... One of the most exciting things that I find about teaching is that in the space of fifty minutes you can end up doing things or

heading in directions that you didn't even conceive of at the start of the lesson. Now a lot of people would condemn a teacher for that. They would say that's ad hoc and here, there and every-where. But I think that a lot of kids generally find classes deadly boring and mundane. Providing changes of tack and things like that makes the class interesting and exciting and a good place to be for that fifty minutes.

Peter's decision not to plan to teach the content of the grade 10 course was based on a system of priorities. As well as teaching two grade 10 general science classes, he also taught one grade 11 biology class and two human biology classes (grade 11 and 12, respectively). He regarded his upper school teaching (that is, grades 11 and 12) as more important and allocated most of his out-of-class time to preparing for these classes and marking associated work. In contrast, he endeavoured to do most marking for his grade 10 classes in class time.

Because of a desire to spend time with his wife and young family, Peter was keen to restrict the amount of time allocated to school work after 5 p.m. As a consequence, he minimized the time for planning and marking student work for the grade 10 general science classes and maxi-mized the time for biology and human biology, which were perceived to be most important. In addition, the demands of an external examination involved a higher level of accountability with respect to the grade 11 and 12 courses.

Sandra's Planning

Sandra's planning and preparation were detailed and more than adequate to prepare for teaching. In her role as head of the science department, Sandra had responsibility for coordinating the course, planning equip-ment needs and sequencing of topics throughout the year. Thus, she had a long-term view of the science program and knew how the topics related to one another. Similarly, she planned her own topics thoroughly and anticipated the amount of time that she expected to allocate to core activities and how many of the optional activities most students would cover. In the day-to-day planning, she always was prepared in terms of equipment to be used and the content to be covered. When laboratory activities were scheduled, the materials were on hand at the beginning of the lesson and there was no need for her to leave the classroom to locate additional equipment. As a part of her planning, Sandra made effective use of the school laboratory technician who assembled the necessary equipment on a tray and sometimes assisted in the classroom.

When asked how she prepared for her classes, Sandra said that she first referred to the workbook and read the activities. Also, she looked at the equipment required for each activity and examined the textbook to see if it contained the information needed to complete each question or task. She then estimated the time needed for each activity. The time schedule was reviewed on a weekly basis as students completed the activities.

Sandra's science content knowledge was strong and, because she was an experienced teacher, there was no need to spend too much time preparing content in a formal manner by writing lesson notes and the like. A brief note on a sheet of paper was sufficient for her to recall the necessary content. Furthermore, because the major resources in Sandra's classes were the workbook and the textbook, most of the questions and directions were pre-planned. Consequently, Sandra was able to concentrate on planning for the management of activities. However, Sandra's planning for student engagement did not appear to take account of major problems that occurred in her classroom each day. Certainly she thought about her problems, and worried about them too, yet during the two topics she did not implement strategies to overcome major difficulties. Day after day, she taught in the same way, despite the fact that student learning opportunities were not optimal.

Discussion of Teachers' Planning

The differences between Sandra and Peter were most evident in their planning to teach. Sandra planned with student learning in mind. She prepared laboratory and learning experiences that would allow students to develop an understanding of the science being studied. Both teachers were reliant on the workbooks to prescribe the work to be done, but Sandra always had prepared herself to be a resource and had the necessary materials available in the room for student use. In contrast, Peter did not appear to plan in a substantive way. His knowledge was limited, yet he did not spend much time planning to assist in content presentation. Furthermore, during the Nuclear Energy topic, he did not move too far away from the student text. Instead, Peter spent a significant amount of time in planning excursions and competitions which were ancillary parts of the science course. He always was willing to plan an excursion and be the bus driver or organize school science competitions, yet most of his lessons appeared to be 'off the cuff', laboratory activities were conducted in an ad hoc manner and films were used as a form of entertainment during the course. During Nuclear Energy in particular, Peter often used the workbooks to get the lesson started and did his planning during the lesson. As a consequence, it was often necessary to leave the classroom several times per lesson to obtain materials and books which were needed, and during instruction Peter sometimes made content errors and failed to develop the science content in a manner which would facilitate student understanding.

The Implemented Curriculum

Peter's teaching role placed him as a major source of the science content which students were to learn. Consequently, the strengths and weaknesses exhibited as he taught the content of both topics were a feature of the implemented curriculum in his class. In contrast, Sandra emphasized students working from the workbooks and assisting one another to learn and understand the science content. Her role was as a resource person who helped as the need arose. This style of teaching focused attention on classroom management, which was the feature of the implemented curriculum in Sandra's class.

A term that is useful in describing and contrasting Peter's and Sandra's teaching is *pedagogical content knowledge*, which has been described by Shulman (1987) in the following terms:

> The teacher can transform understanding, performance skills, or desired attitudes or values into pedagogical representations and actions. These are ways of talking, showing, enacting, or otherwise representing ideas so that the unknowing can come to know, those without understanding can comprehend and discern, and the unskilled can become adept. Thus, teaching necessarily begins with a teacher's understanding of what is to be learned and how it is to be taught. (p. 7)

Discipline-specific pedagogical knowledge, or pedagogical content knowledge, was inferred from interviews and observations of teaching. During interviews, we endeavoured to focus our discussions on specific instances which were observed in the lessons and, as a consequence, we were able to probe particular classroom events.

The Implemented Curriculum in Peter's Class

Peter taught quite differently in each of the topics, but careful analysis of the data from each component of the study indicated that he had limitations in pedagogical content knowledge in each topic. In an important sense, his limitations in pedagogical content knowledge reflected his limited science teacher education and his lack of substantive planning before lessons.

Peter perceived his main role in terms of knowledge dissemination. He familiarized himself with the content to be learned and presented it to the class in a form which he felt could be memorized. Thus, the role of students in Peter's class was to listen intently, to copy what Peter said or wrote on the board and, at a later time, to complete activities from the workbook.

Peter regarded himself as in-field when he taught Vertebrates and out-of-field when he taught Nuclear Energy, and his approach to teaching the two topics reflected his perceived level of expertise. During the Vertebrates topic, he appeared confident and was not reliant on the student text as a source of knowledge. He used a university text as a source of information and frequently referred to knowledge gained from his anatomy courses at university. Peter's teaching was focused on the acquisition of low-level cognitive outcomes and little emphasis or value appeared to be attached to learning with understanding and using the facts that were presented in order to develop concepts. Science was presented as a body of facts and in so doing Peter was vulnerable because of his knowledge limitations. Frequently errors were made and the environment which prevailed in his class was not conducive to meaningful learning. Peter's approach to the Vertebrates topic was encapsulated in the following comment from an interview:

> I just wanted to get through it. It really doesn't hold a lot of interest for me. Because it doesn't hold a lot of fascination, I basically wanted to cover the work in those workbooks and I didn't want to extend beyond that.

Peter taught in a less confident and less expansive manner in the Nuclear Energy topic, which he had not taught for five years. In this case, he relied on the student text for his knowledge and avoided explanations of key concepts such as nuclear instability and half life. Instead, he focused on the social aspects of nuclear energy in his whole-class activities and provided students with much more time to work in an individualized manner. Consequently, in the Nuclear Energy topic, students were much more reliant on the workbooks and textbooks than was the case during the Vertebrates topic.

During the Nuclear Energy topic, Peter appeared to avoid the science content involved in the topic by emphasizing social and affective aspects of nuclear energy. For example, Peter began the nuclear energy topic with the comment that: 'I must confess that Nuclear Energy is not a favourite topic of mine'. He then explained that there was no future for nuclear energy in the state or the nation. He noted that every day nuclear energy was in the news and he cited examples of protests about testing nuclear weapons and visits of nuclear powered ships. He then described how he once lived near a nuclear power station in Canada, how the British brought an atomic bomb into a harbour near Dalton, how the people in New Zealand were making the kinds of decisions that Australians would need to make in the future, and how people in Australia were questioning the whole business of nuclear power and weapons. After a brief interaction with students on nuclear weapons and warships, Peter told the class about the capabilities of the USA and the USSR with respect to nuclear weapons. Each could destroy the world ten times over). Finally, he informed the class that the Curies had died of cancer because they had worked with radioactive sources.

Following this strongly anti-nuclear introduction, Peter began to tell students about gamma radiation. Although he related gamma radiation to other forms of electromagnetic radiation, he did not discuss its origin or its properties. However, he did draw a diagram depicting a radioactive substance, a key and a photographic plate. He informed the class that an imprint of the key would form on the photographic plate. There was no discussion or explanation of how this process occurred, nor was there a comparison with the effect of visible light on a photographic plate. Students were simply given the facts. Subsequent interactions between Peter and students indicated that misunderstandings were widespread. However, Peter did not deal with students' incorrect responses and he did not reteach effectively. The following example indicates that, even though some students misunderstood, Peter was concerned primarily with providing an answer to the question that he had asked:

Peter: What does it say about the radioactive substance?
Diane: It'll get burnt away (a thick sheet of brown paper).
Peter: It's strong enough to pass through the brown paper but not the key.

Soon after the above interaction, Peter gave a workbook assignment which described an experiment similar to the one which he had described in class. There was no prior discussion of the problem or the experimental design. Four students, including Diane, indicated that they did not understand enough to start to answer the questions. At that point, Peter called the class to attention and explained how photographic film reacts to light. He then provided answers to the questions in the assignment, told the students to write the answers at home and explained that they would not do the experiment in class because it was 'not wise to have radioactive sources lying around the place'. This example of Peter's teaching behaviour was typical of a tendency to reduce the cognitive demands of science. He consistently avoided laboratory activities in both topics, preferring to disseminate content to be rote-learned. In addition, ne frequently provided verbatim answers to workbook questions whose purpose was to have students apply knowledge to different contexts. Having been furnished with the answers, the students were left to recall what the teacher had said and write it into their notebooks. In most instances, Peter's explanations were incomplete. For example, he explained radioactive decay and half life in just under a minute at the beginning of one lesson. During that minute, there were several instances of student misunderstanding; however, Peter continued with his lesson and did not reteach the concepts. Thus, in Peter's classes, the work had a low level of cognitive demand.

During both topics, Peter made numerous important errors in presenting content and his pedagogical content knowledge was inadequate in other ways as well. For example, in both topics, he confused the terms dependent and independent variable. During the Vertebrates topic, many facts were incorrect and several concepts were not fully explained. However, in the Nuclear Energy topic, errors were much more frequent and, in many instances, Peter did not explain concepts needed for the understanding of later content. For example, he did not assist students to understand key concepts such as radioactivity, unstable nuclei, strength of radioactive sources, radioactive decay, half life, fission and fusion. In response to a question posed in the workbook, which requested the number of protons contained in a radon nucleus, Peter provided the following response:

> Radium, when it is converted to radon, loses an alpha particle and the alpha particle contains ... well the alpha particle in this instance is a helium atom which contains two neutrons, two protons and two electrons. So, in the conversion of radium to radon, 88 is changed to 86. And so the answer is 86 and that's how you should derive that answer.

The above response only gave the answer and did not provide students with sufficient breadth to understand the changes associated with alpha emission from radium. For example, no mention was made of the mass number changing from 226 to 222 and no reasons were offered for mentioning the two electrons associated with a helium atom. Additional discussion of these factors would seem reasonable because students could not answer the question. In fact, when Jenny provided an answer of twenty, Peter remarked that he liked her reasoning but did not point out why she was wrong.

During a demonstration in which Peter used uranium ore, cobalt, strontium and americium as sources to demonstrate radioactive emission, alpha, beta or gamma radiation were not mentioned and he did not control any variables in a demonstration in which a geiger counter was used to compare the strength of the radiation from each source. Throughout the lesson, Peter did not inform students of the properties or sources of alpha, beta and gamma radiation, even though he read an extract from a text which indicated that an electric field could be used to separate the three types of radiation.

Frequent errors of fact were undoubtedly an impediment to learning. However, a tendency to avoid reteaching after an error had been made and was detected was a problem that was of greater importance. During one lesson, Peter taught the class about carbon dating. He commenced with a diagram showing the sun converting carbon-12 to carbon-14 and he informed students that carbon-14 was a radioisotope and that there was an equilibrium between the amount of carbon-14 and carbon-12 in the atmosphere. He then explained that the equilibrium was upset when 'we cease to live'. Needless to say, the students demonstrated considerable confusion about the carbon dating method. However, Peter was unable to resolve or diagnose misunderstandings. Diane asked about the source of carbon-14, but Peter simply repeated what he had said earlier concerning the sun and carbon-12 being converted to carbon-14.

One week later, during a review lesson prior to the test, Peter asked Robert a question about the origin of carbon-14. Robert replied that carbon-12 was converted to carbon-14 when it was exposed to the sun. Peter immediately said 'No' and called on Jeffrey who affirmed Robert's response. Peter then stated:

> In fact it is nitrogen as a result of cosmic radiation that converts or is converted to carbon-14. Nitrogen is converted to carbon-14 and then carbon-14, through natural decay will form carbon-12. I mean that there is an enormous amount of carbon-12 anyway and it's just the radiation of nitrogen that gives you carbon-14.

Later in the lesson, he noted that 'carbon-14 loses a couple of neutrons and becomes carbon-12'. He gave the class a new set of facts to replace the other incorrect information, but did not point out that there was a difference and he did not explain any of the processes involved in the nuclear reactions.

At the end of the review lesson, Peter explained to members of the research team that he realized his error about carbon dating when he taught the process in a grade 12 human biology course. He did not reteach the facts to his grade 10 class because he did not regard learning facts to be as important as learning process skills. The irony of this remark was that there was no evidence of an emphasis on process skills in any of Peter's lessons during the study.

At the end of the Nuclear Energy topic, most students were still confused about the carbon dating process. Most stated that carbon-12 was converted to carbon-14 as a result of the sun's radiation. In addition, concepts which are necessary for an understanding of the carbon dating process were not clearly understood. For example, few students had operational understandings of nuclear instability, alpha, beta and gamma radiation, neutron emission and the role of photosynthesis in carbon dating.

Peter behaved in a similar manner when other errors were made in class. Two of these involved arithmetic and the concept of half-life. In order to obtain the answer to a problem involving half-life, Peter had to multiply $3 \times 47 \times 10^9$ years. After considerable thought, Peter wrote 141×10^{27}. Jeffrey stated that Peter was wrong, other students were visibly confused and Peter appeared flustered. Quickly he assigned students some work to do and, while they were working, he referred to his notes and a reference book. After speaking quietly with Louise, he corrected his error on the blackboard and, although he discussed the change privately with Jenny and Louise, he did not bring the error to the attention of others in the class. Less than one minute later, he erased the problem and the solution from the chalkboard.

Peter was aware of his content limitations in Nuclear Energy in particular and physics generally. During an interview, he noted:

> I didn't have the background in physics to discuss nuclear physics with students. At times I really don't have a clue. I just guess....
> I think there were a number of occasions when the kids weren't convinced with respect to what I was talking about or what I was saying and that worries me as a teacher.

However, despite Peter's awareness of his knowledge limitations for the Nuclear Energy topic, his planning did not reflect the concern.

Feedback and assistance from the teacher was only one of the avenues available for student learning. Equally important were the opportunities for students to learn as a result of their individual efforts and collaborations with peers. Peter allowed students to arrange their own seating in the class. He noted that they sat close to their friends at the beginning of the year and had retained the same seats throughout the year. The practice of students sitting close to friends, the relatively high proportion of time allocated to individualized activities and Peter's belief that students learned most from interactions with peers ensured that there were ample opportunities in each lesson for students to interact and learn from one another. Despite these opportunities, an examination of student work files suggested that they did not learn a great deal from their interactions with peers or from completing the activities in the workbooks. Most student work files were incomplete and contained errors. For example, Greg, one of the top students in both topics, had defined respiration incorrectly and had not completed the sections on digestion or the circulatory system. Failure of students to complete the activities in the workbooks accurately raises questions about the need for so much time to be allocated to this goal. If students are to undertake and complete their work with understanding, they should have correct answers to the activities that they have completed. Although many questions were discussed in class, Peter did not have a mechanism for ensuring that students were aware of errors in their work files. A possible reason for this might be associated with the assessment system which favoured performance on tests, assignments and examinations. During the Vertebrates and Nuclear Energy topics, Peter did not assess the student work files even though they were handed in for his perusal.

In contrast to the work files which were not discussed and corrected in a routine manner, tests and assignments were marked by students in a whole-class activity which was closely supervised by Peter. Thus, they received feedback on the correct and incorrect answers to questions included in tests and assignments. However, the final examinations which concerned all work studied in the topic were not discussed with the class. As a consequence, students were provided with a measure of their general performance on each topic, but were not given feedback on specific understandings and misunderstandings.

The Implemented Curriculum in Sandra's Class

Sandra indicated that the knowledge that she had acquired during her formal degree work was sufficient for her to teach biology and chemistry. Sandra noted that she had gained the pedagogical content knowledge needed to teach Vertebrates by teaching it on earlier occasions and by teaching similar topics such as the human biology course in grades 11 and 12. The knowledge needed to teach Nuclear Energy to grade 10 students was partially obtained from her first year physics course at university and partially obtained from teaching the topic on other occasions. Sandra appeared to be in-field during both Vertebrates and Nuclear Energy and had a knowledge base that was adequate for teaching both topics.

Sandra believed in active student involvement as a means of learning with understanding. Consequently, she embraced the philosophy of self-paced learning which had been a characteristic of Southside High for many years. She emphasized small-group and individualized activities and constantly monitored student engagement.

Despite Sandra's interest in assisting students to learn, almost all of the intellectual activities, including the questions asked, were at a knowledge level. Most questions were initiated by students and were related specifically to completing workbook activities. Sandra noted that:

> The one thing I've not felt satisfied with is the level of difficulty for the student. Whether it's the content of the booklets or the way we use them, the content objectives are very straight-forward. How you can be sure that the kids are going to get the content and still do more interesting work is something I'm still coming to grips with.

Thus, a paradox emerged. Although Sandra wanted to probe student understanding and assist students to learn in a meaningful way, almost all of her time was occupied by answering questions raised by students attempting to complete workbook activities which Sandra regarded as lacking cognitive demand. From a student perspective, the work was at a knowledge level because the answers were either available in the book or provided by Sandra.

The following example of an interaction with a female student who was having difficulty with one of the workbook exercises provides an indication of the extent to which Sandra taught for understanding.

Sandra: What are the control rods doing?
Female student: I don't know.
Sandra: Read that. What are the control rods doing?
Female student: Absorbs excess neutrons.
Sandra: They take up excess neutrons. Keeping in mind that it's your neutrons, here, in your little diagram, that are responsible . . .
Female student: Do they . . . Do they absorb them?
Sandra: They absorb the extra ones. So if you've got no control rods in your reactor what does it do to your number of neutrons?
Female student: It's going to get bigger.
Sandra: Bigger. If you've got more neutrons, what's it doing to your fission? Your rate of reaction?
Female student: It's going to get slower.
Sandra: If you've got more neutrons. More neutrons!
Female student: Faster.
Sandra: Faster. OK.

Through questioning, Sandra endeavoured to have the students understand that control rods absorb neutrons and, therefore, by immersing the control rods into the reactor, more neutrons would be absorbed so that fewer would be left to initiate fission reactions. Initially the student was able to respond to the question concerning the function of the control rods by reading from a textbook. When the student was asked how control rods would affect the rate of the fission reaction, she had a choice of faster or slower. She appeared to guess incorrectly. When she reversed her guess, Sandra appeared satisfied that she now knew the correct answer and moved on to assist another student.

Sandra did not rely on an answer to a single question when she interacted with students. In almost all cases, she asked a string of questions and allowed students to get involved in responding. Usually she initiated an interaction in such a manner that students were required to contribute before she provided information. Sandra probably used this technique so as to determine the extent of student understanding of the concepts involved. Following such interactions, Sandra contributed an explanation designed to clarify or elaborate a concept.

The self-paced nature of the class ensured that Sandra was responding to student questions as they worked on them. This placed considerable pressure on Sandra's knowledge of the content being studied. At times, her responses to student questions and difficulties obviously were unrehearsed and, as she moved to subsequent students and answered similar questions, the quality of her explanations and questions improved. At other times, she made content errors which might have contributed to student misunderstandings. Such occurrences were rare. For example, in response to a question by Craig about what is meant by critical mass, Sandra responded: 'It's the specific size of a specific mass of uranium. If the mass is bigger then what happens? You get a? ... a chain reaction'.

The unrehearsed nature of Sandra's explanations was evident in the following responses to student questions concerning nuclear fission.

Sandra: It gets absorbed by the nucleus and the extra neutron in the nucleus makes it very unstable. And when it gets unstable the energy to repel becomes stronger than the energy holding it together. So it pulls apart. When it pulls apart that's what you're getting.

The one goes in and it's slow enough ... oh fast ... but it's still enough that you've got your big nucleus and it takes it up. So it takes it up and makes it very unstable. And it becomes very unstable ... and it doesn't split into two. It splits into one, two, three, four, five. Just little bits.

So what particles come out of this split? What are the particles that came out? You started with uranium-235.

Female student: Hm.

Sandra: Took up one and became tremendously unstable and it splits. You know it rocks.

Girl: Ha. Ha. Ha.

Sandra: Well that's an easy way to think of it. It splits and you get five things. So that's what they mean. As well as the energy, what particles are they? Don't say what elements these are because it varies depending on how it splits.

In some instances, Sandra's attempts to explain complex phenomena simply trailed off and she did not pursue the issue of whether or not the students understood the concepts. For example, in an attempt at explaining fusion, she stated that '... it creates excess energy that is lost because the helium nucleus requires less energy to hold it together than each of the two hydrogen requires. OK? So it's more stable'. Sandra then moved on to deal with a question from another student. By so doing, she avoided the issue of whether or not the concept of binding energy per nucleon was understood by the student to whom she had been speaking.

In most of her interactions, the contributions from students were short and reliant on a convergent form of questioning from Sandra. The example below indicates how she was able to respond to a student question and provide a framework for the student to respond in writing to the question.

Female student: Why are power stations built differently?

Sandra: Um. What comes out of power stations?

Female student: Nuclear energy.

Sandra: Good. And that's what we use them for. But what else comes out that we don't necessarily want to come out?
Female student: Waste.
Sandra: What kinds of waste?
Female student: Radioactive.
Sandra: ... From a nuclear power station your biggest waste would be radioactive. So you've got your thick walls of concrete ... In the case of your other power stations, like your coal and your gas and your oil stations, what do you get out of those?
Female student: Pollution.
Sandra: Such as?
Female student: Gases ...
Sandra: Gases and smoke and stuff. In which case they have their big smoke stacks.
Female student: Oh. Right.
Sandra: Good girl.

The above extracts are typical of the exchanges which occurred continuously throughout the great majority of the observed lessons. Sandra moved about the class and worked with students, assisting them to complete the activities from the workbooks. In most instances, the interactions were extended in nature, providing opportunities for students to respond, to formulate questions of their own, and to think about the work that they were doing in a broader context than was presented in the textbook or the workbook. However, as is evident from the above interactions, many of the student responses were at a low level of cognitive demand. Efforts to assist students to understand were largely dependent on teacher questions and occasional teacher explanations. Student responses tended to be short and recalled from memory or read from the textbook.

During instruction, Sandra provided constant encouragement for students to produce high quality work. She always seemed able to find something positive to say to students about their efforts or their work. She was never heard to be sarcastic or negative. As she moved about the room, she provided students with procedural information about what work was due, when it was due and the reasons why particular deadlines applied. In addition, she explained her assessment policy and reminded students of what was required of them. If students did not ask her questions, she asked them questions to determine their progress.

During an interview, Sandra identified the major problem with the grade 10 program as being associated with the amount of work that students had to cover. She noted that there was too much to do in five weeks and that she would like to reduce the content and provide students with more time to think about the concepts. She also criticized the emphasis on copying from the textbook that the current approach involved. She noted that more hands-on activities in the Nuclear Energy topic would lead to an undesirable proliferation of radioisotopes in the room, but that there were probably other ways of actively engaging students. Her comments seemed to highlight the importance of having students actively engaged in work of a different kind to that prescribed by the workbooks. However, she did not regard whole-class activities as an alternative.

Knowledge flow in the classroom tended to be from the text to the student. Even though Sandra knew the content that she was to teach and took the time to explain what was happening, many students did not appear to listen in whole-class activities. Although Sandra seemed to be aiming at understanding through her explanations, the work for most students involved search and find activities from the textbook. In view of Sandra's classroom organization, students were placed in a position of having to find other resources to assist in the process of constructing knowledge. Emphasis was given to the workbook because its questions prescribed what students ought to be doing in class time. The workbook was referenced to the textbook, which therefore assumed the position of being the most important source of information.

Two problems arose as a consequence of the focus on the textbook. First, the textbook emphasized facts about science and did not build concepts by relating the facts to one another or by providing explanations of the science underlying important science facts. In addition, the textbook had been written with low ability students in mind. The reading difficulty had been minimized, sentences were short and complex issues were avoided. Thus, for these more advanced learners, the textbook was too easy. In most instances, students only had to locate key words or phrases and copy them from the textbook in order to complete a task in the intended manner. The second problem was associated with the types of questions posed in the workbook. These consisted of low-level cognitive tasks which, in most instances, required students to use the textbook as a reservoir of facts. In addition, the questions presented a distorted view of the nature of science, often with an implication that the answer in the textbook was certain (as distinct from tentative) and that there was only one suitable answer. For example, one question was: 'Why is the tail of a human much smaller than that of a kangaroo?' The question implied that the answer was known and that the answer in the book was correct. Discussion of the degree of speculation and plausibility of alternative answers or hypotheses did not occur in class. Furthermore, when Sandra assessed student work files, she made a brief notation on the two or three points that she was expecting for an answer to this and other questions. Generally speaking, the responses to questions were not discussed in a whole-class activity and the only feedback that students received was from Sandra's written and oral comments.

Sandra assessed student work consistently and thoroughly. Her feedback to students was extensive and should have provided a basis for meaningful learning. For some students, this was undoubtedly the case, although certain other students did not appear to read the written comments provided by Sandra. If they did, the evidence suggests that they did not act in accordance with what she had advised.

Sandra had organized students into work groups with the intention of having them contribute to one another's learning. Unfortunately, the desire for students to deal with their social agendas was usually greater than their motivation to learn about science. Consequently, management of student behaviour became the major issue in the class and, although the reward system ensured that students did complete their work, the cognitive level of the work was low and more time than necessary was taken up in completing assigned tasks.

Sandra believed that students learned most effectively when instruction was individualized and when they shared with peers. Consequently, most of the teaching occurred at an individualized level or in small groups. Occasionally, Sandra gave explanations to two or three students and, on fewer occasions, she spoke to an entire group of up to six students. However, the most common approach was for Sandra to speak in a quiet voice to a single student. She was very diagnostic on such occasions and searched for student understanding. While she was assisting a student in this way, students in the same group were often off-task. The incidence of off-task behaviour in the class as a whole was always high and, as a consequence, few students benefitted from Sandra's extensive pedagogical content knowledge at a specific time.

This situation was exacerbated by the fact that several 'target' students were able to monopolize Sandra's time by requesting assistance more often than other students did. Students in Sandra's class used three procedures to attract her attention. First, students called on her as she came close to them; second, students raised their hands until the teacher noticed and came to provide assistance; and third, students left their seats and approached Sandra for assistance. One group of girls was particularly active in obtaining assistance in this manner. Natalie, Sally and Janila were able to monopolize the teacher's attention for disproportionate periods of time by asking probing questions designed to enhance their understandings of the science content which they were to learn. These students dominated the use of the teacher's time in a manner which was analogous to the target students described by Tobin and Gallagher (1987a) in classes where whole-class interactive activities were emphasized. Students who made the effort to understand the science content were readily given assistance by Sandra and, whereas this was helpful to the students concerned, others in the class were at a relative disadvantage and resorted to rote learning procedures.

At times during the Nuclear Energy topic, Sandra demonstrated a concern for assisting those who were prepared to make the effort to learn.

For example, she spent a considerable amount of time with the five female students who solicited her assistance and she made a special effort to help Gavin who had been uncooperative but had resolved to catch up. Sandra was able to provide these students with extra assistance only by denying quality time to others in the class. In an important sense, Sandra's style of conducting activities made her teaching effectiveness questionable. She seemed to be rushed almost all of the time and, although she was eager to assist students in the learning process, was unable to manage the class effectively.

Sandra's attempts to implement a self-paced approach to learning were unsuccessful for two reasons. First, several boys in the class (Gavin, Wayne, Nigel, Francesca and Martin) were involved regularly in socially unacceptable behaviour. This pattern of uncooperative behaviour constantly diverted Sandra from her goal of teaching for understanding. Sandra was always on the lookout for disruptive behaviour from these boys, and she circulated around the room in order to control their misbehaviour by being physically close to them. As well as continually circulating around the room, Sandra always was scanning the class for misbehaviour, and it was evident that this practice distracted her from offering the high quality personalized assistance that she believed should be provided.

A second management problem was associated with socially acceptable disruptive behaviour. Almost everyone in the class took advantage of the manner in which the students were grouped to socialize. At a given moment, as many as seventy-five per cent of all students were off-task as they dealt with their social agendas. In many cases, students worked at their assigned task and talked with peers in their group. Sandra was aware of this problem and endeavoured to solve it by circulating about the room. Thus, she constantly monitored students for on-task/off-task behaviour as she quickly moved around the room. Her constant movement about the classroom enabled students to seek assistance as required.

Sandra acknowledged that she had management problems with her grade 10 class during both topics. At least some of the problems can be attributed to Sandra's relative inexperience of teaching students in small groups for such a high proportion of the time and to the presence of observers in the classroom. Sandra explained that earlier in the year she had seated students in rows, but had decided to organize them in groups because the content-oriented topics of Vertebrates and Nuclear Energy lent themselves to group work utilizing the workbooks. Under normal circumstances, Sandra felt that she would have changed group membership after the Vertebrates topic. However, because the research team was present, she did not do so in case they would be inconvenienced. Also, she noted that managing the class was similar in some respects to a family visiting relatives. The children in the family are not disciplined for misdemeanours during the visit, but when the family returns home 'you give them a thump'. In an analogous way, Sandra did not want to belittle the constant offenders in her class, such as Wayne, in the presence of the research team. Thus, the observers constrained her from taking discipline measures that ordinarily she might have adopted. The following excerpt from an interview provides an indication of Sandra's level of concern for management in her grade 10 class:

> *Interviewer:* Another thing we talked about is that this group that you have are good kids on a one-to-one basis, but they have a tendency to socialize. Some people watching you closely might think there is an excessive amount of off-task time. Would you just like to talk about that in general?
>
> *Sandra:* It's something that worries me and it goes up and down. It depends a lot on what is happening in class I thought the way around it would be to stop them and resort to a teacher-centred class. It's something I'm not ready to do yet. During the last couple of weeks, I haven't been quite as relaxed as I normally would be. It has meant that, instead of stepping in and chopping off certain behaviours, I instead would stand back and hesitate. Hopefully I'll get over that very soon.
>
> *Interviewer:* My impressions were that a lot of these kids can 'goof off' half of the time and still get their work done. Is that reasonable?
>
> *Sandra:* Yes. What they tend to do if they find that they are falling behind is to spend two nights making sure that they are ahead. They borrow the books at night and they catch up.

The above comments indicate that Sandra was aware of both types of disruptive behaviour. By adopting the educationally sound practice of assigning credit for the activities completed at school and at home, the reward schedule allowed students to work at home and socialize at school. Even though Sandra was aware of this tendency, she did not alter her procedures for allocating marks so as to reward those who worked consistently throughout the class period. In fact, she stated in an interview that, at the grade 10 level, it was important for students to enjoy themselves in their science classes and that it might not be desirable for them to have to work hard throughout the entire period.

During laboratory activities, the students in Sandra's class were involved, particularly the boys. However, their involvement was not scientific in many instances. Most often they messed about with the equipment as if they were playing with toys. For example, in the Vertebrates topic, two boys intermittently fought a mock duel with scalpels for two class periods. During an activity on alternative energy sources, most students played with the steam engine, friction toys, jet propulsion equipment and the bunsen burners. The serious discussion which was needed to develop the science from the experience with the materials only occurred for a small number of the more able and interested students in the class.

Discussion of the Implemented Curriculum

This study provided a context in which two very different teachers could be studied in an intensive manner. Because of this school's science department policies and the arrangement of furniture in classrooms, Sandra and Peter were constrained to teach in a manner which differed from how they would like to teach. For example, the science department produced workbooks to facilitate self-paced learning, prescribed textbooks and provided other text resources to be used in class. In Peter's classroom, the desks were arranged in four rows and he was reluctant to move the furniture into another configuration because of possible inconvenience to other teachers. In contrast, Sandra arranged the desks in her classroom into a formation of eight clusters that allowed up to six students to sit together in groups. Although the configuration of furniture in the room could be offered as an important reason for the differences in the way in which Peter and Sandra managed instruction, fundamental differences in the cognitive characteristics of the teachers were probably more important.

Sandra and Peter differed profoundly in terms of: the metaphors used to conceptualize the teacher's role in science teaching; the images they presented during instruction; the pedagogical content knowledge available to teach general science; and their beliefs about what ought to be in the curriculum, how students learn and how teachers should teach. These differences resulted in the curriculum being implemented in characteristically different ways in their two classrooms.

During interviews, both teachers explained that they had obtained the content knowledge to teach science from their formal courses at university, by teaching science for a number of years and by reading reference books. In addition, Sandra had extensive knowledge which included having worked as a scientist, including being a producer of scientific knowledge. Possibly, as a result of such experiences, Sandra perceived science as a process rather than as a body of facts. This perception of science as a process appeared to have a marked influence on her style of endeavouring to involve students to the maximum possible extent in their own learning. Peter had started a physical education degree and had switched to an education degree with a major in science. Consequently, he did not have the same strong background as Sandra, who had a double major in science. Peter perceived science as a body of facts and taught accordingly. This tendency was consistent with Hacker and Rowe's (1985) finding that lower levels of intellectual engagement occurred when teachers taught outside their specialist disciplines when teaching integrated science. They reported that 'non-practical, informational approaches predominated in the classroom when teachers moved outside their area of specialism, even though they had taught the curriculum for six years' (p. 179).

Both teachers stated that there were no formal sources for their pedagogical content knowledge. The discipline-specific pedagogical knowledge which was needed to teach Vertebrates and Nuclear Energy at the grade 10 level was obtained when the teachers themselves were high school students and by teaching similar topics on previous occasions. Informal discussions with colleagues were mentioned as another source of this type of content knowledge. In Sandra's case, the pedagogical content knowledge was integrated into an extensive network of science knowledge. Peter did not possess such a rich network of science concepts and he usually was unable to elaborate to any great extent on the information included in the students' textbooks.

An important difference which emerged in the study was the extent to which Sandra could explain science content in a manner which assisted students to understand. She appeared to have the knowledge to allow her to provide clear explanations which were illustrated with analogies and were augmented with demonstrations and other teaching aids. Similarly, she was able to use questions to diagnose the extent to which students understood science concepts and could listen to student responses and explanations and follow up in an appropriate way. Peter was unable to do most of these things, and frequently he did not even attempt to do them. For example, his teaching tended to consist of presenting facts and, in many instances, his explanations were flawed.

Sandra's inability to sustain an effective learning environment in her class highlights the importance of classroom management. Even though Sandra had exceptional discipline-specific content knowledge, she was unable to use her knowledge to the general advantage of students. It appeared that Sandra too had knowledge limitations. Her major problems were associated with pedagogical knowledge. Her efforts to conduct effective small-group activities were unsuccessful day after day and her only suggestions for improvement were associated with the use of whole-class activities. Yet the main problem was that Sandra was too busy. Because she spent a considerable amount of time monitoring for misbehaviour and for off-task behaviour, there were few opportunities for Sandra to reflect on her practice during class time. Cooperative learning strategies were not employed in a conscious manner and Sandra allowed herself to become the principal resource for student learning. Clearly, there are limits to the number of students that one teacher can assist in a substantive way in a one-hour lesson. Consequently, there were only a few students who benefitted from Sandra's lessons. In order to improve substantially, students would need to accept more responsibility for their own learning, thereby freeing Sandra to teach in a more considered and reflective manner. Sandra could not cater for the needs of each student in her class. But, class size was not the major problem in that a reduction of four or five students probably would not have led to substantial improvements in the learning environment.

Throughout this study, it was apparent that a major driving force on the implemented curriculum was completing the content in the allocated time. The school had scheduled five weeks for the completion of each topic and it was necessary for each teacher to complete the core material in the allowed time so that their students had covered the content before taking the topic test. Thus, prime importance was given to completing the work in the scheduled time and, within that constraint, learning was emphasized. Sandra was particularly concerned that, although the best science was contained in the options, most time was taken up completing core material. Peter did not seem to have the same concern and did not endeavour to complete the optional parts of the course.

In order to do justice to the relationships among the content areas dealt with in each topic and to obtain most benefit from laboratory activities, there is little doubt that less content would have to be covered. However, if less content were included in the course, there is no guarantee that the teachers would teach differently. The evidence from this study suggests that teachers need to be educated before they can sustain activities that would promote meaningful learning. This outcome of the study presents a substantial challenge for teacher educators who have largely ignored the development of pedagogical content knowledge and have concentrated on information dissemination and learning by absorption in teacher education courses.

Sandra was an enigma in many respects. She was regarded by almost everyone as a first-class person and a first-class teacher. Her colleagues perceived her to be talented, hard working, knowledgeable and conscientious and her students regarded her in similar vein. Yet, in the classroom, she floundered because she did not have the active knowledge to manage student engagement in learning tasks. To be sure, Sandra made conscious decisions to teach in the way that she did, and she knew that students were off-task frequently in small-group activities. However, she also knew that students became disinterested in her whole-class activities. Consequently, she argued that student learning opportunities were at the very least no worse in small-group activities than in whole-class activities. For this actually to be the case, Sandra would need to develop and implement new strategies and routines. Such changes would require a commitment on her behalf and a change in beliefs about learning. She would need to be convinced that the postulated changes would reap tangible benefits in student learning. Possible benefits arising from alternative changes in teaching strategies could be discussed with Sandra as a result of feedback sessions in which she was able to reflect on her teaching practices and trace the probable effects of hypothesized changes in teaching. In Sandra's case, the challenge was how to develop knowledge which actually affected the way in which she taught. In a verbal sense, Sandra might have known how to manage the students in her class, but she had not routinized procedures for effective classroom management and did not appear to have a repertoire of active pedagogical knowledge to address the problems which arose in her class. Additional research is needed to understand how teachers develop knowledge which can influence teaching behaviour.

Conclusions

The focus of this chapter has been on the mind frames of Peter and Sandra and the manner in which these mind frames influenced the planned and implemented curriculum. The analyses demonstrated that the two teachers were very different indeed.

The metaphors used by Peter when he taught related to his management role in the classroom. No doubt Peter had metaphors for his role of facilitating learning, but they were not apparent in this study. Peter's use of two management metaphors dominated his speech about teaching and his actions in the classroom. The two different metaphors were associated with marked differences in the way that the class was managed, and his comments suggest that he had discrete sets of beliefs associated with each management role. When he was Captain of the Ship, one set of beliefs influenced how he acted in class and, when he was the Entertainer, another quite distinctive set of beliefs guided his behaviours.

The Entertainer mode of management was more informal than the Captain of the Ship mode. Consequently, this management style enabled a good many of Peter's projected images to interact with students. Peter's projected images drew attention to himself and, as a consequence, were interactive. Some students appeared to like these images and others did not. In many ways, Peter seemed insecure with people and tried to project himself as a person who was successful, self assured, competent and able to relate to others. In some cases at least, the projected images shifted the focus from the learning agenda to other factors associated with Peter the person. For example, his custom of interacting with females who were more attractive, often in a risque manner, might have been to the long-term detriment of some females in the class. This question is pursued in greater depth by Kahle in Chapter 4.

Some of Peter's beliefs about standards dealt with surface-level features, such as whether students used ink or pencil, whether a margin was ruled on the page and whether or not there were external examinations. These standards did not deal with the adequacy of students' understanding of what they were learning or whether they were engaging in a manner that would promote their own learning and the learning of others. In a similar manner, Peter talked about the standards of teachers and equated his own high standards with a preference to wear a tie when he taught. This tendency might have been associated with his inclination to wear a laboratory coat on some occasions even when a laboratory investigation was not involved.

Although Peter did not say too much about convenience for the teacher during the repertory grid exercise, his actions suggested that this set of beliefs had a major influence on how he planned and implemented the curriculum. Peter did not plan for either topic in the depth needed, even though he acknowledged his weaknesses in some content areas. Furthermore, he did not mark student work in a way that could have given him insights into the extent to which students were doing the work and learning. The reasons for not doing these things appear to be associated with lack of time or with inconvenience to the teacher. It was not that Peter did not put in a full day at the office. On the contrary, he did a lot of additional tasks. The main point is that Peter did the things that appealed to him, not necessarily the things that were most closely associated with improving student learning. Instead of organizing excursions and science competitions, Peter could have been marking student work or planning his activities for grade 10 students. The reasons given for not allocating time for planning usually were related to the need to spend time with his family. Although this is a worthwhile goal, it clearly indicated Peter's priorities.

More information about Peter's roles as a teacher and his beliefs associated with each role could have enhanced our understanding of why he did what he did. We know that he emphasized management of students and the curriculum. Although he talked a lot about the ideal way for students to learn, he focused on content coverage in most instances because of a perception that the work had to be covered for the end-of-topic examination. Greater value was attached to covering the content than to ensuring that students understood it. The rationale for that emphasis probably was that students could take the time to develop understanding at home. What was not clear was the rationale for covering the content without due regard for whether all students understood what they were covering. Despite the fact that Peter believed that students learned best by working together and interacting with the teacher, students simply were not given enough time to work together in groups and to sort out the meaning of the science content.

The constraints perceived by Peter were in many instances associated with his own personal comfort. For example, the head of physical science at Southside High noted that there was no pressure to use the workbooks for any of the topics. Yet Peter indicated that he felt he had no choice but to use the workbooks. An assertion that is consistent with the data is that the workbooks enabled Peter to implement each topic without having to prepare something as an alternative.

Peter's planned and implemented curricula can be explained in terms of his metaphors, beliefs, values and knowledge. Although we have learned a great deal about Peter's use of metaphors to conceptualize his role as a manager in the classroom, there is a great deal more to learn. Why did Peter emphasize management to the detriment of learning? The reason is probably associated with beliefs about his roles as facilitator of learning and as an assessor of learning. However, we do not have much information about these beliefs because, at the time of the study, we were not examining beliefs in relation to specific roles in a conscious manner. Ongoing research in classrooms has highlighted the value of examining beliefs and metaphors in relation to specific roles such as facilitator of learning, assessor and manager. Having gained this theoretical insight, it is impossible to disregard it in the interpretation of the data for this study. Because of Peter's unwillingness to cooperate further in the research after the observation period, we were unable to collect further relevant data from him.

Sandra's teaching was characterized by her impressive personal characteristics. She was a concerned and dedicated teacher. The main question that arises from our investigations of Sandra's teaching involves the reasons why she was so unsuccessful in managing her grade 10 students? Her beliefs about teaching and learning appeared to be internally consistent, and she implemented the curriculum exactly in the manner which she thought appropriate. Yet management problems made it difficult for students to learn. Stronger actions against students who disrupted the work of others, penalties for students who failed to accomplish a reasonable amount of work in a class period, and disincentives for copying the work of others were factors that Sandra might have considered. Similarly, activities that incorporated individual engagement and whole-class engagement might have been used as a source of variety, to control student misbehaviour and to allow students to engage in a different manner.

Sandra's shortcomings with students at the grade 10 level were associated with students' unwillingness to accept responsibility for their own learning. A lack of motivation to learn and a willingness to deal with their social agendas, led to a situation in which even the best students in the class spent a disproportionate amount of time off-task. Sandra knew about her management problems and opted to do nothing differently. She indicated that whole-class activities were not an acceptable alternative because students still would not learn. What was Sandra trying to accomplish? Certainly she allowed her beliefs about her role as a facilitator of learning to drive her behaviour and there was consistency between her beliefs about management and her beliefs about facilitating learning. To Sandra, it made no sense to manage students in a way that was inconsistent with her beliefs about how they learned. Quite possibly, her approach might have been more successful over a longer time interval.

She was concerned for individuals and constantly encouraged them to accept responsibility for their own learning. If she had been successful in assisting four or five disruptive male students to increase their motivation to learn, Sandra would have had more time to concentrate on facilitating learning rather than on managing student behaviour.

Sandra's adherence to the Teacher as Resource metaphor led to situations in which she was not reflective in action. As Sandra dashed around the room, trying to equalize each student's share of the teacher resource, there were things that might have been done to improve the learning environment. Fewer circuits of the classroom and more reflection in action are possible changes for Sandra to consider. In the light of Peter's use of alternative metaphors to change radically what he did in his classroom, it might have been helpful for Sandra to develop alternative management metaphors to guide her teaching. These could have been used on occasions to reduce the amount of social noise and to focus student engagement on important content.

Adoption of an alternative metaphor for handling the manner in which new content is introduced might also have helped to overcome Sandra's problem associated with answering almost all questions on an individual basis. Apart from this practice being time-consuming, each question is in some ways unique and, as a consequence, each response is largely unrehearsed. Therefore, not all responses might provide the cues needed to stimulate learning in the desired manner. This situation might not have been so bad if students had been given the time to discuss the issues at length with Sandra. But most interactions were fleeting and, despite her intentions, Sandra's style of dealing with student questions frequently resulted in a dichotomous choice of answers from which students selected the correct one.

Although Sandra was assertive in not using whole-class activities because of their dubious value for promoting student learning, she allowed several constraints to shape the implemented curriculum in a way that she perceived to be detrimental to students. The most notable of Sandra's constraints was use of the workbooks, which she used because other science staff wanted to use them. In this instance, her belief in being a democratic head of department was stronger than her belief that the workbooks probably were not conducive to learning. Sandra also allowed other constraints associated with the learning environment to influence the implemented curriculum. For example, she expressed dissatisfaction with the style of assessment and the balance between core and optional activities. As head of the science department, Sandra certainly could have exercised leadership with respect to these issues, particularly as she felt that student learning was being jeopardized. Yet she did not appear to try to change either of these constraints. Her role as an academic leader was non-assertive and she permitted the constraints to influence the implemented curriculum. In contrast, Sandra made her own decisions about homework. Despite opposition by some of her colleagues, Sandra set homework regularly, based on a belief that some homework is desirable. An assertion that fits the above patterns of behaviour is that Sandra did not allow constraints to influence the implemented curriculum if the decisions only affected her class. If other classes were involved, such as in the case of assessment and use of workbooks, Sandra adopted a democratic style and followed the majority preference.

References

BLACK, M. (1979) 'More about metaphor', in ORTONY, A. (Ed.) *Metaphor and Thought*, Cambridge, England, Cambridge University Press.

DEWEY, J. (1922) *Human Nature and Conduct*, Rahway, New Jersey, Henry Holt and Company.

EISENHART, M.A., SHRUM, J.L., HARDING, J.R. and CUTHBERT, A.M. (in press) 'Teacher beliefs: Definitions, findings, and directions', *Educational Policy*.

FENSTERMACHER, G.D. (1986) 'Philosophy of research on teaching', in WITTROCK, M.C. (Ed.) *Handbook of Research on Teaching*, 3rd. ed., New York, Macmillan.

GOODENOUGH, W.H. (1971) 'Culture, language and society', *Addison-Wesley Module in Anthropology*, No. 7, Reading, MA, Addison-Wesley, pp. 24–7.

HACKER, R.G. and ROWE, M.J. (1985) 'A study of teaching and learning processes in integrated science classrooms', *European Journal of Science Education*, 7, pp. 173–80.

LAKOFF, G. and JOHNSON, M. (1980) *Metaphors We Live By*, Chicago, University of Chicago Press.

McCUTCHEON, G. (1980), 'How do elementary school teachers plan their courses?' *Elementary School Journal*, 81, pp. 4–23.

MUNBY, H. (1984) 'A qualitative approach to the study of teachers' beliefs', *Journal of Research in Science Teaching*, 21, pp. 27–38.

POPE, M.L. and KEEN, T.R. (1981) *Personal Construct Psychology and Education*, London, Academic Press.

POPE, M.L. and GILBERT, J.K. (1983), 'Explanation and metaphor: Some empirical questions in science education', *European Journal of Science Education*, 5, pp. 249–61.

POWER, C. (1977) 'A critical review of science classroom interaction studies', *Studies in Science Education*, 4, pp. 1–30.

SCHON, D. (1979) 'Generative metaphor: A perspective on problem-setting in social policy', in ORTONY, A. (Ed.) *Metaphor and Thought*, Cambridge, England, Cambridge University Press.

SCHON, D.A. (1983) *The Reflective Practitioner: How Professionals Think in Action*, New York, Basic Books, Inc.

SHULMAN, L.S. (1987) 'Knowledge and teaching: Foundations of the new reform'. *Harvard Educational Review*, 57, 1, pp. 1–22.

STEFFLRE, V.J. (1965) 'Simulation of people's behavior towards new objects and events', *American Behavioral Scientist*, 8, pp. 12–16.

TISHER, R.P. and POWER, C.N. (1973) 'The effects of teaching strategies in miniteaching and microteaching situations where Australian Science Education Project materials are used'. Report of AACRDE project, University of Queensland.

TISHER, R.P. and POWER, C.N. (1975) 'The effects of classroom activities, pupil perceptions and educational values where self-paced curricula are used'. Report of AACRDE project, Monash University.

TOBIN, K., and ESPINET, M. (1989) 'Impediments to change: An application of coaching in high school science', *Journal of Research in Science Teaching*, 26, pp. 105–20.

TOBIN, K. and GALLAGHER, J. (1987a) 'The role of target students in the science classroom', *Journal of Research in Science Teaching*, 24, pp. 61–75.

TOBIN, K. and GALLAGHER, J.J. (1987b) 'What happens in high school science classrooms?', *Journal of Curriculum Studies*, 19, pp. 549–60.

Chapter 4: Real Students Take Chemistry and Physics: Gender Issues

Jane Butler Kahle

Interviewer: Is there something in boys that is beneath them to like biology?

Peter: Well, that's part of the macho thing — that real students go on and do physics and chemistry and that's the way it's been ever since I can remember — ever since I went to high school. Now, a lot of that is being broken down, but it's very gradual. The thing is that girls, for example, didn't go into physics and chemistry. To a large extent that is still par for the course. I think that, underlying it, is the fact that a lot of girls don't have the confidence and don't feel they can do chemistry and physics.

Introduction

Peter strides into class, distinguished looking in his laboratory coat and carrying a stack of reference materials and equipment. Intent and business-like, he deposits his load on the front demonstration table and arranges a dissecting pan and a few instruments. He turns and faces the now quiet class and slowly — one finger at a time — pulls on protective rubber gloves. He has everyone's attention; Peter is ready to teach. Peter demonstrates the teaching beliefs and teaching patterns of many of his colleagues. He enjoys kids and he wants them to like and respect him. He has a basic background in science and he wants to be perceived as a scientist. He likes his job and he hopes to advance and reap the rewards of successful teaching. In order to facilitate his hopes and ambitions, Peter applies a series of principles to guide his behaviour in the classroom and his interactions with students and other teachers both in and out of school.

On the other hand, Sandra unobtrusively begins her class. Several times she quietly states 'still waiting', hoping to calm the students seated in groups of four around square tables. She doesn't raise her voice, but she moves from one noisy area to another until the students have settled down. Now, Sandra is ready to teach. After a few instructions concerning schedules or procedures, Sandra allows the students to work in their groups or individually. During the hour, she never raises her voice and she tirelessly answers the same knowledge-level questions asked by various students. Sandra is confident in herself as a teacher and as a scientist. She has attained the recognition of being the only woman science department head in the city's state education system at the time of the study. She is concerned about students individually and collectively. However, what students learn or don't learn in her class depends to a large extent on the students themselves.

This chapter first explores both Peter's and Sandra's teaching in terms of their educational and experiential backgrounds, of the organizational and social aspects of their schools, and of their teaching tools, texts and workbooks. The principles guiding Peter's teaching, and their effect on learning by his students, are constrasted with those guiding Sandra's instruction. Next, what actually happens in Peter's and Sandra's classes is compared and contrasted with observations from other high school science classes and with data collected in similar schools. Last, the chapter focuses on gender issues in science, in school and in Western society.

Peter's Principles

Peter's observed grade 10 general science class consists of twenty girls and eleven boys. Four students sit at long tables arranged in horizontal rows. Although some table groups are mixed, most consist of only boys or only girls. The atmosphere is casual yet orderly. As noted in Chapter 3, Peter displays two different teaching patterns. In one, he is Captain of the Ship, holding forth at the front of the room with a demonstration or using rapid-fire questions to review or to ascertain answers for the workbooks. In the other mode, he portrays the teacher as Entertainer. As he says, 'A teacher is like an actor; he has to sell his performance'. In his Entertainer role, he might wander about the room, stopping to assist individual pupils with their work. The level of the instruction, regardless of teaching style, is rote learning. In addition, in both styles, Peter fits Galton's (1981) description of an informer. Galton's three styles in teaching are: *Problem Solver*, which involves a high frequency of teacher questions and a low frequency of pupil initiated or maintained activities; *Informer*, which uses teacher delivery of facts and an infrequent use of questions except to recall facts; and *Inquirer*, which uses pupil initiated and maintained experiments as well as inferring, formulating and testing hypotheses.

Peter's Teaching Styles

Each of the above styles of teaching appeals to a different type of student. Both the Problem Solver and the Informer styles involve public interactions and are more often enjoyed by students who are risk takers. On the other hand, the Inquirer style is preferred by students who are not risk takers, because public exchanges could expose their lack of knowledge as they work through a problem or as they respond to a question (Tobin and Gallagher, 1987; Tobin and Garnett, 1987). Many girls are disadvantaged in classes conducted in either the Informer or Problem Solver mode because, on the whole, girls take fewer risks. Use of the Problem Solver or Informer style in teaching science is a particular problem because girls typically have less positive perceptions of their abilities and aptitudes in science (Kahle, 1985; Whyte, 1986). Girls' reluctance to take risks is reinforced by their lower self-concepts, resulting in reduced participation in science classes. The Inquirer style used by Sandra, however, particularly appeals to most girls. Her use of that style and its effect on student attitudes and achievement levels are discussed later.

It is clear that one of Peter's principles is that the Informer style of teaching is both effective and efficient. For example, Peter assists students in completing their notebooks and in reviewing for tests by conducting whole-class interactive lessons during which he fires off many questions. In this teaching mode, he frequently calls on students who have not raised their hands to answer. Both of those behaviours — using rapid questioning and calling on non-volunteers — create an atmosphere of competition and encourage students who display risk-taking behaviours. Neither the competitive nor the high-risk atmosphere is preferred by most girls (Meece, 1987).

There were daily examples of Peter's use of the Informer mode of teaching. For example, Peter began a lesson on respiration by emphasizing the difference between breathing and cellular respiration. During the fifty-minute period, his students listened to his summary, participated in a demonstration, answered questions concerning the demonstration and worked in their notebooks.

Table 4.1 shows the amount of time devoted to each of five types of activities, namely, whole-class non-interactive, whole-class interactive, individual, small-group and transition. Clearly, Peter used the Informer style of teaching, spending sixty-eight per cent of the class time on the whole-class activities.

The questioning component, which composed a large segment of the whole-class interaction, revealed several patterns (see Table 4.2). First, Peter more frequently called on students who did not have their hands up (that is, who had not volunteered to answer). Second, his reinforcing comments tended to be more frequent for boys' than for girls' responses.

Table 4.1: Time allocated to types of instruction in Peter's class

Type		Minutes	Per Cent	Nature of Instruction
Whole-class	(wc)	3	6	Summarize lesson
Whole-class interactive	(wci)	35	68	Demonstration/questions
Individual	(ind)	4	8	Complete notebook
Small group	(sm)	0	0	
Transition	(trans)	9	18	Obtain equipment
Total		50	100	

Table 4.2: Student/teacher interaction pattern in Peter's class

Students	Cognitive Level		Teacher Reinforcement		
	Recall	High	Positive	Neutral	Negative
Boy (HU)		4	1	2	
Boy (NHU)	8	3	5	5	
Girl (HU)	1	6		3	1
Girl (NHU)	7	4	1	3	2
Chorus	6				

HU 'hand-up' (students volunteer)
NHU 'no hands-up' (students do not volunteer)

For example, consider a representative sample of his comments to boys and girls:

Sue, you might just find this interesting, believe it or not.

Diane, could you possibly lift your head to a more vertical position? Thank you, Diane.

Come on, Robert, we need brilliant young minds.

Robert, can we get on with it? I realize, Robert, that Peta is disturbingly alluring. We have to ignore disturbances in life ... maintain our equilibrium.

Each comment is innocuous in itself, but each one suggests that science is okay for boys, who are rough, tough and bright, but that it is questionable for girls, who are lovely, charming and bored. In addition, the last comment clearly introduces sexism into the classroom. (Sexism is defined as using traditionally sex-role stereotyped examples, humour, roles or behaviour within the classroom setting.) Both types of behaviour — calling on non-volunteers and reinforcing male answers — set a certain type of classroom climate, namely, one which supports the behaviour of the more assertive, and usually male, students.

However, during the observation period, Peter encouraged and enjoyed assertive girls as well as boys. For example, he described his personal reaction to an independent female student in the following response to an interviewer's question about Mary's role within her row:

She is very independent, painfully independent sometimes; very much her own person and makes that very clear — very much a nonconformist. I'm not sure how you describe it nowadays, but I think she has a very definite feminist view of things. She's the sort of kid who enjoys a fight and, yet, we have this incredible love-hate relationship. It is quite extraordinary; every now and then she gets the better of me and she wins. Then I get the better of her and I win. She came out on the yacht with me. Mary's mum showed up, and Mary's mum and I had a chat. Mary was right there and we chatted away, and it was obvious that the mum has this same love-hate relationship with her own daughter that I do. I described her as sometimes being a snappy terrier; sometimes she likes to bite something and so she bites my arm and I walk around the classroom with the kid hanging on to the end of my arm. Mary was just fuming but she didn't say a word, so she will square that one off with me next year probably. But there is a tremendous amount of respect for one another between herself and myself.

And she's quite an extraordinary kid to have in the class. The sort of kid who a less experienced teacher could really make major mistakes with. If given the chance, she would take over, I think. She certainly dominated the kids in that row, and it was rather good that she put herself down there, because if she were not to the front she would have had a more dramatic dominating influence on the class. She is very much her own person. When she wants to provide input, she does; when she wants to do her own thing, she does.

Peter recognized and enjoyed Mary's behaviour and correctly described her as a potential target student. Clearly, he enjoyed interacting with high risk-taking girls as well as boys. In addition, during the course of our observations, there were instances in which Peter used sarcasm to squelch both boys (Robert, Greg) and girls (Helen, Diane) who were too vocal and volatile.

One series of exchanges suggested a subtle message inherent in Peter's questioning behaviour. For example, in response to Craig's description of the exchange of carbon dioxide and oxygen in the lungs, Peter cheered him on with comments such as 'Yea, right' and 'Go on, you've almost made it.' Later, two girls and two boys raised their hands in response to the following question from Peter: 'This is a question for

Table 4.3: Combined data over six occasions for student/teacher interaction patterns in Peter's class

Students		Cognitive Level			Teacher Reinforcement			
		Recall	*High*	*Total*	*Positive*	*Neutral*	*Negative*	*Total*
Boy	(HU)	12	2	14	6	2	0	8
Boy	(NHU)	9	2	11	6	1	0	7
Girl	(HU)	4	1	5	1	0	1	2
Girl	(NHU)	35	0	35	5	7	8	20
Chorus		13						

HU   'hand-up' (students volunteer)
NHU   'no hands-up' (students do not volunteer)

real thinkers. You've all heard of mouth-to-mouth resuscitation. How is it that air blown (out of the resuscitator's lungs) is still good?' Danielle's partially correct answer was accepted with no comment. Robert was called upon next. He corrected Danielle and was praised by Peter. Jeffrey added a point. Peter concluded the series by reinforcing Robert's answer. Although he was unaware of it, the above student/teacher interaction pattern reinforces the stereotype that boys, compared with girls, perform better in science classes.

Table 4.3 shows data for Peter's interaction patterns combined over a period of six occasions. This table suggests that Peter frequently called on girls who had not raised their hands. Over a six-day period, he did not ask a girl to respond to a single higher-order question. Because there were twenty girls in his class, on the average, each one responded twice. The eleven boys averaged 2.2 responses each during this period. Peter seemed to call on boys with their hands up or down about evenly and he provided positive feedback after both boys' and girls' answers. But he criticized the responses of the girls much more frequently than those of boys.

Table 4.4 provides combined data over six occasions for the frequency of each instructional mode in Peter's class. This information supports the pattern found in the respiration lesson in that most class periods were spent in question/answer sessions and managerial activities, while little time was allocated to individual or small-group activities such as laboratories, library research, etc. Yet, case studies of teachers who were successful in encouraging girls to continue in science courses in the USA indicate that laboratories were very important in motivating students to study science (Kahle, 1985). In addition, other studies identified individual work as important in attracting non-traditional students (girls and minorities) to science (Tobin, 1987).

Table 4.4: Combined data over six occasions for time spent on different types of instruction in Peter's class

Type	Amount of Time on Six Occasions												Total %
	min	%	min	%	min	%	min	%	min	%	min	%	
Whole-class	18	45	7	14	24*	34	15	29	3	6	0	0	21.3
Whole-class interactive	13	32	17	33	29	29	10	20	34	68	20	42	60.0
Individual	0		0	0	14	14	12	24	4	8	10	30	8.0
Small group	0		20	39	0	0	0	0	0	0	0	0	6.5
Transition	9	23	7	14	23	23	14	27	9	18	13	28	17.5

* Double period with total time of 100 minutes

The interaction pattern in Peter's class supported the finding that teachers who use the problem–solving or informing mode frequently identified and interacted with target students (Tobin and Gallagher, 1987; Tobin and Garnett, 1987). Unless specifically noted, the interviews quoted in this chapter were not conducted by the author. This precaution was taken in order to avoid bias in both questions and responces. Peter described how and why he selected and used specific students as target students:

> Interviewer: How do you feel about letting the class get involved either in small groups or whole groups in a discussion?
> Peter: Well, I enjoy that as well. I enjoy that immensely and ... I like very much their input. I guess as an observer from the outside you'd find that I probably tend towards those kids who interact with me the most. I possibly favour them.
> Interviewer: What students do you interact with most often?
> Peter: Well, Danielle, Louise, Robert and Kim, Joe to a lesser extent. I guess I find myself leaning towards those kids because they will interact, they will respond straight away. They'll nearly always provide some sort of an answer, but I also make an attempt to drag other kids into it ... But, there are obviously kids who feel very threatened by that and I think it's unfair to dwell on them.

Although Peter named four girls and three boys, observations showed that he more frequently called on the boys and that he asked them more challenging questions. In this behaviour, Peter was the typical science teacher in that studies have shown that the ratio of girls to boys involved as target students in science classes ranges from 1:4 to 1:8. For example, Tobin (1987) noted that male students typically respond to teacher questions by raising their hands more frequently than girls do (ratio of eight boys to one girl) and that target students tend to be boys rather than girls. Such differences were found to occur regardless of the whole-class ratio of boys to girls, regardless of the sex of teacher and regardless of the ability level of the class. For example, Tobin found that, in a grade 11 biology class which contained twelve girls and nine boys, seventy per cent of the teacher questions were answered by the boys. In a grade 9 low ability science class, he reported that boys were identified as all of the target students. Likewise, seven out of eight target students in a grade 9 high ability science class were male (Tobin, 1987).

However, Peter was not aware that he more frequently called on boys and that he routinely addressed higher-order questions to them. Gender-related differences were apparent in the interactions which occurred in Peter's class. Peter noted that he tended to interact with the females in his class to a greater extent than with the males. He stated that he preferred to interact with 'the most extroverted girls, those who knew how to interact, who were beautifully presented, with a beautiful smile, were ready to interact and enjoyed interacting'. During whole-class interactive activities, Jeffrey, Greg and Kim initiated interactions by volunteering to respond to teacher questions and asking questions to obtain additional information. Other students who were involved often in whole-class interactions were Susan, Helen, Diane and Robert. Most students participated by responding to questions when selected by Peter. In most instances, the answers involved recall of factual information. Some students, such as Craig, Alex, Nicola, Karen, Andrea, Rhonda, Joanne and Joanna were not often selected to participate and did not initiate whole- class interactions. When Peter was asked about the interaction patterns in his class, he described his Informer style in the following way:

> *Interviewer:* What percentage would be student-initiated questions? What percentage would be questions you ask of them? What percentage would be, sort of, all the kinds of interactions one has with kids just to maintain good rapport?
> *Peter:* Well, I think one of the indicators of how healthy the learning environment is in a class is how many questions the kids do ask. And I think that kids in that class ask a lot of questions. I mean sometimes I can be completely bombarded with questions to the point where there is so much sensory input I sort of feel, hey, I've got to get out of this room and have a break from it. . . . And there are some kids who are so spontaneous like Danielle and Michelle and Greg and Jeffrey that they will just fire continuous questions. You feel you've got to tone it down a little bit. In fact, I think Michelle loves the one-to-one interaction and she likes to control that. She will fire continuous questions and she'll just keep

that going because it's Michelle demonstrating to the rest of the class that she has this ability to interact with the teacher. I think there's a lot of that, maybe fifty to sixty per cent of the interaction is student-initiated interaction. Maybe forty per cent of it is teacher-initiated and maybe ten per cent of it is just rapport-maintaining interaction.

Interviewer: What about the initiation of questions when you're having a whole-class presentation?

Peter: Well, there I would dominate the situation. I would probably dominate it maybe eighty to ninety per cent. It could jump to that high. I often have sessions where I'm firing questions at them. Just spraying them all over the room. And they're sitting there, you know, wondering when they are going to get one?

Interviewer: Do you have any particular thought-out strategy in mind as you're spraying questions around the room?

Peter: Well I want the kids to think. I want them very much to think about what we've been doing and the questions will go right back to classification, which is what we covered at the very beginning.... I love to go off on tangents, a lot of lateral thinking.

Although Peter suggested that many interactions were student-initiated, he described an Informer style in which he 'sprayed' questions around the room. His Informer style of teaching was derived from a management metaphor which drove his teaching and which allowed him to handle effectively a variety of classroom situations.

Another favourite mode of teaching, supported by the data in Tables 4.1 and 4.4, was individualized instruction. In that mode, Peter often combined his perceived roles as Informer and as Entertainer, on one hand, stopping to joke with students and, on the other hand, correcting their notebooks and answering questions. For example, on some occasions, Peter used individualized activities to interact with students on matters unrelated to their work and, on the other occasions, to assist students with activities from the workbooks. The students who interacted with the teacher most often were Rachel, Nicola, Mary, Susan, Helen, Danielle, Britta, Louise, Mandy and Jenny. Of the males, Jeffrey, Joe and Robert were most likely to be involved with the teacher during individualized activities, but not to the extent that the named females were involved. Peter moved about the room in order to maintain discipline and to provide assistance. He paused longer and stood closer to the girls whom he had identified as attractive in comparison with other girls and boys. He usually paused by boys in order to monitor or to modify behaviour. In this teaching mode, Peter encouraged students who were not risk takers. During his stops, his voice was low so that questions, admonitions and responses were private and non-threatening.

Peter's Interactions with Students

Another principle guiding Peter's behaviour was his belief in interpersonal relationship with students. He talked disparagingly about the tendency of some teachers to walk into the class, pile their books on the front bench and teach from behind the teacher's demonstration bench. 'And then they wonder why they have problems with student behaviour', he commented. When he moved around the class a lot, he felt that the kids were more comfortable in interacting with him and he liked that. 'The more interaction the better', he said. His belief in the value of personal interactions between students and teachers was supported by his willingness to organize and conduct field trips. However, it also affected his attitudes as well as his evaluation of several of his students.

For example, during our study, a representative group of students was tested for level of cognitive developoment using the Piagetian tasks discussed in Chapter 5. Earlier, we had requested both teachers to identify the most and the least able students in their respective classes. Peter's nominations of the most able or best students included the ones with whom he interacted regularly. Peter described the best boys as 'smart' and 'a real mate', while he mentioned the physical attributes of the best girls. For example, 'Jenny, she's a lovely girl' or 'Peta has beautiful eyes' or 'Nicole is a rather gorgeous kid'. When the results of the Piagetian tasks were compared with Peter's list of most able students, discrepancies were noted. The research team sought clarification from Peter, who discussed his attitudes towards and evaluation of three students, Diane, Helen and Jeffrey, whom he had ranked low in terms of ability, but who had performed at the level of formal reasoning on the researchers' Piagetian task measures.

> *Interviewer:* Three kids come to mind who are worth pursuing for me. Diane is one; Helen would be another; and I think Jeffrey would be the third. In each case, my view would be that they are very capable kids; and yet, I am not sure that that is your view. How do we sort of match there?
>
> *Peter:* Well, I thought that Diane was lazy; that she could have done a lot more. I guess my views are slightly coloured because my wife actually taught her music and we discussed Diane. . . . The point in question was a major presentation that the music students were providing, and Diane was a part of the orchestra, playing one of the instruments. Two days before the performance, mum rang school to say that Diane feels she can't handle it and to withdraw her from this performance.
>
> Helen, I think, is also very lazy. In fact, I made comments on her report to the effect that she will have to work a lot harder next year, especially in the subjects she is taking, if she wants to

succeed. But, again, I think it is probably a certain amount of personal bias because of her size. I find it disagreeable when kids are as overweight as she is and I find it difficult to understand and to appreciate. I really think she needs to get up off her backside and do a lot more. She really didn't do a lot in the classroom situation to impress me; yet, she seemed at times to be very critical and sarcastic. So, Helen was one of the few kids in that class about whom I didn't write a favourable report.

Actually, my feelings about Jeffrey changed considerably through the year, because at the start of the year I thought he was the classic classroom clown, and every class has got a couple. Even though, Jeffrey didn't modify that behaviour himself and I did have a minor clash with him because Jeffrey did have a bad habit of sort of mouthing off. . . . On parent/teacher night, I actually did mention it to his parents and said that I didn't appreciate that and that Jeffrey ought to be very careful about some of the things he says. Jeffrey came to me afterwards and completely denied having said it. . . . He went away and must have thought about that because he was very careful in the future about mouthing off, and I think we began to see each other in quite a different light. I think we actually finished the year on quite a high note, Jeffrey and I. He came away on the yacht trip and had a fantastic time and threatened all day to throw me in the water; yet it was funny.

Peter's attitudes towards and evaluation of student abilities and performances reflected other concerns such as parental interference, physical appearance and questionable behaviour. Often his opinions also reflected sex-role stereotypes of appropriate behaviour.

Peter's Out-of-School Excursions

Another of Peter's principles was a strong belief in the value of out-of-school excursions. Peter's roles as Captain of the Ship and as Entertainer were supported by such activities. As he expressed it, 'I personally am very much into establishing a relationship with kids in a non-school environment. I like to get kids away from the school for camps and trips'. The excursions were all nature- or science-oriented, yet establishing rapport rather than increasing learning seemed to be their main purpose. Furthermore, Peter did not capitalize on them as opportunities to interest less-motivated students in science. In an interview with two other researchers, Peter elaborated on one of the irritations of providing out-of- school experiences for his students:

Peter: I can clarify my point of view just a bit further. I mean there are teachers now walking around this school, whenever you take an excursion for example, who want to know if there are equal numbers of boys and girls. That is really starting to get right up my nose.

Interviewer: It is hard if you've got different numbers in the class, isn't it?

Peter: Yeah, well, those yachting excursions are an example. Going out on the yacht, being thrown around for the day and sitting in the sun all day aren't probably everyone's cup of tea and, yet, here was a teacher who wanted to know what the gender split was. I mean, I am running the excursions. I am assuming all the responsibility. I am collecting the money and organizing the whole thing. And a rinky outsider wants to know whether the numbers match or not.

Peter was convinced that his external activities with his students built rapport, encouraged admiration and led to a genuine liking. However, his belief in the value of excursions was firmly rooted in the present, rather than in the future. They were a means of impressing kids, of establishing rapport and of being liked. They were not a mechanism for providing additional learning opportunities for girls, who typically have fewer out of school science experiences (Kahle and Lakes, 1983; Parker, 1985; Sjoberg, 1986). Near the end of the study, I questioned Peter about the potential of his science-related excursions for remediating the different number of out-of-school science experiences of boys and girls. The following passages indicate how Peter chose to ignore the thrust of the question:

Interviewer: What you want to do with kids (that is, informal learning) is so popular right now in the States. From my perspective, it is one of the key things that young women need because they don't have those experiences.

Peter: What do you mean by informal learning? The way Sandra and I teach?

Interviewer: No, I'm sorry. That's another interpretation of informal learning. I was talking about teaching out of the school environment.

Peter: Ah, right ... I am taking two classes out on a fifty-foot ketch, and I am pleased to say I think it is a fifty per cent split between with girls and boys

Peter had answered the criticism of some of the staff about the participation rates of boys and girls. I do not know if both sexes participated equally in science-related tasks during the excursion. Generally, though,

Peter did not link school science with the out-of-school activities in order to augment student learning.

Influencing Peter's Principles: Gender Issues

In an interview with the schools' equity officer (Sue), several plans and strategies for involving more girls in upper-division science and mathematics classes were discussed. That discussion, as well as Peter's new appointment as school leader for grade 10, provided the basis for a lengthy interview concerning gender issues. At the outset, both the interviewer and the interviewee were nervous. The interview was carried out after the observation period in order to reduce its impact on the overall research. During the interview, Peter and I discussed the sex-role stereotypes which were evident in the course selection pattern. In Coastal Australia, all students take grade 10 General Science, which includes topics in biology, chemistry and physics. Lower school ends with grade 10 and many children leave school at that point. Those who remain select their upper school subjects, which in science include physics, chemistry, physical science, biology and human biology. Admission to most science and/or engineering programs in the State require both chemistry and physics as well as Mathematics II and III. Therefore, subject selection is extremely important to a child's future options. Lesley Parker (1987) has referred to the selection of upper school courses, which occurs in grade 10, as the 'choice point'; that is, subject choice in grade 10 determines future goals and careers. Therefore, I queried Peter about his perception of his role as grade 10 leader. What would he do to encourage students, particularly girls, to elect physics and chemistry? Did he have a responsibility in that area? Unfortunately, the interview revealed little, partly because Peter did not directly address the issue in spite of frequent questions:

> *Interviewer:* Sue (equity officer and chemistry teacher) said that she tried to encourage tenth grade girls by having physics and chemistry students come down and talk to them. If you were doing that coordinating (grade 10 leader), you could be very instrumental.
>
> *Peter:* In the few instances I have had, it has been girls in particular who wanted to get out of the advanced classes. It has usually been the mother at home who has been pushing it — it's too hard for my daughter, she can't handle it, she doesn't like it, I want what is best for her — that sort of thing.

In the above sequence, Peter avoided the direct question, commenting rather on the home influence. Later, I tried another tack:

> *Interviewer:* I am interested in gender issues as you see them because of my own research.

Peter: I am sure things are changing. There were a lot of teachers who were very racist in the teaching system (black and white and even Australian versus other nationalities). But I think a lot of that has gone by the way.

Interviewer: Is gender bias the same? Is that gone?

Peter: I like to think that I give the girls more of my time, for example; and I think I do, but an independent observer in the classroom could totally disagree with me. You might be giving girls more time, but you may be responding to them differently. A lot of that could be subconscious.

Interviewer: Do you do anything differently with girls to keep them encouraged and interested?

Peter: I like to take a personal interest in girls more so than boys, because I am basically a heterosexual sort of person, if you know what I mean. I am attracted to girls and I think that is sort of the normal way that it should be. The other side of that, with respect to the boys, is that often I have a sort of a mateship which I establish with a lot of them. I walk up to some boys and thump them on the back, or I drop my shoulder and bump them, and a lot of them will drop their shoulders and try and bump me back. I can't do that with the girls. You can't thump a girl on the back. You see, that is missing in the relationship you have with girls. I often will compliment a girl on how she is dressed, but you don't compliment a boy on how he is dressed.

Interviewer: Do you know of any teaching things you do specifically that would interest the girls in going on in science? Are you conscious of anything?

Peter: I think that, in a school like this, subjects are often timetabled to be on at the same time, so a kid has to make that decision. If you had the situation where a kid could take chemistry, physics and biology, that would ease the pressure a bit. You might get more girls taking it (physics and chemistry) that way.

Throughout the interview, Peter addressed important and substantial issues (for example, parental pressure, racism, personal relations and curriculum organization). However, in spite of repeated attempts to rephrase the gender-related enrolment question, Peter did not respond to questions about sex-role stereotyping in course selection and a possible proactive role which he might take as grade 10 leader. Peter perceived himself as particularly encouraging to girls. Yet, the interactions he described, and which were observed daily over a ten-week period, suggested that Peter's behaviours reinforced traditional sex roles for girls as well as for boys. Intellectual challenges through higher-order questions directed at girls, intervention opportunities through encouraging girls to participate in his excursions, and advisement activities through the recruitment of girls to physics and chemistry were not part of Peter's repertoire.

Although Peter professed to believe in and to support an inquiry approach to science, his laboratory activities were teacher dominated; that is, demonstrations or closed-ended experiments were used. During the few hands-on activities observed, there were clear differences in the participation rates of the girls and the boys and the observed differences related to the content of the lesson. In the Vertebrates unit, the girls initiated the use of the microscopes and it was not until later that they were used by rather disinterested boys. However, in the Nuclear Energy unit, the boys rushed to the laboratory benches, monopolized the equipment and destroyed the reagents by mixing them. During several laboratory sessions, many girls had no opportunity for hands-on science — either there was no time or no uncontaminated materials left. Similar differences were noted in Sandra's classroom and have been reported in the four-year Girls into the Science and Technology (GIST) project, conducted in Manchester, UK (Whyte, 1986). When Peter was questioned about the different participation rates of girls and boys in the biological versus the physical science activities, he agreed with the noted disparities. Although he worried about the boys' lack of interest in biology, which was his field, his concern did not translate into positive intervention.

> *Interviewer:* Now, the boys (Robert, Kim, Steven) you're talking about would not be going on in biology. They want to go on in chemistry by preference.
>
> *Peter:* Yeah ... Well, Steve and Robert and ... Kim, I think they're doing physics and chemistry and mathematics. I am not of the school that says that kids going through science do only biology or physics and chemistry. I think that's an absurd notion, but many many teachers are like that.... It concerns me that kids get it into their minds that they're not interested at all in biological science and they're going to ignore it, or forget about it, or block it out, or whatever. I see that as a part of a weakness ... that I haven't been able to sell it. Although, when we did genetics much earlier in the year, of course, there was a sort of mathematics basis to genetics with quadratic expressions if you want to go into dihybrid crosses. I didn't feel that there was that opting out that appears to be evident with those three boys (Steve, Robert, Kim) in particular with that topic.

Indeed, Peter believed in and perpetuated the masculine image of science, particularly of physical science. He did not relate science and mathematics competence with increased opportunities for students. Although he expended much energy providing unique field trips for his students, he did not feel that it was his place to challenge or change any stereotypes.

Peter truly thought that real students (that is, males) took chemistry and physics. He would support Garratt's (1986) notion that:

> Biology is perhaps perceived as being relevant to girls of all abilities, but only appropriate for boys of average ability. Conversely, physics may be seen as suitable for a broad ability band of boys, but only for girls of higher ability. (p. 68)

Peter expressed his concern and his culpability during the following interview.

Interviewer: What about the greater interest on the part of the girls in vertebrates? Do you think that's attributable to the fact that they have a greater interest in biology, for example?

Peter: I don't know. I mean, the girls seem to have a bias against chemistry, in particular. We did almost a whole term of chemistry and some of the girls towards the end were simply saying 'I can't do it, that's it.' And, they wouldn't even talk about it. I mean other girls thrived on it. Sue for example, thrived on it. But ... Jenny and Danielle to an extent have this in-built escape clause when it gets too difficult. 'I can't do it, therefore, I won't get a good mark and it's all hopeless.' And that's it, end of story. That really surprises me because I would put Jenny as pretty close to being one of the brighter kids in that class. I'd put her, probably without doubt, in the top ten if not the top five. She's very bright, witty; you know, she strikes me as being quite an intelligent kid.

Interviewer: The girl you mentioned, was it Sue? Is she one of those who's going on in chemistry?

Peter: Oh, I can't tell you, I don't know. I can't remember offhand what her selection of choices will be.

Interviewer: Is the apparent lack of willingness to work hard on chemistry by people like Jenny and Danielle because they're unsuccessful, do you think?

Peter: Well, that's obviously part of it. But, in the final test, Jenny and a couple of the other girls, who were making noises about not being able to do it ... did extremely well, including Kristine, who's Danielle's big friend. I think Kristine scored 100 per cent on the last chemistry test. They actually were genuinely surprised at how well they did in that final test. It's a sort of an in-built escape mechanism that they've got in their brain somewhere.

Interviewer: What about things that you do or don't do towards girls who have that attitude about chemistry?

Peter: I just tell them point blank, you know, that in my humble opinion I think that they can do it. . . . In chemistry you've got to go through a series of steps in order to get right to the end of the chemical calculations that we did. Step one is learning first of all the symbols and then learning the valencies. Then you sort of build your way up and up, and you can balance equations. And, then from that, you use the mole concept to solve problems and so on. I emphasize to the kids that it all starts with the initial learning of the symbols. Now, the boys seem to handle that better than the girls ... and from then on it's a sort of a natural progression for a lot of the better boys, the more able boys. They just go from strength to strength, while for a lot of the girls just a little bit of failure creeps in; and then, all of a sudden, it's throw your hands up in despair and let's not even go on. In my other grade 10 advanced class, I had girls who were coming to me and insisting that they be removed from the class....

Interviewer: Do you feel you have any special responsibilities to try to change girls' attitudes towards physical sciences?

Peter: Well, not a special responsibility, but it's interesting. Early this year they did an assignment which was based on a famous scientist of their own choice. This was my idea of wanting to emphasize the contribution that scientists have made. Mary is quite a feminist in many ways and she lets me know that every session. That doesn't worry me, I just let it bounce off me and every now and again, you know, we have a snap at one another, but it's pretty friendly sort of stuff. I think we've established how far we can sort of push one another. She wanted to do Madam Curie which I thought was tremendous; she did Madam Curie and she did it very well. They actually had to get up before the class and talk about the scientist of their choice. Even though the overwhelming number of scientists were male scientists, it was her personal input which reminded the rest of the kids in the class that there were, and there are, famous female scientists who climbed to the absolute zenith of their particular discipline. And, so, I encouraged that. I actually helped her get information on Madam Curie in order for her to do that assignment. But, no, I don't see that as a personal responsibility of mine to try and push particular kids. I think some teachers do too much of that already. I've actually worked with physics and chemistry teachers who have pushed into physics and chemistry girls who had demonstrated most adequately in lower school that they had no hope of doing them in upper school. They did that purely to make up numbers in a second class or a third class so that would give them an extra upper school class and keep them away from the thirty plus students per class that you tend to get in lower school.... Human biology would have been far more relevant, so I think you've got to be very careful when you start pushing kids in particular directions.

Interviewer: For example, if girls were thinking of going on into nursing and if you were making a recommendation to a student like that concerning the relative merits of physics and chemistry to human biology, what would you advise?

Peter: Well, I'd advise biology — human biology — because of the physiology and the anatomy that they cover in human biology and to a lesser extent in biology.

Interviewer: How about medicine?

Peter: Well, medicine has to be physics and chemistry. (University enrolment in all academic science majors requires secondary school physics and chemistry, but not biology or human biology. Enrolment in medicine has no science prerequisites but is a very selective and prestigious program.)

Interviewer: Ecology?

Peter: Well, I'm not sure what the prerequisites are for ecology courses at University, but I think they're more general in what they want or who they will accept than say for medicine, for example, which is very cut-throat.

Although Peter's knowledge of women's contributions in science might not be limited to Madam Curie, his encouragement of girls to pursue science was limited by his views, perspectives and principles.

Sandra's Dilemma

Sandra's teaching behaviours, based on her beliefs and principles, provided a sharp contrast to those of Peter. She was confident and knowledgeable. She perceived her teaching role as a facilitator of learning. Day after day, she demonstrated the Inquirer mode of teaching. Sandra's only deviation from the classic Inquirer style was that her students did not initiate the experiments and/or activities. Rather, they followed the activities presented in their workbooks and they were responsible for pacing themselves through the materials. Nevertheless, the classroom was student oriented and, to a large extent, student controlled. Therefore, students were seldom placed in a risk-taking or competitive position. Essentially, all records of student/teacher interaction during the observation period revealed an identical pattern consisting of short transition, brief announcements, individual activities and short transition. One of Sandra's principles was that students were responsible for their own learning. However, as expected, different students assumed that responsibility in different ways.

Activities of One Group

Because of the way that her class was organized, we had to focus our observations on one group or follow an individual. The following three examples demonstrated the dilemma which Sandra faced as a teacher. During one week, observations focused on one laboratory group which usually consisted of four girls, Janila, Sally, Natalie, Sarah, and one boy, Steven. However, since the observation began, Steven had been sitting at the back bench. Two explanations were offered: first, Steven and Sarah had a tiff; and, second, Steven did not like all the attention that the group was getting from the observers. The intent was to focus on one group in order to identify specific teaching/learning behaviours. Sandra had indicated that Steven recently had joined the laboratory group when she had split up a group of obstreperous boys (Steven, Wayne and Gavin). During the observed period, he remained at the back bench in partial isolation. The girls, on the other hand, were busy gossiping and working at the front table. Although two of them (Janila and Sally) were academically outstanding, another one, Natalie, dominated the group as she often did the class. In a subtle way, those students were 'target' students (see Tobin and Gallagher, 1987), requesting and getting much of Sandra's attention and initiating and responding to many questions.

Let's follow the girls at Table 1 during our typical day in Sandra's room. Natalie orchestrated the activities at her table; she urged one student to skip the options and asked another to hurry to catch up with her so that they could work together. When they settled down to work on the day's topic, sexual reproduction, Natalie responded to Janila's question, 'Didn't your mother ever tell you anything?' At 9:27 a.m., Natalie announced that she hadn't done any work, although class had started at 9 a.m. In general, the girls spent the hour copying factual information from source books to their own notebooks. Janila had one source, *Biology Resource Book*, from the curriculum section of the Education Department of Coastal Australia. It appeared to be an interesting and well illustrated book; for example, there were colour photographs of human fetal development, which usually were of great interest to students. Janila was the only one to use the book. When I asked how she was using it, she said she used it to answer the questions in her workbook. I noted that the *Biology Resource Book* consisted basically of questions, but received no further insights as to why it was being used. Interestingly, no-one seemed either to read it or to enjoy the excellent illustrations. Although the girls were motivated and interested, only rote learning was occurring. The girls continued to copy information and answers into their notebooks. Other students were doing a laboratory activity involving identifying food groups. One question asked them to explain the breakdown of fats, carbohydrates and proteins. I asked first Sarah and then Sally if the question had anything to do with the laboratory activity. Both said no. Sarah was answering the question by copying the text's drawings, which consisted mainly of little circles, of the structure of the three substances. Again, although the girls were on-task, probably little learning occurred.

When she commenced class, Sandra announced that they would have a film. Peter, who was in her class to collect equipment, remarked that the projector was not working. Without any request or indication of need from Sandra, midway through the period Natalie stopped Sarah and insisted that she leave class with her. In a few minutes, when they returned with a second projector which was needed, Natalie loudly announced that Sandra 'doesn't know how to work the other one'. During the film, Natalie and Janila were both very attentive. Both Sarah and Sally continued to work in their notebooks. However, at the end of the film, Janila could not tell the observer what it was about.

When asked about the learning system which they were using, the girls defended it vigorously. Sally, Natalie and Sarah all insisted that one learned better by writing, as shown in the following comments:

> *Sally:* What I don't like is that you don't have time to think about things. So, I get the notebook done, and then read the textbook and try to have four days to ask questions.
>
> *Interviewer:* Do you have a group session in which to ask questions of Sandra?
>
> *Sally:* No.

But Sally indicated that she could get enough attention to get her questions answered individually. Clearly, the girls at Table 1 were target students. Although they accepted responsibility for their own learning, on many days little learning occurred.

Some Students Cause Problems

Another observation during the same lesson illustrated what occurred when students did not assume responsibility for learning. This observation involved the workbench which was set up for a food composition experiment. As soon as Sandra finished with her announcements (9:10 a.m.), Wayne and Nigel rushed to the laboratory station. They proceeded to occupy that space and to control most of the equipment until 9:53 a.m. Nigel began to do the experiment, then pinched out the burner and pulled out its wick. He then soaked the wick in the alcohol and completely dismantled one of the two lamps. As a result of his actions, few students were able to do the experiment. Domination of the equipment by boys in both Peter's and Sandra's classes corresponded to Judith Whyte's (1986) descriptions of boys 'hogging' resources, while girls were left to 'fetch and carry' in many of the classrooms observed during the GIST project. In Sandra's classroom, the lack of one student accepting responsibility for learning also affected the possibilities for learning by other students. That problem, which posed Sandra's dilemma, was illustrated by closely following a very recalcitrant and reluctant learner, Wayne.

Wayne sat alone at the back bench in Sandra's classroom. He had been separated from the others by Sandra prior to our observation period. Wayne was as mature physically as most of the other boys. But his face was boyish and his voice had not changed. A lock of blond hair tumbled into his eyes as he played the class clown.

On Friday September 3, Wayne managed his buffoon role well, avoiding reprimands and work as well. Sandra began class by reviewing the papers on respiration which she had carefully marked. During this period (eight minutes), Wayne rested with his head upon his folded arms. Once Phoebe tried to get his attention, but she must have decided to 'let sleeping dogs lie'. When Sandra finished, the students began to move about the room, collecting books and preparing to complete their worksheets and notebooks. Wayne took advantage of this period to talk with Jody and to call out to Nigel. Soon he was asking all the girls at Table 7 about what grades they received on their returned papers. 'I got one and a half', he said with a guffaw.

Watching Sandra, he moved to talk with Nigel, returning to his seat a minute later when Sandra arrived on the scene. Again watching her, he returned to Nigel and socialized with him. Next, he ambled to Table 4. 'I got one and a half', he repeated. He made a short stop back at Table 7, then moved on to visit Rod at Table 5. Sandra arrived and reprimanded Wayne by shaking her finger at him. He returned to the back bench — laughing visibly — and put his head down. 'Oh, Jesus', he moaned. Mark reinforced his behaviour by calling to him.

After only one minute in his seat, he set off for Table 4 to talk with Michael. He cruised by Sandra to request some worksheets. She sent him to the demonstration table for them. Ambling by Table 2, he stopped to talk. Mark called across to him. Finally, Wayne arrived at the demonstration table, a trip which required three minutes and four stops. He then doubled over with laughter, glancing back over his shoulder to make certain that he was observed.

Carrying the text, he began to wind his way back to his seat, stopping off at Sandra's seat, then at Cliff's seat. Martin arrived at Cliff's to share in the fun. Finally, Wayne cruised back to Table 7, where he had moved his chair. He continued to call to Cliff and Rod, giggling and gesturing. Unable to contain himself, he retrieved a book from Rod and moved to share his joke first with Mark and then with the girls at Table 7. A photograph of a boy watering with a hose (side view) was the source of humour. 'It'd be alright for an elephant' (hose as penis), he explained to Petrina, Jody and Phoebe, who concurred that 'he is disgusting' and returned to their work.

At 2:42 p.m. (32 minutes after class started), Sandra arrived to check if he was working. Wayne grabbed a book away from Phoebe; Sandra moved on. Wayne wrote on Phoebe's notebook; she punched him. Wayne finally began to fill in a diagram of the heart by grabbing Jody's and copying it. In a few minutes, however, he tired of that effort and engaged all students at Table 7 in conversation about bleach — for hair, for cleaning. During the discussion, Sandra arrived at Table 7; they paused; she left; they continued discussing bleach.

On Sandra's next stroll by, she asked Wayne about when his father was coming home. 'Today', he replied. 'Then you'll want to take home a book?' He nodded yes. Wayne continued to chat away and the girls complained that they could not work. He strolled to Table 4 to borrow a ruler, returning to his seat briefly before he threw the ruler, without using it, back to Digby. Finally, Phoebe tried to get him to move. 'Sandra told me to stay', he protested.

Next, he discussed rock and roll, calling back and forth to Martin. Crouching, he slid over to Nigel for a little conversation. Sandra arrived and Wayne returned to Table 7. The girls by now had decided to talk with him and they passed the remaining minutes chatting. When Sandra tried to quieten the class (unsuccessfully), Wayne giggled and said 'Watch Sandra, in another minute she'll say "still waiting, please, still waiting."' And she did.

Sandra's Teaching Style

Because day after day passed in Sandra's class with similar activities and organization, interactions within small groups and between Sandra and one or more students best described actual teacher behaviour and student learning. Sandra's teaching style, although dramatically different from Peter's, involved different interaction patterns and different learning situations for girls and boys. The Inquirer mode, which was both modelled and practised, provided opportunities for individualized learning and created a non-threatening involvement. Quiet girls, such as Phoebe and Sarah, were comfortable in Sandra's room, yet assertive students, epitomized by Natalie, Nigel and Wayne in the vignettes above, could command both her time and attention.

Sandra's influence on the girls at Table 1 (Sally, Janila, Sarah and Natalie) was strong and supportive. When I asked the girls what careers they wanted to follow, Sally replied 'obstetrics', Janila replied 'veterinary' and Sarah replied 'veterinary, until I went on field experience and found veterinary science boring; now I'm thinking about marine science.' Natalie wanted to be a high school science teacher. Three of the girls (Janila, Sarah and Sally) were scheduled to take three science courses. Sally will take chemistry, physics and human biology. The other two will take chemistry, physics and biology. Natalie discussed her course options, noting that she was taking the exact sequence as an older friend, who had given her all of her notes, papers, etc. Natalie also said that Sandra had talked her into taking biology next year. Natalie further commented that her mother had enrolled her in the following year in a community college, where she would be a boarding student. However, she doubted that she would attend. Next, we discussed the type of mathematics that they would be taking. All three of the science majors were enrolled in Mathematics I. (Students may enroll in one of two levels of academic mathematics, Mathematics I or II and III; the most capable students usually select Mathematics II and III which places them on an accelerated track.) They indicated that all advanced students are encouraged to take Mathematics II and III. They mentioned that the mathematics teachers and science enrichment teachers had discussed the mathematics choices with them. Sally, who had been encouraged to take Mathematics II and III, said that the guidance officer had told her that she didn't have to do it for entrance into medical studies. Sarah mentioned her parents as a source of advice. When asked what they said, she replied that they had told her that she could take any mathematics that she thought she could do.

In that series of exchanges, it was clear that Sandra had provided an image of a scientist who is feminine, attractive and pleasant. The girls were all motivated towards science-related careers. In addition, she personally had advised them and had interceded with Natalie, who academically was the most limited one of the group, when she thought that a wrong direction was being taken. An American national study of teachers who were successful in encouraging students, particularly girls, to elect to take optional science courses (chemistry and physics) all provided both subject choice and career advice to their students (Kahle, 1985). In fact, over two-thirds of all students in their classes noted that behaviour. Some girls also stated that no other teacher ever had advised them concerning subjects needed for potential college majors and jobs. Sandra's advice was important in another way because Sally and Sarah suggested that many guidance officers and parents did not understand the value of quantitative subjects for girls. Sandra's presence and directed intervention were important in keeping options open for all four young women.

This point was reinforced by the reactions of all girls to the next question. It was unusual that Sally, Janila and Sarah elected to take the physical science track, yet they opted to continue to study biology. (In Australia, students specialize in subjects in grades 11 and 12; there is both a biological science and a physical science track.) When asked who they would like to have as their biology, or human biology, teacher, they all replied, 'Sandra'. Their reasons were that: she's understanding; she cares and she helps; and she makes it all personal. Sally expanded on her response by noting that she had talked with Sandra in order to make the choice between biology and human biology. Her actions indicate that Sandra considered it her role and responsibility to provide options and to keep doors open for her students.

When Sandra was asked to identify her top achieving students, she first mentioned Janila, Sally, Sarah and Michael and then immediately followed that listing with the names of Clarissa and Nigel. She briefly pointed out each student's achievement level and related it to ability and motivation levels. She did not refer to any personal attributes of either the boys or girls named. When queried about with whom she interacted the most frequently, Sandra responded, 'Janila and Sally and, most recently, Craig'. Although she did not expand on why the interactions were high with the students mentioned, both Sally and Janila were named as top achievers, sat in the prominent first laboratory group and functioned as target students. Craig, on the other hand, was not named as a high achiever. But Craig and his more able friend, Paul, were both members of Sandra's electronics class. Although Sandra did not identify him as one of the best students academically, she responded positively to Craig's newly expressed interest in science.

Informally, Sandra encouraged all students to work hard and to expand their potential. Her dilemma was related to her inability to create and maintain a maximum learning environment for all students. Her constraints were a dated, restrictive curriculum and her own management style. The observations of the girls at Table 1, Sally, Janila, Natalie and Sarah, illustrated the first constraint; Wayne's wasted day focused on the second constraint. Both Sandra and Peter worked within a specific school, community and society. Although schools and teachers can be agents of change within a culture, both frequently reproduce, rather than transform, the sterotypes of their culture (Kelly, 1985). Sandra and Peter saw their roles as teachers and as change agents differently. For example, Sandra tried to transform the sex-role stereotypes commonly held by her students; Peter, on the other hand, reinforced sex-role stereotypes frequently. Their different roles as change agents interacted with their teaching strategies and styles to produce very different classroom climates for girls and for boys, as described in the next section.

Classroom Climates: Causes and Consequences

Sandra and Peter held different beliefs about teaching and they followed different metaphors in teaching. Sandra was a facilitator of learning while Peter was a director of learning. In addition, both interacted with different types of students in different ways. Because I was interested in possible gender differences, I focused on teaching interactions and instructional strategies which might provide different classroom climates for boys and for girls in Peter's and Sandra's rooms. As described earlier, Peter and Sandra used basically different styles of teaching. If all else had been equal, those different styles alone would have resulted in two distinctive classroom climates. The prevailing effect of those different styles (Informer and Inquirer) masked the lesser effects of Sandra's and Peter's personal beliefs about student learning and their conscious efforts to involve both girls and boys. In addition, because Sandra and Peter did not teach in a vacuum, the climates of their classrooms were affected by the school and community environments. What classroom climates were found and what were their causes and their consequences?

A national study in the USA revealed both teaching strategies and teacher behaviours which produce a positive classroom climate suitable for girls as well as for boys (Kahle, 1985). Researchers identified biology teachers who had been successful in encouraging girls as well as boys to enroll in optional, upper-division chemistry and physics courses. (In the United States, biology is taken by virtually all tenth grade students. Chemistry, which can be taken in grade 11 or 12, is taken by 39 per cent of boys and 30 per cent of girls, while physics, a twelfth grade subject, is elected by 24 per cent of boys and 14 per cent of the girls, according to 1986 data.) Then, both qualitative and quantitative data were collected for teachers, students, administrators and parents. The teachers selected taught in diverse geographic locations as well as in urban, suburban and rural schools. Briefly, the results revealed that these teachers commonly: maintained well-equipped, organized and perceptually stimulating classrooms; were supported in their teaching activities by the parents of their students and are respected by current and former students; used nonsexist language and examples and included information on women scientists; used laboratories, discussions and weekly quizzes as their primary modes of instruction and supplement those activities with field trips and guest speakers; and stressed creativity and basic skills and provide career information (Kahle, 1983).

Peter's Classroom Climate

For a variety of reasons, Peter and Sandra differed in demonstrating those identified attributes and behaviours. For example, Peter, in his first year of teaching in this school, moved from room to room during the day. His room, therefore, did not have the characteristics noted. Peter attempted to add interest by posting examples of neat work on the bulletin board, but that attempt was brief. Because he was in his first year of teaching at the school, he did not have a system of parental/community support established. As noted earlier, Peter complained about parental (mother) interference with his decisions and activities. Peter wanted to be liked by students. Therefore, he tried to be a 'mate' to the boys and he flirted with many of the girls. In both friendly and disciplinary interactions, Peter relied upon sex-role stereotyped comments and personal innuendos which usually were greeted with giggles and guffaws. Whether because Peter moved from room to room, or because he prepared inadequately, or because he enjoyed being the Captain of the Ship,

Peter used laboratory activities infrequently and did not have the skills to lead discussion sessions effectively.

The American teachers who were successful in encouraging girls all reported that they quizzed their students every week. By using that strategy, they were able to identify students who were confused or behind. Assistance was provided and students were brought into and kept in the mainstream of the class. It was agreed by the researchers that this strategy was important for students who were not risk-takers. As Tobin describes in Chapter 3 of this volume, Peter felt considerable time pressure in his teaching. He was often poorly prepared to teach general science and he devoted little time to grading students' work. Therefore, Peter did not quiz or test his students frequently and he provided minimal feedback on their written work (workbooks). Although he made verbal comments as he handed back student work, an examination of the workbooks showed only ticks (checks) in the margins. There were no written comments and he did not 'catch' missing information or pages. His verbal comments were brief and pointed; for example, the following ones were noted as he distributed the notebooks for the vertebrates unit:

Excellent set of notes, Jenny, A

Top stuff, Joanna, A

Very poor, Greg, D

Very good, Craig, B

Well done, Mary, A.

At the conclusion of that particular period, Robert approached Peter and asked why his hard work during the Vertebrates unit resulted in the same low grade, C, that he had received earlier when his work was incomplete. Robert protested that he had done all the work, which Peter confirmed. Peter then remarked, 'Yes, but your presentation wasn't very good, was it? You ought to look at the presentations of some of the girls'. Although Peter used the returning of the notebooks as an opportunity to praise more girls, compared with boys, he did not provide substantive comments or feedback. Some workbooks were incomplete and others included errors and inaccuracies which Peter had not found. The praise, or the reward, for the girls was based mainly on neatness. Although Peter did not realize it, that pattern as well as his comments to Robert reinforced a sex-role stereotype. Peter did not test or quiz once a week and his grading of assigned work, which might have provided feedback, was cursory.

The researchers in the USA identified three types of basic skills: first, developmental skills such as the ability to rotate three-dimensional figures visually (visual-spatial ability); second, process skills such as the ability to observe, hypothesize and analyze (hypothetico–deductive reasoning); and, third, quantifiable skills such as the ability to transform and interpret data (tables, charts, figures). Peter's teaching strategies did not stress any of those three skill areas. For example, in most laboratory sessions and demonstrations, the students did not transform the data and had few opportunities to improve their spatial abilities by manipulating the tools and equipment of science. In Chapter 5, Nordland discusses another problem with quantification, namely, that Peter made errors which went uncorrected or unacknowledged.

One opportunity to build visual-spatial ability, however, presented itself during the dissection of the sheep's heart. Although Peter felt confident and comfortable in teaching that laboratory activity, several problems arose which resulted in a poor learning experience. First, sections were cut before the students had a spatial orientation for the whole structure. Second, the dissection did little to reveal the internal anatomy of the heart and resulted in confusion when students tried to compare the actual heart with the diagrams provided in the workbooks. At the back table, Helen simply refused to participate in the dissection, noting her loathing of touching raw flesh. In my opinion, she quickly grasped the futility of the work (the workbook drawing, not the sectioned heart, would be on the test), and she (and several other girls) did not want to get her hands dirty. Although there was a sink in the room, there were no paper towels for drying hands.

Basic skills generally were not emphasized in Peter's class. Likewise, the research team did not note examples of creativity in Peter's approach to teaching, and his career information was usually personalized. For example, he would describe his own courses when he was at university. Although I noted that Peter often commented positively when he was asked to sign either a boy's or a girl's course request for upper division science classes, Peter did not include among his responsibilities the provision of career information.

In summary, Peter did not demonstrate the characteristics and attributes which build a supportive classroom climate for girls as well as for boys. Yet, Peter's comments clearly indicated that he enjoyed teaching and interacting with some of the girls. In fact, our observations repeatedly showed that he favoured some girls with more praise, more time and more rewards. However, Peter's style of teaching and his instructional stagies favoured boys relative to girls. The overriding effect of his Informer teaching style and his use of sex-role stereotyped examples, humour and behaviours was the creation of a classroom climate which was less favourable for girls than the one which he thought he was providing.

Sandra's Classroom Climate

Sandra, on the other hand, revealed many of the teaching behaviours and had many of the community/school relationships which were identified in the sample in the USA. Although Sandra was relatively new to Southside High School, she had a strong reputation as a teacher, as evidenced by her move to the school as head of one of the science departments. Her classroom provided a pleasant atmosphere; she knew many of her students' families; and, for others, she sought out personal information which would help her teach them.

During an interview with both Sandra and the school's equity officer, Sue, Sandra discussed her personal experiences in working as a scientist. From first-hand knowledge, Sandra understood the negative effects of sexism and of sex-role stereotyping. She, therefore, used equitable language and examples. Sandra did not provide readings or information about women scientists during the observation period, but she set the tone — the example — that a woman could be successful in science.

When Sandra's students were asked to draw a scientist, using the Draw-A- Scientist approach suggested by Chambers (1983), several drew likenesses of Sandra. Figure 4.1 illustrates one of the student drawings which resembled Sandra.

Sandra's Inquirer style of teaching included many laboratory activities. Although she did not hold class discussions, she held mini-discussions with individual or small groups of students incessantly. Sandra, too, did not quiz students weekly, yet she did assess their progress by collecting notebooks on a weekly basis. In addition, her grading was thorough and her comments were based on accuracy rather than on neatness.

Certainly, Sandra provided career information, as shown earlier in the description of her interactions with Sally, Janila, Sarah and Natalie. She also encouraged boys to continue in school and science, and she fairly badgered Wayne to work up to his potential. Sandra felt, and the researchers concurred, that the workbooks constrained creativity in her teaching. In the area of her greatest expertise, chemistry, Sandra abandoned the workbook. Because we did not observe during that unit, I cannot assess the extent of inclusion of creative activities.

On the other hand, even with the limitation of the workbooks, Sandra attempted to build basic skills. She provided additional worksheets, she graded tables and graphs of data carefully and she stressed observation as she moved from group to group. However, many of Sandra's attempts to build basic skills were lost due to poor classroom management. For example, during the food experiment as noted earlier, two boys destroyed the materials so that others could neither observe the process nor collect the data. Because students were free to copy each other's work, many individual experiences in quantifying observations or information were lost.

In summary, Sandra's Inquirer style provided a science classroom climate that had been found to be particularly appealing to girls. Using the inquiring mode, Sandra persisted in small-group activities and

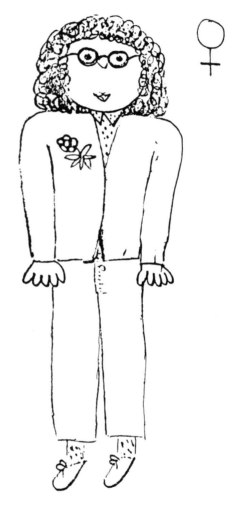

Figure 4.1: A student's drawing of a scientist resembling Sandra

eschewed whole-class sessions. She lowered the risk level in her classroom and she personalized both science and scientists. She supported and encouraged both male and female students, yet she disadvantaged both because of her lack of classroom control. For example, obstreperous boys were relocated and placed with functioning groups of girls as a management technique, and she spent a disproportionate amount of energy moving to place herself beside students who presented potential behavioural problems. In Sandra's case, her adherence to the Inquirer style, unsupported by firm management techniques, interfered with effective teaching of and learning by all students in her classroom.

School and Community Climates

In the USA, the national study of biology teachers who were particularly successful in encouraging girls to continue to study science and to seek non-traditional careers identified common, positive behaviours and practices. (As discussed above, Sandra and Peter exemplified some of the behaviours and used some of the practices.) Also factors which discouraged adolescent girls from continuing in science were identified via student interviews, comments written on student surveys, teacher observations and other research studies. These factors were (1) high school counsellors not insisting on further courses in science and mathematics; (2) lack of information about science-related career opportunities and the prerequisites for them; (3) sex-stereotyped views of science and scientists which are found in texts, media and many adults; (4) lack of development of spatial ability skills, which might be fostered in shop and mechanical drawing classes; and (5) fewer experiences with science activities and equipment which are stereotyped as masculine (mechanics, electricity, astronomy) (Kahle, 1983). Similar factors were identified in the state of Coastal Australia, in the city of Dalton and at Southside High School, as well as in Peter and Sandra's classrooms.

Several lengthy interviews with Sue, the school's equity officer, as well as extensive exchanges with a variety of city, state and national people concerned about the entrance and retention of women in the non-traditional workforce, provided a societal reference point for assessing the presence or absence of the identified factors. (A job is considered traditional for either males or females if eighty per cent or more of the workers holding it are of one sex.) Likewise, informal interviews with students in Sandra's and Peter's classes, as well as formal interviews with several teachers and administrators, provided a local perspective. In addition, texts were analyzed and students were asked to complete Chamber's (1983) Draw-A-Scientist test.

Because of the country's need for more scientific and/or technological expertise, efforts were being made nationally and locally to attract girls to science courses and careers. That is, the importance of factors one and two listed previously as deterrents to girls continuing in science and mathematics had been recognized. Networks of equal opportunity officers had been established in state and national departments of education as well as in secondary and tertiary institutions. Governmental monies were available for projects and for salaries. The activities initiated by Sue directly related to the first and second factors listed previously; that is, they encouraged girls as well as boys to take advanced science and mathematics courses and they provided career information to students. Sue, an upper school chemistry/physics teacher, was in a unique position to provide counselling and career information. In her role as a department head, Sandra also was in a position to effect change. Sue and Sandra described some of their activities in the following interview:

> *Interviewer:* The figures ... showed tremendous increases in the number of girls in upper division courses — mathematics, chemistry and physics — between grade 11 and 12. Is that when you [Sue] began counselling for grade 11?
>
> *Sue:* No, no, I didn't.
>
> *Interviewer:* Well, what happened? What do you attribute it to? And you, too, Sandra.
>
> *Sue:* I think that one of the factors might have been (this is probably a very small factor) that I started teaching physical science that year. Previously it had been all male physical science teachers. So when I was able to say I was teaching chemistry next year, it could have had some sort of impact in suggesting that women can do physical science. That also was the year that Dennis (senior master) did his research on why grade 10 girls chose to do their subjects.
>
> *Sandra:* The way that we want to do it next year is to set up a session and have girl students from grade 12 physics come in and talk to all the classes. Then the male students from grade 11 and 12 biology would come in and talk to all students. Then we'd set up a library with textbooks and syllabuses so that kids actually can go in and leaf through them and look around and have us available [to talk with them].
>
> *Sue:* See, that is something I tried this year. I got two girls who were doing physics, chemistry and mathematics II and III to talk to my grade 10 class, [which was] primarily girls ... The girls in my chemistry class are very outspoken and very committed to their studies and to the future. Grade 10 students have no concept of the future. One of those girls stood up and said, 'I was an advanced student in grade 10, but I have been really struggling with chemistry and physics (in grade 11), but I am getting through. I am studying real hard and I am doing well. Now, I want to go on and do chemistry at university and build a future in the food/nutrition area working for companies.' The other one said she wanted to go into a commerce degree. They [my grade 10 girls] were just stunned and they asked a lot of questions. That needs to happen on a bigger scale next year.
>
> *Sandra:* The only way that it will happen is if we organize it. Right? If we don't organize it, it's not done.
>
> *Sue:* You have to get the students out of classes and they may not necessarily be science classes you are withdrawing them from. So, you have to make sure that you don't antagonize their subject teachers.

Sue and Sandra were both committed to providing course information and career encouragement to all students. They wanted to ameliorate the feminine image of biology/human biology as well as the masculine image of chemistry/physics; that is, they hoped to expand opportunities for all students.

Although there was a supportive atmosphere in the science department because of the leadership of Dennis and Sandra, Sue preferred a low profile for her equal opportunity duties. She was aware of both school and community resistance, which she described in the following way:

> *Interviewer:* Sue, do you feel any antagonism because you took the EO job?
>
> *Sue:* From staff?
>
> *Interviewer:* Yes.
>
> *Sue:* I was very worried about it in the beginning. Dennis asked me to address the staff council about my role very early, because the staff were going around saying, 'Hey, what is this — this equal opportunity thing?' I am used to being ribbed by my colleagues about all sorts of things, and this was just another focus. I said to Dennis that I'm not sure if I can take all the jokes.... I have taken a very low profile, because I think that if you stand up and say, 'Hey, we've got to do this because ...' or 'You are doing the wrong thing', you are going to arouse a lot of antagonism. I have heard of examples of that happening in other schools with other equal opportunity coordinators and I was very careful of it. There are some disappointments, like when I told them about the research option. I had been to the talk which you gave to the coordinators and, not mentioning any names, you get comments like, 'So girls don't want to do science. Why push them?' This is from a science teacher. 'What's the problem? Just let them do biology if they don't want to do physics and chemistry.' 'Who do you think you are, forcing them to do something they don't want to do?'

Sue's efforts, as well as those of Sandra, could help to provide information and encouragement, as well as to breakdown the sex-role stereotyping of courses and jobs. However, the new principal of Southside High School chose not to provide support for the continuation of the equal opportunity position. Sue's and Sandra's efforts were relegated to their own classrooms and to those of other cooperative teachers. Because there was no support and no time provided for a coordinated effort, one can assume that the lack of course and career information could continue to affect the enrolment patterns of students, particularly girls, in advanced science and mathematics courses at Southside High.

The third discouraging factor listed previously involves sex-role

Table 4.5: Analysis of illustrations in science texts (Source: Kahle, 1987)

Country	Date	Text	Percentages		
			Male	*Female*	*Unknown*
UK	(unknown)	Nuffield Combined Science (activity books)	78	14	8
UK	(unknown)	Science for the 20's	62	31	7
UK	(unknown)	Science 2000	62	21	17
USA	1983	Holt, Modern Biology	63	30	7
USA	1983	Scott-Foresman, Biology	58	35	7
USA	1983	Merrill, Biology	57	34	8
USA	1985	BSCS, Blue	51	49	0
USA	1985	Scott-Foresman, Biology	60	32	8
Australia	1981	Fundamental Science, BK 2	85	15	0
Australia	1981	Essentials of Science, BK 3	54	38	8
Australia	1982	Tomorrow's Science	90	10	0

stereotyping of science and scientists by texts, media and adults. Table 4.5 provides data illustrating how various science texts use a greater proportion of male illustrations than female illustrations. Australian science texts generally portray science as a masculine activity done by males. For example, two of the three Australian texts used as resource materials in Peter's and Sandra's classes showed males in over 85 per cent of their illustrations. It is obvious that some Australian texts perpetuated the male stereotype of science and scientists. This view was not ameliorated by the teacher-developed workbooks because few photographs or human drawings were used in them.

On the other hand, excellent posters of girls (and boys) in non-traditional jobs and sports were provided free to all teachers, especially science and mathematics teachers, by the Equal Opportunity Branch of the Education Department of Coastal Australia. A booklet of facts about the life patterns of women, educational requirements for scientific and technological careers, and non-traditional work opportunities was another free and excellent source of information for teachers. In Coastal Australia, therefore, efforts were being made to change the sex-role stereotype of science as masculine and of scientists as men. However, the overriding image from public media and texts still portrayed men in a male occupation.

Influencing the Classroom Climate

Sandra often bemoaned the fact that she had no girls in her electronics class; she also stated that the technical craft subjects were sex-role stereotyped. Yet, the GIST (Girls Into Science and Technology) study had shown that girls' scores on a test of visual-spatial ability could be improved significantly by enrolment in just one semester of a technical crafts subject such as woodworking, mechanical drawings, electronis, etc. (Whyte, 1986). Therefore, Sandra's concern was legitimate. As noted earlier, due to the lack of preparation (Peter's classes) and the lack of management (Sandra's classes), neither teacher provided frequent learning opportunities which would increase a student's spatial ability. (Sandra wrote enthusiastically after the study that a girl had elected to take electronics and that three girls had enrolled in technical drawing.) Therefore, low spatial ability might continue to discourage some students at Southside High from enroling in elective mathematics and science in upper school.

Differential enrolments by girls and boys in chemistry, physics, mathematics and electronics indicate that factor five from the previous list — lack of experiences with science equipment and activities — could have influenced students' attitudes, achievement levels and retention rates in science courses at Southside High School.

Sandra's and Peter's actions and attitudes also had an effect on students' enrolment patterns. Both encouraged students and informally counselled them to take additional science and mathematics. However, because of time problems in Peter's case and management problems in Sandra's situation, neither provided sustained activities which could foster the development of a student's spatial ability or increase his/her familiarity with the tools and instruments of science. However, they differed in one significant way: Sandra was committed to a proactive role, whereas Peter preferred a reactive role.

Who Wins: Who Loses?

Although Sandra and Peter adopted different metaphors about teaching and these influenced their personal instructional styles, both worked within the same cultural milieu and within the same societal constraints. In different ways, both were conscientious and both displayed a love of and enthusiasm for teaching. Yet, in both of their classes, some students were winners while others were losers. Who wins, who loses and why?

The Effect of Peter's Principles

As Tobin discusses in Chapter 2, originally the majority of the research team did not find gender differences in student-teacher interaction patterns in Peter's classroom. However, after a time, all concurred that there were consistent differences in the manner and frequency of Peter's interactions with some girls and some boys. That is, Peter did not interact in the same way with every girl or with each boy; yet two different patterns were discernible.

What were the effects of Peter's differential behaviour towards boys and girls? First, although Peter stated that he preferred to interact with girls 'who were beautifully presented', observational records showed that his whole-group interactions were primarily with boys who raised their hands and were called upon to respond to most of the higher-level cognitive questions posed. Second, because many of his interactions with girls were on a personal level, academic or scientific competence was not reinforced for even the brightest girls in Peter's classes. Third, Peter's Informer style of teaching, which favoured the risk-takers and which relied on masculine references (football, archery, sailing, etc.), also encouraged boys compared with girls.

One of the basic problems was that even an enthusiastic and well meaning teacher such as Peter had difficulty overcoming sex-role stereotypes and societal expectations of appropriate behaviour. For example, a science teacher related an exchange which occurred early in the year between Peter and Sue in the science teacher office area. Peter arrived and announced that a 'delightful young lady' was waiting to see Sue in the corridor. Sue responded, 'Well, actually, she is a physics student'. To this, Peter replied, 'She is, *and* she is a delightful young lady!' Sue became irritated and explained that the person waiting was a student who had come about a physics problem and that her appearance and attractiveness were irrelevant. Peter persisted, saying 'Well, she *is* delightful'. Sue repeated her statement and walked out angrily.

Peter was not a change agent. In his classroom, he transmitted the cultural message of gender differences. Kelly (1985) argued that, when schools play a reproductive rather than a transforming role in transmitting the culture's sex-role stereotypes, differences in subject ability, subject confidence, subject anxiety, risk-taking behaviour and skill competence increase between girls and boys as they progress through school. Peter's teaching behaviours played a strong reproductive role in fostering sex-role stereotyped behaviours and interests among the boys and girls in his classes.

In one area, namely, the acceptance of biology as an appropriate topic of study for males, Peter wished to play a transforming role. He saw himself as a real man, a mate, a good father and husband; and yet he had studied biology. Although Peter stated 'that real students ... do physics and chemistry', he wished that the study of biology could be feminized. When asked about the different levels of student interest in the various units, he responded in the following thoughtful way:

> *Peter:* Robert and Kim, in the chemistry and the motion units, definitely sparkle. Now they have been considerably subdued

throughout this topic [Vertebrates], I'm sure that Robert looks upon it as a bit of an ordeal and Kim just looks upon it as another task that he has to plough his way through. Even Steven [the American kid who sits in the front row] is almost solemn and yet, in physics and in the motion and the chemistry [units], I think he was far more ready to interact. I find that frustrating. The girls, a lot of the girls, are obviously enjoying Vertebrates immensely, and I find it frustrating that the boys aren't as engaged and enjoying it.

The Effect of Sandra's Dilemma

Sandra, on the other hand, clearly saw her role as a change agent. She felt that she had experienced discrimination and she consistently endeavoured to be a transformer, not reproducer, of sex-role stereotypes which promulgated gender differences. The following passage describes Sandra's response to a question about why she was a teacher:

> My parents are both teachers, but my brothers aren't teachers ...
> I decided when I was about twelve years old that I was going to be a secretary, because I wasn't really into education. By the time I was fifteen, I wasn't going to be a teacher, but I wasn't going to be a secretary either. By the time I had finished university I had gone for three degrees. In 1969, and at that stage, inevitably there would be two or three of us left, and we would all get all the royal treatment in looking over the plants in terms of being a chemist. I always had the best marks, but I didn't get a scholarship. So, instead, I got a Commonwealth cadetship and took a job in Sydney. They had biochemist type jobs for chemists. I took a biochemistry cadetship. I did three months research here, and then I went over there to join the research team that was working on a polyacid cycle and electrophoresis and that type of thing. In the mornings, you did normal clinical work and, in the afternoons, you did the research work. I was the only lady. All the other girls were technical officers who had gone through the technical education system.

> There were two things: I was bored stiff; and they were all men. They probably contributed to each other, and it was very obvious from the clinical pathologist in charge that the guys were there forever and were doing their PhDs that way. I wasn't going to be invited to do my PhD. I was so sick of a laboratory; there were so few people to talk to. You did the same tests continuously and it was so tedious. I decided that I preferred to be with people.

Similar explanations were proffered by several of the women teachers in the study in the USA (Kahle, 1985). Generally, the American teachers who had their own career opportunities limited actively tried to expand horizons for their students.

Sandra's metaphor of teacher as facilitator influenced her teaching style as an Inquirer. That style was used more frequently by the American teachers who successfully encouraged girls to take optional physical science classes. Her classroom climate and her advising activities were designed to help all students develop their greatest potential. Yet, management difficulties resulted in certain groups of girls being used to control obstreperous boys. The sex-role stereotype of neat, tidy and hard-working girls was reproduced in Sandra's classroom, while she displayed unusual tolerance of the disruptive and dominating behaviour of some of the boys. Her understanding and patience concerning those behaviours reinforced a sex-role stereotype for the boys in her class; it was expected that boys would be rambunctious and high spirited.

Gender Issues in Science Classrooms

Who wins and who loses? A follow-up study to the one in the USA described earlier revealed that the success of teachers in breaking down sex-role stereotypes concerning science and scientists could be discerned using several types of data (Kahle, 1987). First, achievement in science affected a student's perception of science as an appropriate or inappropriate activity. Second, enrolment in advanced science and mathematics courses demonstrated whether a student saw science as an endeavour congruent with his/her sex. And, third, drawings of a student's image of a scientist indicated whether a student held any sex-role stereotypes concerning science as a career. All three types of data also were collected from Peter's and Sandra's students.

Although Peter praised girls' work when returning the workbooks, a comparison of girls' and boys' grades, shown in Table 4.6 for all of Peter's general science classes (including one that was not observed), indicates that over twice as many males as females received the highest grade. However, in Sandra's class, equal numbers of girls and boys received the highest mark (see Table 4.6). Generally, Sandra's grading favoured girls, while in Peter's classes boys had the advantage.

Grades are particularly important because they influence subject choices in upper school. Very different enrolment patterns were found among the boys and the girls who matriculated in Sandra's and Peter's classes during the period of the study. As Table 4.7 shows, a higher proportion of girls in Sandra's classes, compared to those in Peter's classes, enrolled in chemistry and physics, which are prerequisites for academic science majors in all of Coastal Australia's universities. Although the overall enrolment patterns for boys and girls at Southside

Table 4.6: Comparison of final grades by gender for Peter's and Sandra's students

	Peter's Students[a]			Sandra's Students		
Grade	No. of females	No. of males	% of females	No. of females	No. of males	% of females
Advanced Credit[b]	4	9	31	5	5	50
Advanced Pass	9	9	50	3	0	100
Intermediate Credit	9	18	33	10	7	59
Intermediate Pass	2	4	33	0	1	0

[a] All students in grade 10 General Science classes taught by Peter (N = 64) and Sandra (N = 31)
[b] Grades are listed from highest to lowest, according to State-wide grading in Coastal Australia.

Table 4.7: Science course options selected by Peter's and Sandra's students (in all classes)

	Peter's Students[a]			Sandra's Students		
Subject	No. of females	No. of males	% of females	No. of females	No. of males	% of females
Physics	3	18	14	5	6	45
Chemistry	7	13	35	5	5	50
Physical science	2	4	33	0	0	0
Biology	8	7	53	3	5	38
Human biology	20	4	83	12	4	75
Science	0	5	0	0	1	0

Peter: N = 91; Sandra: N = 46

mirrored the ones found in the city of Dalton, five per cent more girls at Southside High, compared to girls in Dalton, enrolled in chemistry (see Figure 4.2). That figure supports the importance of positive intervention and, perhaps, is related to Sue's and Sandra's activities and presence.

The third way of assessing any stereotyping of science as masculine is by asking students to draw a scientist. This simple activity reveals a student's perception of what a scientist looks like and what he or she does. Internationally, drawings have been collected, analyzed and reported by Mead and Métraux (1957), Chambers (1983) and Schibeci (1986). In all studies, few women scientists have been drawn and the few found have been done by girls. Even after a sustained intervention program, designed to address the masculine stereotype of science and scien-

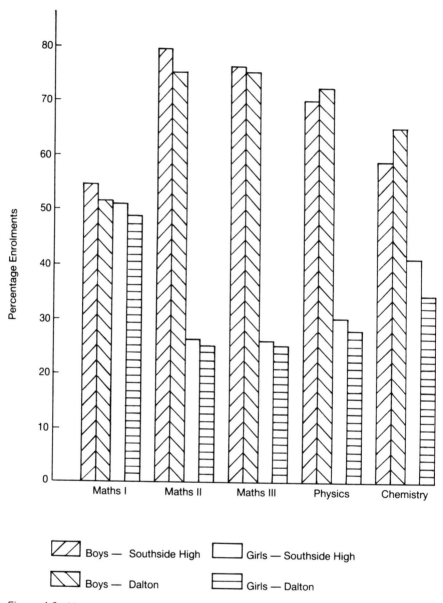

Figure 4.2: Year. 11 enrolment numbers in science and mathematics subjects at Southside High and in Dalton

Table 4.8: Summary of findings from draw-a-scientist test

Indicators for the Standard Image of a Scientist	Percentage of Indicators	
	Sandra	Peter
Laboratory Coat	58	71
Glasses/goggles	81	97
Facial hair	45	55
Symbols of research	45	32
Sex of scientist		
male	87	97
female	3	3
unknown	10	0
Pencils/pens	19	32

Sandra's Class: N = 31; Peter's Class: N = 31

Table 4.9: Percentage of male and female scientists drawn by secondary science students in Coastal Australia

School	Teacher	Students	Sex of Scientist		
			Male %	Female %	Unknown %
Southside	Female (Sandra)	Boys	80	0	20
		Girls	75	6	0
Southside	Male (Peter)	Goys	100	0	0
		Girls	95	5	0
School 1	Female	Boys	100	0	0
		Girls	100	0	0
School 2	Female	Boys	100	0	0
		Girls	80	0	20
School 3	Male	Boys	100	0	0
		Girls	100	0	0

Southside: N = 62; School 1: N = 16; School 2: N = 16; School 3: N = 66

tists, only ten per cent or rural American boys and twenty-eight per cent of the girls drew women scientists (Kahle, 1987). Salient characteristics of the drawings done by Peter's and Sandra's students are shown in Table 4.8. The gender of scientists drawn by Peter's and Sandra's students, as well as some students at other schools, are shown in Table 4.9, which reveals that some of Sandra's female students saw women as scientists. Because students of other female science teachers in Dalton did not draw any women scientists, probably it can be assumed that Sandra's teaching strategies and behaviours were important in modifying her students' images of scientists.

Summary

Peter was an anomaly in that he was a dedicated, well-intentioned teacher who disadvantaged both girls and boys by reproducing society's sex-role stereotypes in his teaching and in his classroom. Peter thought that he favoured girls, but observations and data indicated that his treatment encouraged boys more than girls. His students continued to perceive science as masculine and they followed more stereotypic enrolment patterns. More boys than girls received high marks in his classes. Peter's teaching style (Informer), as well as his reproduction of sex-role stereotypes in his teaching behaviour and examples, reinforced the gender differences that boys and girls brought to his classes. Research has shown that, compared to boys, girls reach grade 10 with fewer experiences in science, with more anxiety about science and with less confidence in their ability to do science (Kahle, 1985; Kahle and Lakes, 1983; Sjoberg, 1986). Peter's behaviours also reinforced the perception that science was an ordinary interest and activity for boys but an extraordinary one for girls. Yet, studies indicate that girls are encouraged to continue in science by seeing it as a normal endeavour for women and as part of a routine career expectation (Erickson and Erickson, 1984; Kahle, 1985; Kelly, 1985). Although Peter thought that he favoured girls with frequent, positive interactions, in reality his acceptance of boys as equals favoured them. The advantaged female in Peter's classroom became the disadvantaged person who saw no place for herself in non-traditional scientific or technological courses and careers.

Sandra, on the other hand, played a transforming role and used a teaching style preferred by many girls, as well as by boys who traditionally have not been attracted to science. Students were monitored in her classroom and considerable effort was expended in the weekly marking of the workbooks. Yet, Sandra also reinforced certain behaviours and reproduced sex-role stereotypes. For example, risk-taking male students such as Wayne could dominate her classroom and her attention. In addition, she maintained control be reinforcing and using the stereotype of serious, hard-working and orderly girls, while she allowed a few boys to dominate equipment and activities, supporting a masculine stereotype. In spite of those problems, however, girls in Sandra's classes saw the possibilities and potential of science. They perceived science as an appropriate and expected career for themselves as well as for boys.

Partially as a result of this study, Sandra recognized her dilemma. However, Peter did not recognize that some of his principles produced a sexist atmosphere in his classroom and in his teaching. Peter perceived that he advantaged girls, particularly the attractive, well presented ones. Yet, expectations of the opportunities for both the girls and boys in his classes were limited by the stereotypes promulgated as appropriate for them. It is difficult to fault Peter, who simply reproduced for children the role which society had assigned as appropriate for their gender. But it is reasonable to criticize Western culture which, until challenged by economic necessity, consistently undervalues the scientific potential of half of its members.

References

CHAMBERS, D.W. (1983) 'Stereotypic images of the scientist: The draw-a-scientist test', *Science Education*, 67, pp. 255–65.

ERICKSON, G.L. and ERICKSON, L.J. (1984) 'Females and science achievement: Existence, explanations and implications', *Science Education*, 68, pp. 63–89.

GALTON, M. (1981) 'Differential treatment of boy and girl pupils during science lessons', in KELLY, A. (Ed.) *The Missing Half,* Manchester, Manchester University Press.

GARRATT, L. (1986) 'Gender differences in relation to science choice at A-level', *Educational Review*, 38, 1, pp. 67–76.

KAHLE, J.B. (1983) 'Girls in school: Women in science', unpublished report, Purdue University. (ERIC ED 258 812).

KAHLE, J.B. (1985) Retention of girls in science: Case studies of secondary teachers', in KAHLE, J.B. (Ed.) *Women in Science: A Report from the Field*, Philadelphia, PA, Falmer Press.

KAHLE, J.B. (1987) 'SCORES: A project for change?', *International Journal of Science Education*, 9, 3, pp. 325–33.

KAHLE, J.B. and LAKES, M.K. (1983) 'The myth of equality in science classrooms', *Journal of Research in science Teaching*, 20, pp. 131–40.

KELLY, A. (1985) 'The construction of masculine science', *British Journal of Sociology of Education*, 6(2), pp. 133–53.

MEAD, M. and MÉTRAUX, R. (1957) 'The image of the scientist among high school students: A pilot study', *Science*, 126, pp. 385–90.

MEECE, J.L. (1987) 'The influence of school experiences on the development of gender schemata', in LIDEN, L.S. and SIGNORELLA, M.L. (Eds) *Children's Gender Schemata*, New Directions for Child Development, No. 38, San Francisco, Josey–Bass, pp. 57–73.

PARKER, L.H. (1985, December) Non-sexist science education: An issue of primary concern, paper presented at the Science Teachers Association of Victoria Conference, Monash University, Melbourne, Australia.

PARKER, L.H. (1987) 'The choice point: A critical event in the science education of girls and boys', in FRASER, B. and GIDDINGS, G. (Eds) *Gender Issues in Science Education*, Perth, Curtin University of Technology.

SCHIBECI, R.A. (1986) 'Images of science and scientists and science education', *Science Education*, 76, 2, pp. 139–49.

SJOBERG, S. (1986) *Naturfaq oq Norsk Skole* (trans. Science and the Norwegian school), National Report of the Second International Science Study, Oslo, University of Oslo.

TOBIN, K. (1987) 'Gender differences in science: They don't happen here!', in FRASER, B. and GIDDINGS, G. (Eds) *Gender Issues in Science Education*, Perth, Curtin University of Technology.

TOBIN, K. and GALLAGHER, J.J. (1987) 'The role of target students in the science classroom', *Journal of Research in Science Teaching*, 24, pp. 61–75.

TOBIN, K. and GARNETT, P. (1987) 'Gender differences in science activities', *Science Education*, 71, 1, pp. 91–105.

WHYTE, J. (1986) *Girls Into Science and Technology*, London, Routledge and Kegan Paul.

Chapter 5: The Cognitive Level of Curriculum and Instruction: Teaching for the Four Rs

Floyd H. Nordland

Peter is positioned in front of the demonstration desk expounding on the human respiratory system. The students are seated behind long horizontal benches. They are quiet and attentive to Peter's lecture presentation and many of them are taking notes.

> *Peter:* The nervous system has the most critical oxygen requirements of any tissue of the body. In fact, brain tissue deprived of an oxygen supply for as short a time as one or two minutes will produce irreparable brain damage.

At the front bench to Peter's right, Jeffrey's hand shoots up. Peter continues lecturing either unaware of Jeffrey's insistent hand-waving or studiously avoiding it.

> *Peter:* Are there any questions?

Peter carefully scrutinizes the entire class before somewhat reluctantly calling on Jeffrey.

> *Jeffrey:* I was watching *Sixty Minutes* on the television recently and they talked about an American kid who was under water for a long time. I think that it was about fifteen or twenty minutes. When they pulled him out, they were able to revive him and apparently there was very little brain damage. How can you explain this?
> *Peter:* Well, I don't know anything about that as I don't watch *Sixty Minutes.*

Peter continues with some disparaging comments about the negative aspects of watching too much television and Jeffrey's excellent question is never acknowledged intellectually. Thus, an opportunity to teach and learn at the application, synthesis or analysis level is lost and the instruction continues at the lowest possible cognitive level.

Although the above vignette presents an extreme example, the exchange is typical of the instruction in Peter's grade 10 science class. Regardless of Peter's attentiveness to students or of his attempts to relate school science to real life, low cognitive levels of learning prevailed during most, if not all, classes observed. This chapter analyzes the cognitive level of teaching activities and of learning outcomes in both Peter's and Sandra's classrooms. It focuses on three aspects of the teaching/learning process: the cognitive levels of the curriculum and instruction; the cognitive levels of the students; and the criteria for assessing the cognitive level of curriculum and instruction. References are made to both classrooms and specific examples from observed situations are used to represent the cognitive levels of teaching and learning of grade 10 science at Southside High.

An Analysis of the Cognitive Levels of the Curriculum and Instruction

During the ten-week period of observation in two grade 10 science classrooms at Southside High School, the students, many of whom were advanced level achievers, were taught units on Vertebrates and Nuclear Energy. Instruction at Southside High was organized around workbooks which included a set of objectives, a series of activities intended to be completed through a self-paced, small-group or individualized learning format and several optional activities. The workbooks were geared to specific textbooks and students often were directed to specific pages in the text. Answers to questions usually were taken directly from the text; and, if they were not found there, the teachers often would supply the 'correct' answer. Two texts were used as primary references; they are called *Essentials of Science* and *Tomorrow's Science* for the purposes of this chapter.

The science staff at Southside High were committed to individualized and self-paced teaching and learning. They believed that it was an effective and innovative approach to the teaching and learning of science. They shared the collective opinion that it resulted in higher levels of achievement and produced higher-level cognitive outcomes than more traditional approaches did. This chapter focuses on the cognitive level of the curriculum materials and of the daily instruction, as well as on the cognitive outcomes achieved by students. In addition, an assessment of students' levels of cognitive development and an analysis of students' potential for learning relative to their actual learning are presented.

Curriculum Materials

A careful analysis of the objectives, activities and questions found in the workbooks indicates that student learning associated with completing the exercises largely would be restricted to low-level cognitive outcomes. The instruction required rote memorization of answers copied into the workbooks followed by short-term recall of their contents. The following examples of workbook content are taken from the unit on Vertebrates. The first passage illustrates the cognitive level of instructional objectives, while the second one presents an actual activity. One of the learning objectives for the Vertebrates unit is stated as follows:

> Students will be able to describe the structure and function of the vertebrate skeleton and be able to relate the two to one another. Know the main bones of the human skeleton.

From reading the above objective, one can assume that an emphasis on the important concept of structure and function might require students to examine carefully the structure of the bones of the vertebrate (human) skeleton and infer from those structures their probable functions. However, the latter part 'know the main bones of the human skeleton' is clearly a memorization activity. After one examines in detail the material in the workbook which is designed to satisfy the above objective, it becomes evident that the knowledge level is the focus of the entire activity.

Next, consider the cognitive level of the following workbook activity related to the three functions of the skeleton: 'Use reference books to find out what these are and write notes on them. Refer to *Essentials of Science*, p. 91'. When students turn to the textbook, they find the three main functions identified and listed on the page indicated. In that manner, a potentially interesting and thought-provoking activity is reduced to copying facts from one source to another. The principal textbook, *Essentials of Science*, initially was written for low-ability students. The sentences are short, the vocabulary level is low and, of particular importance, the book presents science as an encyclopaedic body of absolute facts. Little attention is given to describing how information is generated, to discussing the relative nature of truth or to elucidating the conceptual structure of the discipline. An example from the textbook illustrates its limited approach to science:

> Bony fish such as herring and goldfish have a skeleton of bone.
>
> Bone is produced by bone cells. These cells deposit calcium and phosphorus between the cells. This makes bone hard. Look carefully at the diagram of the fish skeleton. Identify the main parts. (*Essentials of Science*, p. 92)

Another example of the low level of the texts is taken from the alternative text:

> The internal skeleton, consisting of limb bones, ribs and skull, is attached to the backbone. The muscles and organs are attached to, or supported by, this skeleton. The skeleton itself is attached

together by strong pieces of fibre called ligaments. Ligaments allow joints to move so that the body is not too rigid. (*Tomorrow's Science*, p. 126)

An analysis of the texts' contents, samples of which are shown above, revealed that neither text contained current information; in fact, most of the information included had been known for at least fifty years. The descriptive style of the texts also detracted from opportunities for teachers to include open-ended questions which could lead students into inquiry or problem-solving activities. Furthermore, the reader was left to conclude that *either* nothing of importance relating to vertebrates had been discovered during the past fifty years or that the traditional treatment of the topic provided the relevant information needed for meaningful learning.

If one followed a typical activity, the rote learning process fostered by the workbooks became obvious. The following passage shows how the student was guided to specific answers as part of an activity on the bones of the skeleton:

Collect a copy of the worksheet Human Skeleton and fill in the names of the bones which are numbered. Locate these bones on the skeleton and learn them. What is the smallest bone in the body? What is the largest bone in the body? How many bones are there in the human skeleton?

Clearly, the above activity focused on low-level cognitive learning. The highest level of inquiry observed during the unit involved one of the bones which was to be labeled on the worksheet and which was not identified in either text. However, in Sandra's class, when several students asked what it was, she supplied the correct answer. A few students checked another reference book, but they simply were interested in finding the name of the bone, not in seeking additional information.

An examination of another activity illustrated the potential for higher-level learning by using the workbooks. In Activity 4 involving comparison of two vertebrate skeletons, for example, students were asked to analyze and synthesize:

Many of the vertebrates have different ways of moving (running, jumping, flying, etc.) and different ways of protecting themselves. Their bodies and skeletons have adapted to suit their particular requirements.

Collect a copy of the Worksheet. Compare two of the skeletons or pictures of skeletons available in the lab and note their differences and any reasons that you can think of for these differences.

Why is the tail of the human so much smaller than that of the kangaroo?

The activities had the potential for engaging students in higher-level cognitive activities and outcomes. However, when students were working on these in Sandra's class, their work involved a superficial examination of several specimens and/or copying responses from books. Unfortunately, most students treated the class time primarily as a time for social activity. They understood that they were required to complete the activity, but they acted as if they would not be held accountable for the quality of their responses. They also knew that examination questions on the unit would be factual and that appropriate answers could be found in the textbook. The above question, which could have led students to higher-level cognitive thinking, also was attacked in a factual way; students only sought *the* correct answer in their textbooks. Again, students were able to avoid an opportunity to engage in inferential reasoning. Furthermore, the continued emphasis on the textbook as the source of knowledge improperly suggested that the answer to the question was known and that the answer was correctly stated.

Almost all of the required activities in the workbooks were similar to the ones given above. Furthermore, problems usually were stated at the lowest cognitive level. Regardless of the cognitive level of the activities and problems, students were required only to find 'the correct answer' in the book and then to write it on the worksheet or in their notebooks. Several of the workbooks' optional activities required higher-level thinking and they had the potential for producing higher order learning. Unfortunately, such exercises seldom were required of the students and, when they were, often they too were reduced to memorization activities. In summary, the students were given curriculum materials which virtually assured that only low level cognitive outcomes would occur. Activities requiring application, analysis, synthesis or evaluation were seldom found and, if present, they were either reduced in cognitive level or ignored by the instruction used. In order for students to attain higher cognitive levels of learning, the teachers would have had to supplement their curriculum with resources and activities other than the ones found in the workbook and the textbooks.

Instruction

Sandra had an excellent background in the science that she was teaching and she was universally liked by her students. During a typical class period, the students worked in small groups while Sandra moved from group to group. When she was not distracted by interruptions or management issues, she consistently enriched the quality of the instruction for students by making appropriate comments, pointing out applications and often asking higher-order questions. Unfortunately, as has been reported in other chapters, Sandra had serious management problems, which meant that she rarely had time for meaningful intellectual interactions with students. Because she was constantly involved in maintaining classroom control, the cognitive level of the instruction remained at the level of the workbook and the textbooks. Her involvement with management reduced the cognitive level of the instruction to copying facts from the textbook into the notebook.

Peter was much more of an authoritarian. He often lectured and frequently wore a white laboratory coat when addressing the class. He delighted in performing demonstrations such as dissections and he often would gather his students around him as he performed. He frequently engaged in a running commentary concerning the activity, and this often was spiced by sarcastic humour and lively exchanges with the students. For example, when Peter's students worked on completing the workbook activities, Peter moved around the room talking with students. During those exchanges, he was more likely to be discussing extra-curricular excursions than the activity on which the student was working. In fact, he indicated that he perceived completing the worksheets and workbooks as busy work. Therefore, he felt free to use individual study time to interact with his students socially and personally. He would check to see that questions were being answered, but he seldom made any effort to evaluate the quality of the work.

Although Peter collected the workbooks periodically, it was obvious to both the observers and the students that Peter would check primarily to determine that the workbooks had been completed rather than to evaluate the quality of the responses. Grades were determined largely by scores on examinations which stressed rote recall of information. The questions were based directly on the revision sheets which contained review questions at the recall level. Peter's favourite time in class was when he was at the front being the centre of attention, disseminating information, directing questions, telling anecdotes, etc. At those times, he described himself as Captain of the Ship (see Chapter 3).

Evaluation

Towards the end of the five-week unit on Vertebrates, students were supplied with a list of review questions, which were intended to help them assess their understanding of what they had learned as well as to prepare them for the unit exam. Few of the questions posed required anything beyond the recall level of memorized facts. For example, the following questions, concerning objectives and activities related to the skeleton, were typical: 'Is an internal skeleton a feature of the vertebrates?' 'Give three jobs done by the skeleton'. Of the fifty-nine questions given to the students on the revision sheet, fifty-five required recall of memorized information. Immediately prior to the examination, Peter went over each of the fifty-nine revision questions, providing students with the correct answers; there was essentially no opportunity for discussion or student questions.

The examination on the Vertebrates unit, which all students in grade 10 science at Southside High were required to take, consisted of thirty multiple-choice questions and three short-answer questions. Questions relating to the bones included the following examples of multiple-choice items:

What is the name of the bone labelled X?
    a. radius
    b. humerus
    c. ulna
    d. femur

What are the bones labelled Y called?
    a. phalanges
    b. metacarpals
    c. vertebrae
    d. tarsals

An example of the 'short answer' questions was 'Name the parts labelled on the diagram below showing a dissected female rat'. The unit exam consisted of memorization questions. There were only three questions at the application level. However, during the review sessions, answers for even those questions were provided. In summary, all relevant aspects of both the curriculum and the instruction (that is, the textbooks, the workbooks, the learning activities and the evaluations) were conducted at the lowest possible cognitive level of learning which usually required only rote memorization.

A Piagetian Analysis of the Cognitive Level of Students

After a few weeks of observation, it became obvious to all members of the research team that the cognitive demand of the teaching and learning in the two classes was very low. As discussed, the textbooks, the workbooks, the revision sheets, the tests and the instruction all contributed to learning characterized by rote memorization and recall. Yet, the students in the classes had been described as advanced-ability students.

As a research group, we agreed that students in advanced-ability classes should be engaged in science instruction that is experientially based and required inquiry. Furthermore, the instruction should emphasize how we know something is true, how we generate knowledge and the relative nature of what we know. During interviews and discussions, both Sandra and Peter professed to value the same type of inquiry-oriented instruction which was espoused and valued by the research group:

> *Sandra:* Students should set up experiments where they start with an idea, test the idea and then use the results to reinforce a principle — then, ideally and on a broader scale, this is how they actually learn.
>
> Things will change as a result of the way scientists work. It's not something that's static. Kids ... need to be reminded constantly that this is where it's at at the moment. They need to do experiments, even though they're not really doing them as a scientist; at least they can see that it's not a static subject. In science, in particular, information does change.
>
> *Peter:* Well, one of my hobby horses that I got on to last week involved how we never really immerse kids in the experimental method.... I mean it's strictly ... a cookbook approach, and the kids do set labs and they come up with set results. But that's not really how science in the laboratory works and it would be great to try to get kids to try and solve a particular problem, you know, a very mini, little problem using an experimental design approach and having it as a topic that ran for four or five weeks.

There were a few optional activities in the workbooks which had the potential for requiring higher-level cognitive thinking. One such activity was recommended by Sandra to Peter, who subsequently was observed conducting the activity. The activity was intended to investigate and/or demonstrate the relationship between carbon dioxide concentration in the blood and the length of time that it is possible to hold one's breath. In preparation for the activity, Peter selected six students who were to come to the front of the classroom and to serve as experimental subjects. He paired each of them with another student who had a timing device. He explained that they were going to determine how long each of the students could hold his/her breath after three different treatments: (1) after normal breathing; (2) after a short (timed) period of hyperventilation (rapidly breathing in and out); and (3) after a timed period of breathing in and out of a plastic bag.

Peter explained both the activity and his reasons for including it in the curriculum during an interview:

> *Peter:* My purpose in conducting the activity was to demonstrate that the level of carbon dioxide present in the blood is the factor which determines the differences in breath-holding time.
>
> I also like to engage my students in experiments involving data collection. Exposure to the scientific method is important and I try to do this whenever I can. That is why, for example, you'll recall that I discussed the terms dependent and independent variable.

Peter had begun the activity by a discussion of the terms dependent and independent variable. Because Peter believed that students remembered best those things for which a teacher could provide some anecdotal comment or story with which they could associate the term, he related the terms to everyday phenomena:

> *Peter:* From my educational experience as a kid in the classroom, the things I remember the most were the comments the teacher made that made a lot of it relevant, and so you find in my teaching a lot of comments . . . and they are the things that stick.
>
> The sorts of things that I hang my coat on are a lot of the little, personal insights that I try and give through the course of the lesson. When I did the dissection of the lung and I made comments about smoking . . . and I described in great detail just what smoking does to the lungs.

Peter's attempts to relate the terms independent and dependent variable to the student's relationships to friends and family was a good instructional technique and consistent with his beliefs: 'When you hear the term dependent variable, just think of someone who is dependent on you'. Unfortunately, his next example was contradictory and presented the students with an unfortunate misconception: 'An independent variable is one which you have no control over'. Peter continued to reinforce this idea with another example which was both logical to him and consistent with his misconception. This example helps to illustrate why many beginning students have a difficult time remembering the proper use of the terms, dependent and independent variable:

> *Peter:* I am going to ask you to hold your breath as long as you can. Since you will have no control over how long you can hold your breath, that is the independent variable.

It was obvious from observing the students' behaviour during the respiration activity that their interest levels were high. Peter, with his excellent classroom management skills, controlled the boisterous behaviour sufficiently to collect data representative of the phenomenon being observed and capable of meaningful interpretation. He recorded the results on the blackboard, providing the class with the data in Table 5.1. The blanks in the data were caused by students giggling or breaking into laughter, which made it impossible to measure their breath-holding time. No attempt was made to repeat the procedures in order to fill in the missing values. An athletic young man named Robert was the clear 'winner' in all three categories. In fact, it appeared to both observers that he cheated a bit in order to demonstrate the value reported after rebreathing. Robert clearly wanted to be tops among his peers in an activity which was related to physical conditioning.

Consistent with Peter's previously stated purpose of demonstrating

Table 5.1: *Breath-holding time in seconds for six students*

Student	Normal Breathing	Hyperventilation	Rebreathing (Plastic Bag)
1	41	72	14
2	—	60	15
3	91	120	70
4	—	86	40
5	49	92	35
6	—	60	31

the role of carbon dioxide in determining the length of time for which breath can be held, Peter next returned all of the students to their assigned seats, took chalk in hand and directed their attention to the data which he had recorded on the board. He then provided students with the following information:

> *Peter:* The purpose of this activity was to demonstrate the role of carbon dioxide concentration in regulating the respiratory rate. As I mentioned previously, when you hyperventilate, the rapid breathing speeds up the rate at which carbon dioxide is removed from the lungs. This has the effect of lowering the carbon dioxide concentration of the blood. As you can see from the data, all of you were able to hold your breath longer after hyperventilation. This is because, when you began holding your breath, the carbon dioxide concentration was very low; therefore, you could hold your breath longer.
>
> After rebreathing the air from the bag, the carbon dioxide concentration of the air in the bag would continue to increase and, thus, the carbon dioxide concentration of the blood would be much higher than after normal breathing. And, as you can see from the data, all of you had the shortest breath-holding time after breathing in and out of the bag.
>
> Let me emphasize again what we can conclude from this. It is the carbon dioxide concentration in the blood which controls the rate of respiration or, in this case, how long you can hold your breath. The reason that you can't hold your breath long enough to become unconscious is that, once the carbon dioxide concentration reaches a certain crucial level, you lose your ability to hold your breath voluntarily and you begin to breath involuntarily again.

In keeping with his belief that anecdotal points made by the teacher were the most important aids to memory, Peter went on to make the following statement:

Peter: This is why accident victims being treated by paramedics after a near drowning or an accident are not given pure oxygen. Enough carbon dioxide is added to stimulate the respiratory neurons to fire.

Although students clearly enjoyed the activity and although Peter managed its logistics well, he did not frequently use experiential instruction. In fact, the example presented was the only time during the five-week unit on Vertebrates that an activity was conducted which involved the collection of data.

Both the refreshing departure of the respiration activity from the usually low-level cognitive activities of the class and the subsequent analysis and discussion of what was observed catalyzed the research team to consider the following questions:

1　What are the cognitive levels of the students in the classes?
2　Given the opportunity, are the students capable of demonstrating an understanding of terms such as dependent or independent variables, of applying them correctly in concrete and hypothetical problem-solving situations, and of demonstrating the logical, formal-reasoning skills required to understand both the design of experiments and the interpretation of data?
3　To what extent do misconceptions and misinformation affect student learning?

Assessment of Students' Piagetian Stages

It was decided that one member of the research term would engage students from Sandra's and Peter's classes in individually-administered Piagetian-style interviews. Because Peter had conducted a brief discussion of dependent and independent variables as an introduction to the respiration activity, it was decided to administer the Separation of Variables Task. This task is designed to measure a student's ability to identify and control variables. The apparatus used contained six flexible rods of varying length, diameter, shape and material, as well as an assortment of weights. The students were asked to identify the variables which might affect the bending of rods and then to use the apparatus to demonstrate proof of the effect of each variable on the amount of bending found in the rods. The demonstration required understanding of the need to control all variables with the exception of the one being tested or manipulated.

A student, who consistently demonstrates his/her understanding of the need to control variables in problem-solving activities, demonstrates one characteristic of the Piagetian stage of formal operations; such a student is coded as being at Stage III B. Students who do not demonstrate an understanding of the need to control variables demonstrate thought

Table 5.2: Number of Sandra's and Peter's students at each Piagetian stage of cognitive development as determined by the separation of variables task

Piagetian Stage	Number of Students			
	Peter's class	Sandra's class	Total	%
II B	5	3	8	19
III A	8	4	12	29
III B	9	13	22	52

patterns characteristic of the Piagetian stage of concrete operations, and they are coded as being at Stage II B. Concrete operational students apply a particular mental action, or operation, only to concrete objects which are immediately present. Their thought processes are much less flexible and, therefore, less effective in solving new problems. For example, students at the concrete operational level are unable to consider all possible outcomes, and they often overlook factors of importance while concentrating on one aspect of the problem or task (for example, focusing on the thickness of each rod, rather than focusing on multiple aspects of the rods such as thickness, type of material, etc.). Students who demonstrate the need to control variables some of the time, but who are inconsistent in their performances, are considered to be in transition from the concrete operational stage to an early stage of formal operations. This intermediate stage is sometimes referred to as the transitional stage and it is coded as Stage III A (Inhelder & Piaget, 1958). The results of the Piagetian testing, shown in Table 5.2, categorize Sandra's and Peter's students according to Piagetian stage of development.

The fact that eighty-one per cent of the students demonstrated formal reasoning abilities (III A and III B) was not surprising; they were students who had been assigned to advanced classes. This finding suggests that the selection criteria used to assign the students was successful in identifying students capable of utilizing formal reasoning skills. Furthermore, the results indicated that only curriculum and instruction which consistently required the application of higher-level cognitive skills would be appropriate and challenging for such students.

In analyzing the meaning of the Piagetian levels of cognitive development, one can describe typical student responses to the Separation of Variables Task. For example, the difference in performance between students classified as III A and III B primarily is one of consistency. Students classified as III A try to hold all variables constant, but fail to do so in at least one attempt. For example, when attempting to demonstrate that the diameter of the rod is a factor, the student selects a thin brass rod and a thicker steel rod. Although the student controls weight, length and shape, s/he varies two factors, diameter and material. When a transitional student is asked, 'How do you know that it's not the type of material causing the difference in flexibility?', s/he immediately will choose two brass rods of different diameters and will correctly complete the task. Such behaviour indicates that there is little, if any, real difference in the student's intellectual skills when compared to those of a student classified as III B. Both types of students (III A and III B) need and deserve curriculum and instruction which both permits and requires the use of formal reasoning skills.

In comparison, when a similar question is posed, a concrete thinker might select a thin, round, brass rod and compare it to a thick, square, steel rod of a different length. When questioned about the material (or shape, length, etc.) difference, s/he simply will reiterate that the thin rod is bending more and that this demonstrates 'the thinner the rod, the more it will bend'. A concrete operational student fails to recognize the absence of logical reasoning and the need to control all variables except one. Assuming that the student is relaxed sufficiently to perform in a manner representative of his/her developmental level and assuming that s/he is trying, concrete operational characteristics are easy to recognize in students (Nordland, Lawson & Kahle, 1974). Participation in science classes where recall and memorization are stressed does nothing to improve a concrete-operational student's development of reasoning skills. However, instruction which starts with hands-on activities and proceeds to problem- solving activities which require formal thought does contribute to such students' intellectual development. A class in which eighty per cent of the students demonstrate formal reasoning ability provides an ideal peer environment for developing improved reasoning skills.

Student Interviews Regarding Problem-Solving Strategies

Because students from Peter's class had participated in the respiration activity and because Peter had introduced the terms dependent and independent variable, it was decided to ask the students from his class a series of questions which related to the respiration activity and which involved problem-solving strategies concerning a hypothetical experiment. Therefore, after completing the flexible rods task, his students were shown a copy of the data collected during the breath-holding activity; next, the experimental procedures followed in collecting the data were reviewed. It was obvious from observing the students' behaviour during the activity that their interest levels were high. During the interviews, it was apparent also that the students recalled the activity clearly from the standpoint of what procedures had been followed and, in general, what results had been collected. The students were shown a copy of the data collected in class and they were asked, 'Why don't you tell me what you think this means?' or 'What can you conclude from these data?'

Although six to ten weeks had transpired since they had observed the activity, all but three of the students were able to give an adequate interpretation of the data. They were able to generalize that, after hyperventilation, the students involved were able to hold their breaths for a longer period than they could after normal breathing. They observed also that breath-holding time after rebreathing from a bag was shortened in comparison to breath-holding time after normal breathing. Interestingly, all three students who gave inadequate explanations of the breathing experiment had demonstrated concrete operational thinking on the rods task.

Peter had described in an interview that his purpose in conducting the breathing activity was to demonstrate that the level of carbon dioxide was *the* factor which determined differences in breath-holding time. He had pointed out to the class on two different occasions that hyperventilation lowered the carbon dioxide concentration in the blood and that rebreathing from a bag caused the carbon dioxide level of the blood to rise. At the end of the activity, he stated clearly and emphatically that 'carbon dioxide concentration is the factor responsible for the differences in breathing-holding time and in controlling the rate of respiration'. In addition, he added some anecdotal comments intended to help students remember the critical role of carbon dioxide concentration in regulating the rate of respiration. However, during the interview sessions concurrent with the Piagetian task analysis, only three students (14 per cent) were able to identify correctly the level of carbon dioxide as the causal factor. An overwhelming majority of the students, seventeen (78 per cent), identified oxygen as the causal factor, while two students (9 per cent) identified air as the important factor.

The students' responses were consistent with findings reported from the area of misconceptions research. Students were aware that oxygen was essential for life. They arrived in Peter's class with that knowledge, and it was properly reinforced during the discussion of respiration. Therefore, they were prone to select oxygen level in the blood as the probable cause of the difference in breath-holding time; and, six to ten weeks after instruction, obviously they had forgotten that Peter had told them otherwise. These results occurred in spite of the fact that most of the students had selected the correct response to a recall item concerning breath-holding on the unit test, that almost all of them had exhibited a high level of interest during the instruction, and that many had a clear recollection of the procedures followed and the results obtained. Although the actual, incorrect knowledge exhibited is not particularly important from the standpoint of teaching and learning, it is important that being told the correct answer was not a sufficient process to alter misconceptions which were firmly established in students' minds. The difficulty in correcting misconceptions is particularly severe when there is an obvious, or intuitive, logic to the incorrect answer. It demonstrates, also, that using the laboratory to illustrate concepts will be equally unsuccessful unless a lot of time is devoted to discussion and directed towards remediating the misconception. Telling students the answer, asking students to fill in the blanks in a workbook or having them select the memorized correct response on a recall test are simply ineffective techniques for effective learning — no matter how relevant are the comments made by the teacher during the lesson. It should be equally obvious that not only is it a waste of time to memorize and forget facts from the standpoint of correct information, but also this type of classroom activity does little to improve a student's reasoning or thinking skills.

Of course, there were differences in the quality of student responses to the interview questions concerning respiration. Some of the students provided more complete explanations and engaged in more extensive discussions than others did. However, all of the students demonstrated some degree of uncertainty and some level of difficulty in responding to the questions posed. All of the students interviewed would have profited from classroom activities which required them to consider alternative hypotheses, to analyze and interpret data and to formulate conclusions.

Because Peter had introduced the terms dependent and independent variables, a subsequent series of questions was asked during the interviews. That is, students were asked if they remembered Peter's use of the terms in class. Most of the students (91 per cent) remembered the terms being used. However, when asked if they remembered the definition of the terms, only one student even attempted an explanation. Their complete lack of recall of Peter's explanation illustrates the inefficiency of most verbal exposition in promoting learning.

Next, the students were given definitions of the terms by the interviewer; those definitions were available to them during the rest of the interview. The following definitions were provided:

Manipulated or Independent Variable: The variable that is manipulated or varied during the experiment such as a treatment.

Responding or Dependent Variable: The variable that is not manipulated, but presumably responds to variations in the independent or manipulated variable.

Controlled Variable(s):   A variable or variables which is/are held constant or unchanging during the experiment.

Then students were asked to apply the above terms to the separation of variables task and then to the respiration activity. When asked to identify the manipulated or independent variable in a proof of the rods task, seventeen out of twenty-two (77 per cent) correctly identified it.

Furthermore, sixteen out of twenty-two (73 per cent) were able to identify the flexibility of the rods, or the amount of bending, as the dependent variable. However, students who were classified as concrete thinkers on the rods task experienced the greatest difficulty in correctly applying the terms.

Next, students were asked to identify the independent variable in the respiration activity. Fourteen students (64 per cent) correctly identified the type of breathing as the independent variable, while only ten (45 per cent) correctly labeled breath-holding time as the dependent variable. As expected, this request was a more difficult task, compared with identification of the terms with the Piagetian exercise, for most students.

Why did students experience increased difficulty in correctly applying the above terms to the respiration activity? When that activity is analyzed carefully, it reveals a level of difficulty that might not be immediately apparent. For example, consider the problem which a concrete operational student would face in applying the terms to the differences in carbon dioxide levels produced by the three breathing regimes. If one considers the conditions which caused the differences, then the type of breathing is the manipulated variable, while the carbon dioxide level is the responding variable. However, if one approaches the problem in terms of breath-holding time, then carbon dioxide level in the blood becomes the independent variable and breath-holding time remains the responding or dependent variable.

The quality of the students' responses clearly indicated that Peter's introduction of those terms did not clarify student understanding of how respiratory rate and breath-holding time are controlled. In fact, the terms were incorrectly defined and, for most students, served only as a source of confusion. If terms are to be meaningful, they must be defined precisely and accurately and sufficient time must be given to assure student understanding. Later, students must be asked to apply these terms correctly to new activities. This particular teaching technique is expressed as 'the idea first and then the term'. Clearly, Peter's students intellectually were capable of understanding and applying the terms. However, in practice, they could not do so. Generally, complex terms should be used only if they aid student understanding of the concept being investigated; and, under any circumstances, sufficient time must be allotted to peer group discussion of the application and meaning of new terms.

As the last part of the interview, each student was presented with a hypothetical problem. Students were asked to formulate a hypothesis and to describe the design of an experiment intended to test it. In introducing the problem, students were told that four factors known to stimulate respiratory neurons are oxygen level, carbon dioxide level, pH or hydrogen ion concentration and the degree of stretch of the lung tissue. The interviewer, then, posed the following problem:

Interviewer: Suppose that you wanted to design an experiment to determine which one among these four factors is the primary determinant of respiratory rate and/or breath-holding time. Assume that you can measure anything that you want to and that you can control or manipulate anything that you might wish to at any level. How would you design such an experiment?

None of the students was able to describe an experiment designed to provide an answer to the problem. It was hoped that they would indicate an understanding of the need to control three of the four variables and to manipulate only one variable at a time until the causal factor was identified. Instead, they resorted to concrete-operational tendencies and described poorly conceived experiments which often paralleled the demonstration which they had observed in class. Yet, their answers to the Piagetian tasks indicated that most of the students should have been capable intellectually of describing an appropriately controlled, hypothetical experiment which could have provided an answer to the problem. However, the students had experienced few opportunities to participate in problem-solving activities considered prerequisite for the solution. Instructional practices which provided clearly delineated assignments, carefully and critically evaluated performances, and thoughtful and meaningful inquiry would have allowed most, if not all, students to perform at an acceptable level on new problem-solving tasks. Adequate time for peer group interaction, followed by verbal and written descriptions of the experimental design including the rationale for the design, would have been an important requirement for all students.

Suggestions for Increasing Cognitive Demand

How could the cognitive demand placed on students by the described respiration activity have been raised? The answer to that question is based in the following philosophical context (Arons, 1973). Science is not a discipline in which the primary emphasis is placed on memorizing what is known. Rather, the opposite is true, and scientists cannot memorize what is not known. Science is an objective, problem-solving process during which scientists strive to understand new problems. Equally important in the process is that scientists understand why they think that they have arrived at a solution. If an instructional activity is to be consistent with the nature of science, it must engage students in attempting to generate answers to questions, rather than merely illustrating what is pronounced by assertion to be true in the textbook. When laboratory activities or demonstrations are used to illustrate the validity of what is known, the emphasis is placed disproportionally on what we think we know rather than on how we know it. In such situations, students are deprived of opportunities to think, predict, analyze and discuss; that is, they are deprived of opportunities to do science.

For a teacher to instruct in the processes of science rather than about the established facts of science, a fundamental shift in activities and priorities is required. The teacher must move from:

1 conducting an exercise to illustrate what is asserted to be the correct answer by the textbook, to
2 assigning problem-solving exercises during which students are asked to consider specific questions by testing a particular hypothesis or alternative hypotheses.

As long as the emphasis remains on the correct answer, students will not become engaged in the inquiry process. It was observed in Peter's class that students, if selected, participated in demonstrations and activities or they watched with varying degrees of interest and waited to be told what it all meant. Most importantly, they sought to find out what they were supposed to remember for the test. Instead of students engaging in rigorous problem-solving activities during the respiration demonstration, they casually observed it while continuing with their social agendas.

What could have been done to raise the cognitive demand of the activity and to provide instruction which was more representative of the nature of science? Prior to conducting the activity, a whole-class discussion could have been held in order that certain points could have been made through Peter's careful asking of questions. For example, the following ideas needed to be introduced and discussed prior to the demonstration:

1 What is the difference and/or relationship between breathing and respiration?
   (a) What is the difference between the oxygen concentration of inspired and expired air, and between blood entering the lungs and leaving the lungs? Why do you think those differences exist?
   (b) What is the difference between the oxygen concentration of inspired and expired air, and between blood entering and leaving the lungs? Explain those differences.
   (c) Are the differences the same in all individuals? Are the differences within one individual always the same? What factors might affect it? Why do you think those factors are important?
   (d) If there are changes in concentration of carbon dioxide (or oxygen), are they caused by breathing, by respiration or by both? Why?

2   After describing the three breathing regimes (normal breathing, hyperventilation and rebreathing from a bag), students are asked to consider the following aspects of each condition.

    (a)   Compare and contrast differences in oxygen and/or carbon dioxide concentration resulting from each of the above conditions.

    (b)   Are any differences due to respiration, breathing or both? Explain your answer.

    (c)   What, if anything, does lung capacity have to do with any differences? Conditioning? Does it affect breathing, respiration or both? Why?

It is important for a teacher to feel comfortable when raising or entertaining relevant questions, even when the answers are not known. They simply should permit the students to provide answers and let the students discuss the logic or lack of it for any answer given.

The next instructional steps should set the stage for the actual activity. First, the teacher should describe carefully how the exercise would be conducted and provide important information (for example, time for each of the breathing regimes emphasized). The teacher could ask the following questions:

1   What do you predict will happen to breath-holding time after each of the breathing regimes? Why do you expect each to happen?

2   If a student proposes the oxygen level as the probable stimulus, ask how s/he knows that it is not the carbon dioxide level or vice versa.

3   What does lung capacity have to do with the phenomenon? Why do you think that it does or does not affect it?

4   What patterns do you expect to observe in the data within and between individuals?

Next, the teacher and students would conduct the activity and collect the data. With six timing devices available, it is possible to collect data on all of the students. After the data are collected and recorded on the board, students could be organized into small groups in order to analyze the data and to check them against their predictions and explanations. They should be cautioned that their conclusions will be challenged. Every student should be asked to write out his/her own interpretation of the results. During the resulting small-group discussions, the teacher should monitor the groups to be certain that they are on task and to raise questions such as, 'How do you know it's oxygen, not carbon dioxide or lung capacity?' If terms such as independent and dependent variable are considered important, the groups should be asked to identify them by correctly applying the terms and explaining why they think that they have applied them correctly. Again, their answers should be written out in order to reinforce learning. It is important to provide sufficient time for the activities described above even if it means spending an extra period on the pre-activity and post-activity discussions as well as providing more time so that all students are involved in data collection.

Last, a whole-class discussion should be held. The teacher's role in it is to permit each group to report either consensus or lack of consensus. From the student responses during the interviews, it is likely that oxygen concentration would have been the consensus response. The key question to be posed by the teacher, therefore, is: 'How do you know that it is not the carbon dioxide concentration or hydrogen ion concentration?' At that point, it is important to establish that students could not 'know the correct answer' based only on what they have done.

The conclusion of the group reports provides a reasonable time for the teacher to ask what the text says about the control of respiratory rate and/or breath-holding time. It is a reasonable time also to provide students with the information that respiratory neurons are known to respond to at least four factors, namely, (1) carbon dioxide concentration; (2) hydrogen ion concentration; (3) oxygen concentration; and (4) degree of stretch of the lung tissue.

Last, after all of the above information, the teacher could pose the following question for a written homework assignment: 'What type of experiments must have been conducted in order to determine that carbon dioxide concentration and hydrogen ion concentration are the primary determinants of respiratory control? 'If the text has not provided that information, the teacher can provide it from another source. At the completion of the activity, the students should understand that their written answers to the above questions will be collected and that the quality of their responses will be evaluated for grading purposes. Preferably, the written homework should be collected at the beginning of the next period. It should be followed by assigning students to small groups to consider the same questions. This activity should be followed by group reports and a thorough discussion of how to design an experiment intended to provide an answer to this question. After the discussion, students should be provided with data which have been collected from an experiment investigating the phenomenon. The *Web of Life* textbook (Australian Academy of Science, 1983), with which both teachers were familiar, presented pertinent data which could have been used.

The preceding discussion suggests an alternative method of conducting the respiration activity, which would have involved students actively and which would have led to more meaningful learning by students. The need for an alternative strategy is based upon the following student comments and classroom observations:

1   Several students suggested oxygen concentration as the stimulus for one type of breathing, with carbon dioxide concentration as the stimulus for another type of breathing. This response suggests that those students did not understand the regularity which underlies control mechanisms in nature. They failed to realize that, if carbon dioxide concentration is the primary determinant of breath-holding time after rebreathing, it almost certainly is the primary determinant after hyperventilation as well. This type of logic is consistent with a mechanistic view of life and was much more apparent to a formal thinker than it was to a concrete thinker.

2   Although the vast majority of the students appeared to have the cognitive structures to make them capable of demonstrating formal operational reasoning, they often resorted to concrete operational tendencies when faced with novel problem-solving situations.

3   Asking students to understand the logic of experimental design and the conclusions resulting from an analysis of experimental data is a common procedure in many science classes. Yet, the opportunity for students to design either real or hypothetical experiments is seldom an instructional requirement. Without the hands-on, concrete experiences which were part of the respiration activity, it would have been impossible for a concrete thinker and difficult for a formal thinker to consider the design of the hypothetical experiment posed. Instruction which required students to progress from tasks requiring concrete operational thinking to tasks requiring formal reasoning is an example of good pedagogy for students at all intellectual stages of development.

4   Interacting with peer groups and requiring students to express their ideas both verbally and in writing is an important component of problem-solving activities which are designed to improve formal operational reasoning performance.

Inquiry of the type described above requires additional time. Expanding the respiration activity as suggested would require at least one, and possibly two, additional periods, followed by some carefully graded homework. However, if our goals include raising the cognitive demand of our science instruction above the level of rote memorization, attacking misconceptions and improving the formal reasoning ability of students, there is no alternative. Students listening to lectures, filling in blanks in workbooks and worksheets and memorizing short-term recall items on tests neither will alter their misconceptions nor improve their reasoning abilities — the aspects of learning which comprise the definition of meaningful learning advocated in this chapter.

Rather, teachers could consider approaching the topic of respiration by posing the following questions to advanced-ability students:

> *Teacher:* If you wanted to answer the question about respiratory control, would you have to do the experiments with humans? Or could you do them with other vertebrates such as rats, rabbits, monkeys, etc? With invertebrates? If yes, why would other organisms work? If not, why would it not be possible?
>
> *Teacher:* Does your answer imply anything about the evolution of respiratory control? What experimental results would be consistent with organic evolution and what ones would be inconsistent? Why?
>
> *Teacher:* Why is the presence of a respiratory control mechanism a useful adaptation? Give at least two explanations of how the evolution of a control mechanism might have occurred.

The above examples of higher order questions are of the type which advanced-ability students are capable of addressing. Yet, the instruction observed during the research period did nothing to prepare students for constructing answers to similar questions. Rather, students practised copying answers from one source to another. The issue raised is not a question of content versus process, for there are no scientists and no science educators who do not value content. At issue is whether schooling can help students develop cognitively. During the observations, students memorized, forgot and continued to believe important misconceptions. The questions for Peter are how critical is critical thinking, and to what extent does instruction promote, or permit, the intellectual development of students?

Criteria for Assessing the Cognitive Level of the Curriculum and Instruction

How is it possible that intelligent, hard-working teachers permit their classes to be characterized by rote learning and recall of memorized information? This situation exists in spite of the fact that teachers profess to value and hold as a major goal the achievement of higher-level cognitive outcomes. Clearly, as has been documented in this and other chapters, the type of instruction observed placed low cognitive demands on the students in Peter's and Sandra's classes. Perhaps it would be useful to consider several factors in curriculum and instruction which contribute to the presence or absence of higher-level cognitive learning outcomes. In order to progress towards meaningful learning and the development of problem-solving skills, teaching and learning must use the basic three Rs of reading, writing and arithmetic in order to reach the four Rs (*rigour, relevance, representative structure* and *rational powers*). In the following sections, the curriculum and instruction in Sandra's and Peter's classes is assessed for its promotion of the four Rs.

Rigour

Generally, Peter's and Sandra's classes were completely lacking in rigour. They were characterized primarily by relaxed socializing. They were, in effect, the opposite of what one is likely to observe in a scientist's laboratory or in a classroom in which students are striving to achieve higher-level cognitive outcomes. Although many factors contribute to the development of a rigorous environment, the following ones characterize a good science classroom: type of objectives; amount of time on-task; amount of work; difficulty of task; and, perhaps most importantly, thorough and effective ways of evaluating and grading.

It is hardly surprising that the research group observed a lot of off-task activity in both Peter's and Sandra's classes. The literature abounds with studies reporting the low percentage of student time which is spent on-task. What was surprising about the observations was the extreme amount of classroom time during for which most students were off-task. In Sandra's class, where the problem was more severe, it was usual for students to pursue agendas other than their learning agendas for a large proportion of class time. Certainly, one of the prerequisites for higher-level cognitive learning to occur is that students must be on-task. Such learning does not happen during the relaxed socializing and the 'kidding around' which characterized these classes.

The amount of work assigned and required by a teacher is an obvious component of a rigorous learning environment. During the five-week Vertebrates unit observed in Peter's and Sandra's classes, the amount of work required easily could have been completed by most students in about twenty per cent of the required class time. In essence, a student could spend four of five class periods in socializing or wasting time and then, in just one period, complete all of the work assigned for the week. A common practice for Sandra's students was to do nothing during the entire week, and then to check out a textbook overnight in order to complete the workbook at home. There was no required homework in either of the two grade 10 classes. Effective instruction should involve assignments which compel students to engage in active, sustained work during most of the class period. Furthermore, it is reasonable to expect homework in order for most, if not all, students to complete the assigned work.

Not only was the amount of work insufficient to occupy the student's class time, but also there was virtually nothing assigned which required the students to think or to engage in careful thought and analysis. Labeling the names of the bones of the human skeleton was a typical activity. As has been mentioned previously, questions or activities which had the potential for requiring higher-order cognitive participation routinely were reduced to the level of copying an answer from a book, getting the answer from the teacher or often copying it directly from another student's workbook. Copying terms from one source to another simply does not engage students in a meaningful, intellectual exercise. In fact, it was surprising that the students were as tolerant as they were of the curriculum and instruction. But, perhaps, most students would prefer relaxed socializing to sustained periods of hard work.

Of course, it is much easier to write objectives for the recall of factual information; it is also simpler to evaluate objectives at the same level. One of the problems of a curriculum that is organized around instructional objectives is the difficulty in writing objectives which prescribe higher-order cognitive tasks. Clearly, it is possible to write such objectives and appropriate evaluation items. However, for Southside High's grade 10 science, the objectives were primarily at the knowledge level. Obviously, the use of some knowledge-level objectives is defensible. However, if a teacher and/or school system professes to value higher-order learning outcomes, most objectives should be developed with higher-order outcomes in mind. Furthermore, if instruction is to be consistent with the nature of science, learning activities other than the memorization of facts must be required. Obviously, a scientist cannot memorize what is not known. When scientists arrive at the point where they think they know something, they must be able to identify the evidence and know how strongly it supports their hypothesis and resulting conclusions. Of necessity, they must struggle with the frustrations of insufficient evidence. Furthermore, they always must be conscious of the uncertainties that accompany their ideas, because there exists no absolute truth in science. Therefore, some of the instructional objectives for learning science must direct learning towards the processes of science.

Perhaps the reason that the students tolerated curriculum and instruction which generally did not challenge their intellectual ability was that they were given bad tests. If curriculum and instruction is to rise above the level of rote memorization, the methods of evaluation must require something beyond direct recall. If the quality of a student's ability to reason and to generate ideas is what is valued, then a student's grade must be determined by instruments or methods which measure that quality. During the ten-week period observed, students memorized information supplied by the textbook and/or the teacher, and the tests and their consequent grades were based on factual memorization and recall alone.

Relevance

How does relevance of what is taught affect higher-order cognitive development? For example, should a unit on vertebrates taught in 1986 be significantly different from a similar unit in 1946? Earlier in this chapter, it was noted that the content of the Vertebrates unit was virtually identical to the content of a hypothetical unit taught forty years earlier. Although the names of the bones of the body have not changed, there has been a knowledge explosion in the topic during the forty-year period. In addition, the world in which the students live has evolved rapidly towards an increasingly complex existence. Obviously, the content appropriate in a vertebrates unit in 1940 is not relevant to students in the 1980s.

One example involves the AIDS epidemic. Information about it could not have been included in a vertebrates unit of the 1940s, because the first animal retrovirus was not identified until the 1970s and AIDS was first reported in 1980. But, today, it is virtually impossible to read a newspaper or watch a news broadcast without encountering some reference to AIDS. Although relevance is not the only thing to consider in developing curriculum and guiding instruction, it is important to update content. If instructional materials only emphasize the dissemination, memorization and recall of information, then at least information relevant to the twentieth century should be included. In this example, factual information about the biology and epidemiology of AIDS might save a student's life. However, knowing the names of the bones of the body, even for a short period of time, is of questionable value to anyone.

Not only is society becoming more complex, but also the demands of the work place are becoming increasingly complex. Workers are being replaced by robots, and assembly line jobs are being replaced with jobs that require people who can design, program and maintain automated, computerized equipment of the modern age. The ability to memorize archaic information no longer can be a priority of schools. Although it is not obvious what an appropriate science curriculum for the twentieth century should include, it is fairly obvious what it should not be. AIDS is more relevant than the names of the bones of the body; and the ability to think, reason and engage in independent problem-solving must be valued over recall of rote-learned information.

Representative Structure

Curriculum and instruction which is representative of the discipline is another one of the four Rs for higher-level learning. A consideration of the appropriateness of curriculum and instruction must include what Bruner (1966) has called the structure of the discipline. Most disciplines have a set of major ideas or unifying themes around which information is organized and which serve to guide the direction of research. In each discipline, all of the major ideas are important; however, not all of them are equally important.

At Southside High, the major emphasis of the materials on Vertebrates was on the structures of the vertebrates, with limited reference being made to the functions of those structures. However, evolution, the great organizing principle of biology and the natural sciences, was essentially ignored. Yet, the study of vertebrate structure/function provides many opportunities to explore, question and better understand evolution. The higher-order questions posed earlier in this chapter illustrate one such opportunity. Evolution has developed into the paradigm that it is today because it is a powerful organizing idea which has stood the test of time and the rigorous hypothesis testing which is characteristic of the scientific process. It is an extraordinarily powerful generalization that explains what we observe and successfully predicts results; and, perhaps most importantly, it has been and continues to be extremely useful in designing experiments, solving problems and guiding scientific research. Understanding the principle of evolution has important implications for life in the twentieth century. Curriculum and instruction in biology which ignore the principle of evolution are severely flawed when tested against the structure of the discipline. During the Vertebrates unit, students could have considered the nature of science by analyzing evolution. For example, they could have discussed the nature of scientific theories, realizing that evolution is not 'just a theory' in the speculative sense, as Peter tried to imply in the following comments:

> *Peter:* I've had to think long and hard about evolution, because, if students know you're a biology teacher, you're fair game. They're going to try to score a few points or whatever. I've had people in the past just harangue me with respect to this terrible evolution that we teach in the schools ... Whenever I talk about evolution, I always emphasize that it is just a theory and, in fact, so much in science are what we call theories.

The goal of instruction should be to help students come to understand the major organizing ideas of the discipline. But equally importantly, students should be helped to understand why a theme such as evolution occupies the central role that it does within the structure of the discipline.

Teachers and curricula which stress the dissemination of knowledge should be held accountable for selecting content which is representative of the structure of the discipline. Memorizing the names of bones or providing one explanation of how kangaroos got their tails does not help a student understand the relative importance of ideas or how scholars and scientists make informed decisions about the relative importance of a discipline's major ideas. In this case, the principle of evolution was a much more important and powerful idea to be addressed and learned during the study of Vertebrates than the memorization of vertebral anatomical structures. Therefore, a curriculum unit on vertebrates should reflect properly the relative importance of those two ideas within the discipline.

Rational Powers

The last new R, devoted to helping students attain higher levels of learning, is the development and use of their rational powers. In this case, the science curriculum and instruction observed in Peter's and Sandra's classes would have done little to produce students who understood the nature of science. They could have arrived in class believing that evolution was 'just a theory' or stating that 'I don't believe in evolution', and they would have left making the same assertions. Their intellectual activities were characterized by memorizing what was written or asserted to be true by others. They were required seldom, if ever, to use or to develop their own rational powers. Those powers are central to the ability to think; that is, to the processes of recalling and imagining, of classifying and generalizing, of comparing and evaluating, of analyzing and synthesizing and of deducing and inferring. It is the development and application of rational powers in problem solving, often in opposition to other authorities, which allows one to determine what is known and why one thinks it is known. What are needed in classrooms are curricula and instruction which constantly challenge students to apply their rational powers in logical and critical thinking to scientific problem-solving. Peter and Sandra, along with all teachers, must remember that memorization and recall involve only one small part of students' rational powers.

Basic Skills

Last, how do the classic three Rs provide the base for the four Rs discussed above? The necessity of using and developing skills in *reading, writing* and *arithmetic* must precede any attempt to develop higher-order thinking skills in students. At Southside High, students in Peter's and Sandra's classes did very little reading, limited writing and essentially no mathematics. The curriculum and the instruction severely limited any practice or development of those basic skills.

For example, both textbooks were of questionable quality and students were never required to read them for any purpose other than to find answers to questions in the workbooks. However, students should be required to read extensively as a part of good science instruction. Furthermore, they should read things which are intellectually stimulating both in the ideas presented and in the level of difficulty discussed. Advanced students should have classroom materials enriched and supplemented by reading materials other than the text. At least some of the reading should be selected from the primary literature of the discipline.

In both classes, writing was restricted to copying answers from a book, filling in blanks in the workbooks or, occasionally, writing a short paragraph. However, secondary students need opportunities to write. The precise use of language in reporting scientific results and conclusions is an important intellectual skill. A student who is experiencing difficulty in explaining something often might say, 'Well, you know what I mean'. That response tells the teacher that the student still does not understand clearly whatever s/he is attempting to explain. In order to communicate clearly, the written word always requires precision and, therefore, is an important component of intellectual development and of good science instruction.

Science instruction without applications of mathematics is descriptive and unrepresentative of much of the discipline. In addition, members of the research team considered the lack of mathematics in the grade 10 science curriculum inexcusable. Exactly what form the inclusion of mathematics should take is open for debate, but it is not debatable that the application of mathematics should be an integral part of good science instruction. Clearly established and articulated relationships between instruction in mathematics classes and instruction in science classes is seldom observed and should be a goal of all good programs; for science without mathematics is like a glove without a hand. Good curriculum and instruction in science must be based upon and develop skills in reading, writing and arithmetic. To do otherwise in an advanced science class is indefensible in the author's opinion.

Conclusion

Lower-level cognitive outcomes characterized student learning during the ten-week period observed at Southside High. This result occurred in spite of the fact that the students were advanced science students, most of whom were able to demonstrate formal reasoning ability. An analysis of the textbooks, learning activities (workbooks) and tests revealed an overwhelming emphasis on the rote learning and recall of memorized information. Clearly, the instructional materials were a major constraint to higher-level cognitive learning. Because Sandra was better prepared in both content areas than Peter was, it was surprising that there was no apparent difference in the cognitive level of student learning in their classes. Problems with classroom management prevented Sandra from realizing her potential of raising the cognitive level of the instruction above the level found in the instructional materials. As was observed in this study, teacher-developed textbooks, workbooks and tests often reflect inadequacies in terms of teachers' content and pedagogical content knowledge. Unless drastic changes are effected in curriculum materials, in methods of evaluation and in teacher education, the cognitive level of student learning in most science classrooms will remain mired in memorization.

References

ARONS, A. (1973) 'Toward a wider public understanding of science', *American Journal of Pysics*, 41, p. 773.

AUSTRALIAN ACADEMY OF SCIENCE. (1983) *Biological Science: The Web of Life*, Canberra, Australian Academy of Science.

BRUNER, J.S. (1966) *Toward a Theory of Instruction*, Cambridge, Massachusetts, Harvard University Press.

INHELDER, B., and PIAGET, J. (1958) *The Growth of Logical Tinking*, New York, Basic Books.

NORDLAND, F.H., LAWSON, A.E., and KAHLE, J.B. (1974) 'A study of levels of concrete and formal reasoning ability in disadvantaged junior and high school students', *Science Education*, 58, pp. 569–76.

Chapter 6: Student Participation and Motivational Orientations: What Students Do in Science

Leonie J. Rennie

It is the middle of Period Three and the class is relatively quiet. The science teacher, Sandra, is at Table 8 explaining a point to Mark and Charissa who are listening intently while Nigel looks on. Out of sight behind Sandra's back is Wayne, making silly faces at Petrina to nods of approval and encouragement from Martin. At the far side of the room, Janila and Sally have their heads together in earnest argument about the solution to a problem. Natalie tries to overhear, checking her own answer as she does so. Narelle, Andy, Margaret and Leanne sit around the next table working quietly, heads down to their own work. On the table closest to me, Bronwyn rules up a page and writes a heading, talking all the time to anyone who'll listen about her social activities of the previous evening. Her three table-mates watch and listen passively. Elsewhere in the room, some students are working alone or with a partner while others are off-task. One student is reading an electronics magazine; others are chatting with their friends. It's a typical day in Sandra's class.

In the room next door, Peter is standing at the small chalkboard at the side of the room. The students are sitting behind long parallel benches and many have turned to face him. They watch and listen while Peter jots a few words on the board and then begins to elaborate a point, drawing on his own out-of-school experiences. At the front bench, Steven continues his own work quietly, resisting Jeffrey's attempts to draw him into conversation. Greg raises his hand to ask a question. Sue and Helen whisper together at the back of the room, but the class is generally quiet. It's a typical day in Peter's class.

Over the period of observation in these two classrooms, each student seemed to exhibit a regular pattern of activity during class. In many cases, this pattern was so predictable that a description of the student's behaviour was usually sufficient to identify the student! It seems that, by the age of fifteen years, students have settled into regular patterns of classroom engagement and participation in learning tasks. What are these patterns? Do they vary with the instructional setting in the classroom? How do they relate to students' levels of achievement, attitudes about science, self-perceptions of their own ability and performance in science? These are the issues addressed in this chapter.

Empirical research about students' participation in learning tasks, for the most part, has been focused on student engagement or time-on-task. Following Carroll's (1963) model of school learning, which posited that time is the essential ingredient for learning, the large-scale process-product research of the 1970s began to address academic learning time as the mediating variable between the process of teaching and the product of learning. These studies established time-on-task as a major predictor of achievement apart from ability (Berliner, 1979), and their success has led to descriptions of teaching behaviour associated with effective teaching (see, for example, summaries in Brophy and Good, 1986; Rosenshine and Stevens, 1986). Such teaching behaviours do increase students' time-on-task but they contribute only part of the explanation of student participation in the classroom. Classroom observations indicate that the teacher's management skills are important determinants of student engagement and, together with the nature of the academic tasks assigned to students (Doyle, 1983, 1986), contribute another part of the explanation of why students behave as they do.

Yet another factor affecting students' participation is associated with students themselves, particularly their willingness to engage purposively in classroom tasks and the effort which they put into their academic work. This focus on student participation has been adopted by those investigating the psychology of motivation. Research in the areas of cognition and motivation has advanced sufficiently to allow application of motivational theory to educational settings (see, for example, Ames and Ames, 1984; Paris, Olson and Stevenson, 1983). Theories about academic achievement motivation (Dweck and Elliott, 1983), causal attributions (Nicholls, 1979, 1983, 1984; Weiner, 1979, 1984), self-efficacy and social learning theory (Bandura, 1977) all have made a contribution to the understanding of motivation in the classroom, but the application of these theories is not always straightforward (Brophy, 1983; Corno and Mandinach, 1983). As Brophy (1983) points out, much of the general research on motivation has been carried out in play settings where a person can engage in or change activities at will. In contrast, classrooms are work settings where students are expected to engage in compulsory activities which are subject to evaluation. Discussion of motivation for school learning must take these differences into account.

There has been a tendency to measure motivation at school as an affective variable (Bloom, 1976; Uguroglu and Walberg, 1979), and Steinkamp and Maehr (1984) provide a meta-analysis of motivational orientation towards achievement in school science using primarily affective measures. However, Brophy (1983) argues that attention must be given to both the affective and the cognitive aspects of motivation and to the value that students place on academic activity. Clearly, how students perceive the task in terms of its importance, its difficulty, whether they think they can do it, and the manner in which task performance is assessed and rewarded will bear upon students' willingness to become engaged in the task.

The preceding discussion has introduced the several issues which served as the basis for investigating students' participation and learning in the science classrooms observed in this study. Specifically, what students did in the classrooms was described and interpreted from three viewpoints: the teacher's instructional and managerial styles, the task design and assessment structure, and the students' attitudinal and motivational patterns. Accordingly, the next section of the chapter describes the patterns of student participation in the two classes and these are discussed in the context of the teachers' instructional methods and managerial skills. Second, the nature of the tasks, the assessment structure and the degree to which classroom work contributed towards grades are considered in terms of the kinds of effort which students put into completing the set work. Third, students' own attitudes, beliefs and perceptions about science in the classroom and its importance in their futures are examined and related to their motivation to spend their classroom hours in fruitful enterprise. In the final section of the chapter, pen portraits are presented of six students chosen to represent different patterns of participation, learning outcomes and motivational orientations. The case studies are used as a means of analyzing the ways in which teachers can enhance the extent and quality of student participation in classroom activities.

Patterns of Participation in the Classroom

The nature of the learning activities and sequencing of events by the teacher determine the students' opportunities for participation, and the kinds of participation (both authorized and unauthorized) which can occur. Presumably, the teacher's intention is that every student will spend each lesson engaged in purposeful learning. In addition to his or her skill in organizing the instructional tasks, the teacher's skill in classroom management, particularly skill in monitoring student engagement, will affect the amount of time that students are on task. In the two classrooms observed in this study, the academic content of the lessons in each topic was determined by the workbooks used by students for each topic and supplemented by the pool of available textbooks. The workbooks were designed so that, given access to text materials and equipment, the students would be able to complete the work in a self-paced and self-directed way.

Despite the similarity of the available resources, teachers were free to organize the learning in their classrooms and to adopt different patterns of instructional activities. Sandra invariably devoted a few minutes at the beginning and end of each lesson to structuring comments intended to help students pace themselves throughout the topic. The remainder of most of the lessons was taken up by individualized activities or small-group work during which the students worked their way through the workbooks. In contrast, Peter used a more teacher-centred approach, with most of the class time spent in whole-class expository or whole-class interactive mode. At other times, students could choose to work individually or in small groups. The different approaches used by the teachers were associated with different patterns of activity and engagement by the students. In this section, quantitative data are used to describe the patterns of students' participation and, using field notes from classroom observation, lesson transcripts and interview data, these are interpreted in terms of the teachers' instructional and managerial styles.

Nature of Instructional Activity

The allocation of class time to four types of instructional activity, namely, *transition time, whole-class non-interactive activities, whole-class interactive activities*, and either *small-group or individual work*, is reported in Figure 6.1, separately for the two teachers for each of the two topics. These data, which are derived from field notes for over 80 per cent of the lessons for each topic in each class, describe the instructional modes occurring from the time when the students were ready to begin the lesson until the class was dismissed at the end. As lessons which did not follow a break usually began a few minutes late, the actual lesson length represented an average of 94 per cent of scheduled time.

Nature of Student Engagement

Student engagement was described in terms of whether the student was involved in individual, group work or whole-class activity or was off-task. Observations of students were categorized according to the following kinds of activities:

> *Individual engagement* was recorded when the student was not interacting with other students. *Active* individual engagement included reading, writing, getting and using equipment and talking with the teacher. *Passive* engagement included copying work and watching and listening to on-task groups, but not participating in the discussion or activity.

Group Work engagement occurred when the student was interacting with other students by discussing work, getting and using equipment as a group member, or discussing work with the teacher.

Whole-class engagement involved watching films/slides/experiments or demonstrations, listening to teacher directions or explanations and participating in class discussions or question-and-answer sessions.

Off-Task was recorded when students were clearly off-task. A subjective assessment was sometimes necessary when students were engaged in covert activity. *Off-task alone* was indicated by students gazing into space, doodling, doing non-science work or watching other off-task students. *Off-task socially* occurred when students were messing about with other students, or clearly dealing with their social agendas.

Data were recorded by a single observer during the second half of the Vertebrates topic and at regular intervals throughout the Nuclear Energy topic. Data collection was based on sweeps of the whole class during non-transition parts of the lessons. Sweeps were begun at intervals of approximately five minutes. A letter code was used to record what each student was doing during each sweep. If the student's behaviour could not be categorized immediately, the student was watched for a few seconds until his or her activity could be coded. The engagement data were summed for each topic and converted to a percentage of engaged time in each activity. Student engagement is reported in Figures 6.2 and 6.3 which are graphs of the mean percentages of time during which males and females were engaged in a variety of activities. Data are reported separately for the two teachers and the two topics. Except for five students who were frequently absent, the data in Figures 6.2 and 6.3 are based on over 100 observations for each student. One student, Francesco, who arrived in Sandra's class on the third day of the study, was not included in any quantitative measures. Francesco was visiting Australia for six months, spoke little English, generally did not engage in the class activity and did not complete any written work, although he was sometimes the focus of other students' off-task activity.

Participation in Peter's Class

The teacher-centred approach used by Peter is evident in Figure 6.1, which shows that some type of whole-class activity occurred for more than half of class time in both topics. Whereas Sandra used structuring comments to regulate pace, Peter maintained pace by dealing with activities in the whole-class mode. In a typical lesson, Peter would explain some of the content, frequently using the chalkboard, and conduct a question-and-answer session based on part of the activity, often for the

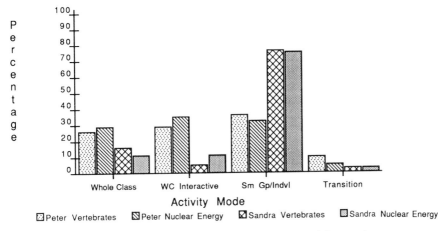

Figure 6.1: Percentage of class time spent in different activity modes

purpose of checking the answers which students had written to questions asked in the workbook. Sometimes Peter went briefly through the activities that students were expected to have completed, giving the answers to questions as he did so. During the Nuclear Energy topic, students were sometimes asked to take turns in reading aloud, with Peter interspersing brief explanations or questions.

Approximately one third of the time in Peter's class was devoted to group work or individual activity. In those instructional modes, students most often worked alone rather than in pairs or groups. During such times, Peter was available for consultation by students and spent his time either helping individuals or groups of students or preparing for the next part of the lesson. On three occasions during the Vertebrates topic, Peter gave students the option of attending to a whole-class activity or working individually from the workbooks. The three whole-class activities included a film, some slides and a demonstration of an activity involving the testing for the presence of protein, sugar and starch. About half of the class, mainly the males, chose to watch, while the rest worked individually. These students 'monitored' the whole-class activity, looking up briefly now and then. The six per cent of class time when this split-mode instruction occurred is graphed in Figure 6.1 as whole-class activity.

Figure 6.2 presents information about students' participation in Peter's class during the two topics. Mean scores for the several categories of engagement are shown separately for males and females. The decision by males to watch the whole-class activity, particularly when given a choice, and the decision of most females to carry on with their individual work is reflected in Figure 6.2. The figure shows that the greater percentage of time spent by females in individual activity during Vertebrates is matched by the greater percentage of males' time spent in whole-class activity.

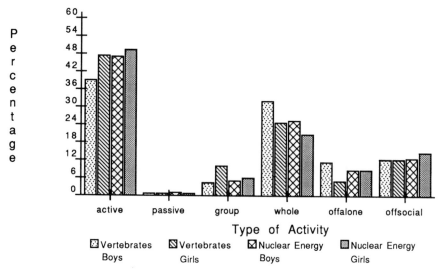

Figure 6.2: Engagement patterns in Peter's class

Other differences between males and females are generally not substantial, particularly for the Nuclear Energy topic. The total time-off-task represents about one fifth of class time, on average, for both topics.

In each of the different kinds of on-task participation, the cognitive level of the learning tasks in which students were engaged was usually low. In individual and small-group activity, the cognitive level of the work was constrained by the content of the workbooks and the textbooks. Nordland's chapter in this volume describes how the resources offered little challenge to students of above average ability. Many of the activities consisted merely of searching for an answer in the textbook and writing it down. Examination of students' completed notes suggested that, even when a question required reasoning, some students' responses showed little evidence of understanding and that usually these misunderstandings went unnoticed.

During the periods of whole-class instruction, Peter's students were cooperative and generally on task. Some continued working individually on their workbooks, half-listening to the whole-class discussions and taking advantage of any information which Peter gave about the answers to questions in the workbook. Many students appeared to find Peter's explanations of the content interesting, particularly when he was able to add examples which were relevant to their experiences. Peter usually was responsive to students' questions and nearly all students asked at least one question during the period of observation. Sometimes these questions were asked to determine the answer to a workbook question, but most often the questions asked for an explanation or information beyond the immediate content of the topic. For example, during a discussion about digestion and the alimentary canal, students showed interest in material outside of the content by asking questions about what happens when you vomit and what causes the taste of vomit. Peter answered these questions and discussed the plight of an Australian child who lost the larger part of her intestine due to suction when she sat on a swimming pool skimmer. Peter explained to the attentive class the effect that such a loss would have on the child's diet and digestion.

Participation in Sandra's Class

Sandra believed that students learn best by interacting with the learning materials. Consequently, as illustrated in Figure 6.1, students were given most of the class time to do the activities in the workbooks. Sandra perceived her role as a facilitator, rather than as a director, of learning. Consequently, during the Vertebrates topic, she spent about 76 per cent of her time interacting with individuals or small groups of students. Most of the 16 per cent of time in the whole-class mode occurred at the beginning and at end of the lessons when she attempted to pace students through the topic by indicating which activities they should have completed and what they should be doing (or have done) during the present lesson. A small amount of whole-class interactive time also was spent in explanation, usually of points that Sandra noticed had been misunderstood in a quiz or assignment. There was a rat dissection and an activity on respiration conducted at the whole-class level during the Vertebrates topic. When demonstrating joint structure and movement with fresh cattle bones, Sandra preferred to demonstrate to small groups in turn. During a film, the instructional mode was graphed as whole-class activity in Figure 6.1, even though many students preferred to continue working individually.

During the Nuclear Energy topic, Sandra continued her structuring comments relating to the pace at which students should work. In this topic, Sandra conducted a number of experiments at the whole-class level in order to minimize the possibility of exposure to radiation sources. The students performed these experiments as demonstrations and recorded the data on the chalkboard while Sandra usually maintained interactive discussion with the students. The 11 per cent of whole-class interactive instruction was associated either with class experiments or with question-and-answer sessions which were used to review concepts such as atomic structure.

In Sandra's class, three-quarters of class time during each topic was available to students for working from the workbooks. During this time, some students tended to work alone, while others worked in small groups. Figure 6.3 graphs the mean engagement data for Sandra's stu-

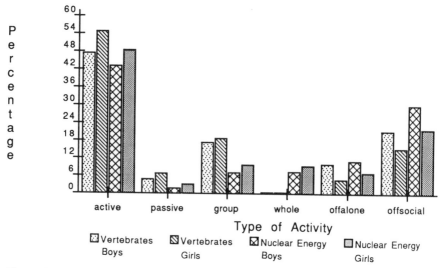

Figure 6.3: Engagement patterns in Sandra's class

dents during the Vertebrates and Nuclear Energy topics. No record of engagement for the whole-class mode is included for the Vertebrates topic because, during the lessons which were coded, the whole-class activity occurred in bursts too short to enable the researcher to complete a sweep.

Inspection of Figure 6.3 shows that on-task students in Sandra's class usually were working either alone or in small groups. The difference of about 10 per cent of time spent by students in group work in Vertebrates compared with Nuclear Energy is a reflection of the several whole-class demonstrations in Nuclear Energy, whereas during the Vertebrates topic demonstrations and experiments were usually done in groups. Comparison of the percentages for the Vertebrates and Nuclear Energy topics shows a general increase of about ten per cent in off-task behaviour to a high 41 per cent for males and 21 per cent for females. This increase is mainly accounted for by increased off-task social behaviour. The least involved student, Wayne, was on task for only 37 per cent of class time during Vertebrates and 24 per cent during Nuclear Energy. In each topic, he spent 11 per cent of his on-task time in the passive task of copying other students' work. Several other students spent some time copying work, but otherwise most of the passive behaviour was accounted for by several students who simply listened or watched other group members working.

Like the students in Peter's class, students in Sandra's class spent most of their on-task time engaged at a low cognitive level. The main reason for this was the constraining nature of the workbooks. Most of class time was spent completing the workbook activities by finding answers to the questions. A few students, like Sally and Janila, found the answers themselves. They actively accepted responsibility for their own learning and produced high quality work. They were able to monitor their own understanding and, when they were not sure, they discussed their answers and/or sought Sandra's help. The majority of students worked through those activities which were straightforward but, when they encountered a difficulty, they immediately requested help, sometimes by getting the answer from a peer or by asking Sandra. If Sandra could not come at once, the students usually filled in the waiting time with social chatter, rather than trying to work out the answer. Two or three students, notably Wayne, did little work of their own and much of their on-task activity was directed towards obtaining the answers from someone else, thus minimizing their own learning opportunities.

Differences in Patterns of Participation between the Classes

The differences in student engagement patterns between the classes are illustrated in Table 6.1. In this table, the mean percentages of time spent by students in the major types of engagement are reported, together with the results of a one-way analysis of variance performed for the purpose of ascertaining the statistical significance of any differences between the two teachers' classes. The significant differences in the nature of the on-task activities are a reflection of the different teaching styles. Peter used the whole-class mode more often than did Sandra, and his students spent a considerably greater proportion of their time in whole-class engagement than did Sandra's students. Indeed, in the lessons coded for engagement during the Vertebrates topic, the periods of whole-class instruction in Sandra's class were too short to complete a coding sweep of the class. In this topic, Sandra's students had significantly higher mean levels of individual and group work engagement than did Peter's students.

During the Nuclear Energy topic, the percentages of time spent in individual and group engagement were similar for both classes. The similarity can be attributed to a change in the patterns of engagement in Sandra's class; on average, students spent less time engaged in individual and group work, more time in whole-class engagement and more time off-task socially during the Nuclear Energy topic. In fact, relative to Peter's students, Sandra's students spent a significantly higher proportion of class time engaged in social off-task behaviour during both topics. An additional point of interest in Table 6.1 relates to the relatively large magnitude of the standard deviations. These values attest to the variation in patterns of engagement among individuals, a point which is discussed more fully in a later part of this chapter.

Students in Peter's and Sandra's classes had different opportunities to

Leonie J. Rennie

Table 6.1: Mean percentage of time spent in different types of engagement

Type of Engagement	Peter		Sandra		
	Mean	SD	Mean	SD	F-Value
Vertebrates Topic					
Individual Active	44.5	11.3	51.2	13.7	5.77*
Group Work	7.9	5.7	18.0	8.3	36.41**
Whole Class	27.3	8.5	—	—	—
Off-Task Alone	7.2	6.0	7.1	6.9	0.22
Off-Task Social	12.5	8.0	17.9	12.6	4.30*
Nuclear Energy Topic					
Individual Active	48.5	11.7	45.9	11.0	0.17
Group Work	5.7	4.7	8.5	5.9	3.94
Whole Class	22.2	6.0	8.4	3.8	138.70**
Off-Task Alone	8.7	5.1	8.7	5.5	0.02
Off-Task Social	13.9	8.4	25.7	11.5	24.21**

* $p < .05$ ** $p < .01$

participate and so they had different patterns of participation. The differences in instructional methods and lesson presentation between the teachers can be traced back to the different beliefs held by Peter and Sandra about their roles. During interviews, Peter several times mentioned his own experiences in science at school. He felt that he remembered best those things which his teacher spoke about and personalized by relating them to the teacher's own experiences and to the experiences of class members. For this reason, Peter thought it appropriate to spend class time expanding and extrapolating the content by presenting relevant information about his own experiences and about aspects which he knew to be of particular interest to students. Sandra posed a direct contrast to this approach — she rarely mentioned her own experiences or interests, although she did draw students' attention to relevant 'real-world' problems and issues and she set an assignment for each topic on such issues. She preferred students to work out things for themselves with the guidance of the workbooks and she gave them most of the lesson time to do this. Lesson transcripts revealed that most teacher-student interaction was structured to encourage students to find out the answers for themselves.

The intention of both teachers was to have students proceed through the workbooks in the time available and to produce their own set of notes/materials for the topic. In Peter's class, students managed to do this in the 34 per cent of the class time devoted to group or individual work. In Sandra's class, students had twice as much time to do the same work, yet inspection of the students' completed topic notes revealed considerable similarity in the final product although, on average, those from Sandra's class were more complete. The reason for this seeming paradox relates to the generally low cognitive level of the workbooks and the usual class textbooks. The above-average students could complete the work in possibly half of the scheduled lesson time, if they were prepared to work consistently throughout the lesson. In Peter's class, the 'surplus' time was taken up by his whole-class presentations and question and answer sessions. Further, Peter went through many of the activities with the class, allowing those with incomplete work to jot down the answers and thus avoid the consequences of working too slowly. In Sandra's class, many students soaked up the excess time with off-task behaviour. Those who got behind due to their low engagement levels were able to catch up by working at home or, in some cases, by copying other students' work. Nevertheless, in both classes, there were some students who had very high levels of engagement and who produced extensive sets of notes, the accuracy and completeness of which bore testimony to the students' industry.

A glance at Figure 6.3 reveals that considerable time was spent by Sandra's class in off-task behaviour, particularly during the Nuclear Energy topic. The high levels of off-task behaviour in Sandra's class, compared to Peter's, were a function of the different instructional methods and management techniques which the teachers used. Peter favoured whole-class instruction. His explanations of potentially difficult or confusing aspects of the work, and the instructions he gave to the students to supplement the directions in the workbooks, reduced possible task ambiguity so that students usually knew what to do. Peter's explanations and his whole-class checking of answers also reduced the cognitive level of the tasks, thus helping students to complete their work. In contrast, Sandra rarely gave whole-class answers or instructions about how to complete tasks. The procedures for many of the activities, as well as the means to find solutions to some questions in the workbooks, were not always clear to students. Lesson transcripts revealed that most students' questions were attempts to reduce the ambiguity of tasks, check that they were on the right track or negotiate with Sandra for more information. Because she could not attend to students' requests for assistance quickly enough, some students cooperated by working together, but others filled in their waiting time with social interaction while others copied answers from someone else.

The consequences of the different task structures on the work flow in classroom activities is well described by Doyle (1988). Because the tasks were made easy and familiar in Peter's class, the work flow was smooth and orderly. Further, the level of order was supported by the physical arrangement of the classroom. With benches in rows and students facing the front, Peter could identify off-task behaviour quickly and ensure that students returned to being on task. The situation was different in Sandra's class in that the tasks were harder in terms of students having to make more decisions about what to do. Such tasks are described by Doyle (1988) as novel and, as he points out, novel work makes the task of classroom management much more complex. Sanford (1987) relates examples of how students in science classes continued to solicit guidance from the teacher when tasks were of higher cognitive level or procedures were not clear; similar behaviour by students was observed in Sandra's class. The physical organization of the classroom also hindered the smooth flow of work. The round-the-table seating arrangement which Sandra used to facilitate group work and interaction also maximized the opportunity for interaction of a social nature. This seating method made whole-class activities very difficult because most students had to turn around to see the teacher. It also made difficult the task of scanning the class for management purposes, because many students had their backs to the teacher. On the occasions when Sandra did use whole-class activities, many students did not turn to face her and, while some looked at their books, others took the opportunity to engage in social whispering.

The personal style of the teachers compounded the management differences between the classes. Peter spoke with a loud, clear voice and no students had difficulty in hearing him. Most interactions with students were conducted in a public way. His desists (the actions directed towards halting undesirable behaviour) were nearly always verbal and, because they were easily heard by all class members, there was opportunity for ripple effects to occur and for other students to take note of the desists. In contrast, Sandra spoke very quietly and always waited for silence before beginning her whole-class deliveries; however, the silence was not usually maintained. In both whole-class and group work instructional modes, Sandra used proximity desists (that is, she moved to stand near the trouble-makers). Her verbal desists were made in a quiet, personal manner and there was no opportunity for ripple effects. The result was that some off-task behaviour was occurring nearly all of the time, and Sandra sometimes had difficulty targeting the problem because the seating arrangement made effective scanning almost impossible. In Peter's class, scanning was much easier, and quick targeting of a student at the beginning of a social exchange enabled the effective use of short verbal desists. Sandra was well able to manage the class in the whole-class mode, and she demonstrated this on several occasions, but during group work off-task behaviour was common. Sandra was aware of, and concerned about, the amount of off-task behaviour in her class. But she found herself torn between allowing the off-task behaviour to continue and changing the seating arrangement, which not only would minimize noise but also would reduce the on-task cooperative group work which Sandra believed was important in helping students to learn with understanding.

Student Assessment and Grading

Students were assessed in their science work on cognitive outcomes. At the end of the academic year, they received a letter grade for science based on their achievement level during the year. The Vertebrates and Nuclear Energy topics each contributed one quarter of the assessment for the second semester. Peter's and Sandra's record books contained marks for interim quizzes, exercises, assignments and class notes for the various topics, but each teacher used a different method of combining the marks. Peter based students' final grade for each topic only on the topic test, whilst Sandra gave equal weighting to the topic test and a composite mark for the students' other work.

The work which students did in class and which could contribute to grading was of three kinds. First, all of the learning activities were designed to build up a record of work done during the topic. This set of notes represented the students' version of the academic curriculum. Second, various quizzes, revision sheets and assignments were given in class. Apart from the quizzes, these tasks could be done at home and often were. Third, at the end of the topic, students completed a topic test which took up a whole fifty-minute period. Because the same topic test was taken by all classes, it had an important role in providing a common link which allowed comparability of students' grades awarded across the classes at that particular grade level.

The notes which students produced as a record of their work in the classroom provided students with a means of revision for the topic test. Thus, there was an incentive to complete them. In assessment terms, the class notes were accorded more importance in Sandra's class than in Peter's class because they counted towards the final grade. This difference in the importance of the class notes was consistent with the way in which students were assessed. In the Vertebrates and Nuclear Energy topics, Peter marked students' work with a letter grade, A through E, with the great majority of the students receiving A or B. The work was collected after the topic test and returned with a letter grade and a short comment, such as 'Excellent set of notes — A'; 'Very good — B'; 'Very poor — D'. Inspection of some of the returned notes revealed little evidence that Peter had done more than scan the pages and occasionally put a check mark. Sandra collected students' work several times during each topic, usually on Monday so that she could mark and return it at the next scheduled class on Wednesday. Sandra explained during interviews that each segment of the work was marked according to accuracy, completeness and presentation. Students could earn extra marks for doing the optional sections of the workbook. Sandra felt that if no marking and correcting of their work was done during the topic, students would not know how they were going and could be learning the wrong things. Sandra's marking was meticulous. Marks awarded for each answer were clearly shown with annotations for corrections and explanations.

The value that teachers gave to the students' notes was reflected in the way in which the students worked on them in class. Sandra rarely discussed answers to workbook activities in the whole-class mode. Although she provided opportunities for students to get the data from whole-class activities and demonstrations, she did not go through the answers in other than general terms. Further, even if Sandra gave answers to students in one group, her voice was so quiet that other students did not benefit from the explanations unless they left their seats to listen in. As a result, the onus was on the students to do the work and complete the activities themselves. In contrast, Peter often went through workbook activities and questions, giving answers and explanations at the whole-class level, even spelling aloud words (such as the names of bones) so that students could write them down. Also, when Peter gave answers to students' questions, he did it in a public way and his loud speaking voice (relative to Sandra's) allowed other students to benefit from the answers. By providing students with frequent opportunities to get the bits which they had missed or had not done, Peter made the task of completing the work very easy. It is therefore appropriate that no weight was given to students' notes in his assessment of their work on the topic; however, discussion with several students revealed that they did not know that their notes did not carry any weight.

The different assessment methods used by Sandra and Peter are congruent with the observed patterns of activity in the classrooms. As recorded in Figure 6.1, Peter's students spent only one third of class time working on their notes and their off-task behaviour did not hold many students back as they usually could get the answers from Peter. Whilst Sandra's students had three quarters of their lesson time available to do their notes, consistent off-task behaviour in her class did have consequences for the students; in particular, students easily got behind. Some students caught up at home while others caught up by copying each other's work. One boy, Digby, did nearly all of his work at home, getting a long way ahead of the class and finishing early. Whilst he could afford his high rate of off-task behaviour (40 per cent in Nuclear Energy and 28 per cent in Vertebrates), his completed notes were the prime target for students wishing to copy work. Other students who made good use of class time with only about 10 per cent of off-task behaviour produced excellent sets of notes.

The achievement tests given at the end of each topic were composed of multiple-choice items with several short answer questions. Nordland's analysis of the tests (see Chapter 5) indicates that they involved predominantly factual knowledge and recall, rather than higher-level cognitive learning. Mean scores on the topic tests were above 70 per cent in each class, and there were only two fail grades — one student in each class failed the Vertebrates test. Boys tended to achieve higher scores in Peter's class, whereas girls tended to score higher in Sandra's class, but these differences were not statistically significant.

The quantitative relationships between students' achievement levels and participation rates in class are not clear cut. Correlations between the two test marks were .60 and .61 for Peter's and Sandra's classes, respectively, suggesting that students have somewhat similar levels of achievement. Further, in each class, there was a correlation of .65 between the total time on-task during the two topics. However, correlations between the test marks and total time on-task varied between .16 and .61. Clearly, being on task during class is at best only a partial explanation of level of achievement. Because meta-analyses of research linking ability with science achievement have consistently revealed positive correlations (Fleming and Malone, 1983; Steinkamp and Maehr, 1983; Willson, 1983), it is likely that general ability played a part in accounting for the correlations between achievement and participation.

Many students with high levels of engagement and good class work tended to get high test marks, but there were some who managed good marks with high levels of off-task behaviour and who disclaimed doing much homework. When asked in a written questionnaire about the amount of homework which they did in science, students' answers ranged between none and up to one hour per night. Some said that they worked only when there was a test or when something had to be handed in. This finding suggests that, for many students, a major reason for doing the work was the extrinsic goal of getting grades or avoiding trouble. The topic test was accorded great importance by students. For example, in an interview with fourteen students from Peter's class, students were asked what made them do the work in class if they didn't like the topic or didn't think that it was important. Five of the nine students who responded said that they wanted to pass the test. The other four mentioned 'threats' as the reason why they would do the work.

It already has been indicated that the cognitive level of the tests was generally low, and this fact, together with the low cognitive level of class work, meant that many of the students in this above-average class who did not work hard during class time were able to pass the test quite comfortably. Therefore, the nature of the learning tasks and the method of assessing them did not seem to provide a motivating challenge for many students. Because, like the classwork, the assessment structure was based on lower-level outcomes, there was neither need nor incentive for students to work at a higher cognitive level, and most did not. However, some students clearly were self-motivated to work harder and at a higher cognitive level than the majority.

Students' Affect and Participation

The attitudes and self-perceptions that students have about science and about their ability to do it are likely to affect the way that students use their time in the classroom. The relationship between students' affect and their participation patterns in science was examined by using several scales from two semantic differential measures. Students' interest in their school science and their perceptions of its importance and difficulty were measured using a semantic differential technique using the concept 'This Science Topic'. A second semantic differential, using the concept 'Me As A Science Student', was used to tap students' attitudes to doing science work in class and their self-perceptions of their ability in science. The semantic differential technique was chosen for use in this study because it provides a measure of the underlying constructs in a short administration time and because, as Heise (1969) has shown, as few as three or four pairs of bipolar adjectives can work effectively. The adjective pairs were chosen on the basis of their successful use in other studies (Rennie, 1986) and were accorded face validity in discussion with the research team. The semantic differential concepts were administered together with the learning environment scales (see Chapter 7 in this volume) during the day after each topic was finished and when students had completed the topic test.

The psychometric properties of the semantic differential instruments were checked using a sample of 194 students from Southside High, and the structure of the scales was confirmed using factor analysis. Students' enjoyment of science and its perceived importance and difficulty were measured using the concept 'This Science Topic'. The three attitude scales named Enjoyment, Importance and Facility had coefficient alpha reliabilities of .93, .93 and .78, respectively. A high score on the Enjoyment scale indicates that students considered the science topic to be fun, enjoyable, interesting and exciting. High scores on the Importance scale are obtained by responding that the science topic is important, valuable, relevant and useful. The third scale, Facility, is the reverse of difficulty. A high score indicates that science is perceived to be simple, easy, effortless and understandable. The second concept, 'Me As A Science Student', was used to measure students' self-perceptions of their ability in science and their attitude to working in science. The two scales named Perceived Ability and Work Attitude had coefficient alpha reliabilities of .87 and .84, respectively. A high score on the Perceived Ability scale indicates that a student perceived himself/herself to be good at science, found science easy and was successful, understanding and confident. A positive Work Attitude involves a student being industrious, motivated, quiet, careful, neat and enthusiastic.

Because the semantic differential scales had different numbers of items, scores for each scale were calculated as mean item scores. Thus, for each scale, the possible range of scores was 1 through 7. Table 6.2 reports

*Table 6.2: Means, standard deviations and correlations with test marks and time-
on-task for the affective scales in Peter's and Sandra's classes*

Affective Scale	Peter				Sandra			
	Mean	SD	Correlation Topic Test	Time-on Task	Mean	SD	Correlation Topic Test	Time-on Task
Vertebrates								
Enjoyment	4.87	1.49	.24	.31	5.42	1.10	.16	.46
Importance	5.07	1.34	.39*	.33	5.65	0.97	.24	.51**
Facility	4.65	1.08	.03	−.12	4.16	1.10	.08	.14
Perceived Ability	5.11	1.02	.64**	.11	5.28	0.93	.25	.28
Work Attitude	5.10	0.91	.22	.43*	5.05	0.78	.03	.44*
Nuclear Energy								
Enjoyment	4.12	1.65	.35*	.22	4.71	1.39	.26	.45*
Importance	5.56	1.32	.42*	.28	5.40	1.29	.21	.32
Facility	4.26	1.33	.47**	.38*	3.62	1.17	.10	.08
Perceived Ability	5.11	0.93	.74**	.31	5.24	1.05	.50**	.18
Work Attitude	4.94	1.05	.59**	.41*	5.16	0.91	.28	.48**

* p < .05   ** p < .01

the means and standard deviations of the affective scales in Peter's and
Sandra's classes. The results indicate positive attitudes about science,
particularly for the Vertebrates topic. The Nuclear Energy topic was not
enjoyed as much, and the means for the Enjoyment and Facility scales for
this topic are among the lowest in the table. The means for Sandra's class
on the Engagement scale were consistently higher than the means for
Peter's class, but the differences were not statistically significant. However, students in Peter's class reported both topics to be easier than did
students in Sandra's class, and an F-test indicated that these differences
were significant at the .05 level.

The quantitative data from the affective scales were used to investigate the magnitude of the relationships between students' affect, achievement and participation. Students' marks on the topic tests were used as a
measure of achievement and total time-on-task was used to indicate
participation. The correlations between these two variables and the affective scales also are reported in Table 6.2. The correlations are mostly
positive but unremarkable. Generally, students with positive attitudes had
higher achievement, but the correlations are not always statistically significant. This finding supports the commonly found result that attitudes and achievement in science have small but positive relationships
(Steinkamp and Maehr, 1983; Willson, 1983). Students with higher levels
of time-on-task also have generally positive attitudes, but most of the
correlations do not reach significance. The one consistent result is the

moderate correlation between the Work Attitude scale and time on-task, a result which might be expected if students' self-perceptions of their classroom work are valid.

Students' Motivational Orientations

In the introduction to this chapter, it was noted that students had rather stable patterns of participation, so that each student tended to participate (or not) in the same way according to the type of learning activities going on in the classroom. The quantitative findings suggest that students' levels of engagement had some association with their achievement, their attitudes to science and their perceptions about themselves as science students, but consideration of these variables fell short of predicting an accurate pattern of how students engage in the learning tasks. Those students who continuously applied themselves to the task at hand and those who spent as little time as possible on-task clearly had different motivational orientations.

There is a number of theoretical positions which can be used to aid interpretations of students' motivational orientations (Brophy 1983; Dweck and Elliott, 1983; Maehr, 1983, 1984; Nicholls, 1983, 1984), and there appears to be a reasonable consensus that three kinds of motivational orientation underlie the behavioural strategies that students employ in the classroom. Students can be task-involved, ego-involved or extrinsically involved (Nicholls, 1983). Task-involved students are described as mastery-oriented, seeking to increase competence by mastering new knowledge or skills. These students are intrinsically motivated, they value learning, enjoy its challenge and are likely to persevere by applying effort and using a variety of cognitive strategies. Ego-involved students are more concerned with performance than learning, are particularly concerned about judgements made of their competencies, and adopt two kinds of strategies (Dweck and Elliott, 1983; Nicholls, Patashnik and Nolen, 1985; Meece and Blumenfeld, 1987). One strategy is to seek favourable judgements of their performance by competing with others, by trying to look smart or by seeking social approval. Attempting to avoid the task is another strategy, because failure, particularly when effort is invested, can result in unfavourable judgements of competence. Ego-involved students often engage in tasks at a superficial level and adopt strategies to minimize effort by guessing, asking others for the answer, copying or rote-learning information likely to be tested. Students who are involved extrinsically are concerned with learning only as a means to an end. Engaging in work to please the teacher, achieve some reward or avoid punishment are examples of extrinsic involvement. Whilst learning can occur, it is accepted that extrinsic involvement is not an effective means of sustaining motivation, and so researchers usually urge the development of task-oriented, non-competitive classrooms as a means of increasing student motivation to learn (Ames, 1984; Brophy, 1983; Corno and Mandinach, 1983; Dweck and Elliott, 1983; Maehr, 1983, 1984; Meece and Blumenfeld, 1987; Nicholls, 1983, 1984).

The three different states of involvement are not mutually exclusive. They can co-exist and be evident at different times in the behaviour of the same student. The assessment structure of the academic work and the degree of public evaluation in the classroom will be significant determinants of whether the classroom atmosphere fosters task-involvement, ego-involvement or extrinsic-involvement in students' motivational patterns.

In the classrooms observed in this study, it was clear that students' patterns of participation were associated with their different motivational orientations. Evidence has been presented to show that each class, as a group, had a pattern of behaviour which was dependent upon the teacher's way of structuring and sequencing the various activities, and that variation in the nature of engagement and off-task behaviour was associated with the management style of the teacher. However, there was a great deal of variation among individual students in each class, underscoring the importance of the student's role in choosing patterns of behaviour according to his or her perceptions of the tasks and constraints operating within the classroom. The quantitative data from the achievement and affective measures offer only a partial explanation of the levels at which students participate in the learning tasks.

A better understanding of how students' attitudes and perceptions influence their patterns of participation results when qualitative data from field notes, lesson transcripts and interviews are used to complement the quantitative data. In the next section, case studies of several students are presented to demonstrate how students' classroom behaviours can be interpreted in terms of how students participate in the lesson, their personal affect about science and their inferred motivational orientations.

Case Studies of Students

The students chosen for case studies were selected to be representative of groups of students with similar quantitative patterns of engagement. Cluster analysis was used as an empirical method to group students exhibiting similar patterns of on-task and off-task time. The cluster analysis was performed using a hierarchical method with raw data comprising each student's percentage of time spent in the six engagement modes for each topic. These were the variables described earlier in this chapter, namely, engagement in individual activity, and individual passive activity, off-task alone, group work, whole-class engagement and social off-task activity. The analyses were carried out separately for each class because there were very different allocations of time to the various activity modes in each class (see Figure 6.1). There are clear-cut criteria neither for determining which clustering method is appropriate for particular kinds of data sets nor for determining the optimal number of clusters. Further, because the cluster analysis for each class was based on a sample of only thirty-one students, three contrasting clustering methods were used in an exploratory approach. The clustering methods used were average linkage analysis, Ward's minimum variance method and two-stage density linkage (SAS, 1985). The results for each analysis were printed using a tree diagram. After inspection of the results, it was possible to define four clusters for each class according to the commonalties evident.

In each class, one cluster had members high on all kinds of on-task engagement and another cluster had members with high levels of off-task behaviour. The remaining clusters had intermediate levels of engagement and were distinguished by slightly different patterns of group or off-task behaviour. Field observations indicated that, within each cluster, students of similar ability and with very similar patterns of participation appeared to have different reasons for those behavioural patterns.

Six students have been selected for detailed case studies of their patterns of participation. Students were selected in same-sex pairs from three of the total of eight clusters in Peter's and Sandra's classes, to give a broad spectrum of the kinds of participation which students exhibited in the class. In each case study, the student's apparent motivational orientations and learning outcomes are interpreted in terms of their observed behaviour, particularly student-teacher interactions and quantitative measures of their attitudes and perceptions.

Sally and Margaret

Sally and Margaret were in the high engagement cluster in Sandra's class. Both had high levels of on-task behaviour, but Sally spent a little more time in group work (mainly with Janila) than did Margaret, who worked alone or sometimes with Andy who sat next to her. The girls' scores on the affective scales and their achievement data are reported in Table 6.3. Sally scored the highest test marks in the class and her marks for class work were among the highest. Margaret's test marks were among the lowest and her marks for class work were just below average. Sally's scores on the affective scales were among the highest, except for her perceptions of the facility of the topics, particularly for Nuclear Energy which, despite her high performance, she rated as very difficult. Sally responded in a questionnaire that science was her favourite subject, she intended it to be her career and she planned to study both chemistry and physics the following year. Margaret's affective results are close to aver-

Table 6.3: Scores on affective, achievement and off-task variables for selected students

Measure	Sally	Margaret	Greg	Jeffrey	Gavin	Wayne
Vertebrates						
Enjoyment	6.75	5.00	2.50	5.50	2.50	4.50
Importance	6.75	6.00	3.25	5.00	4.00	3.75
Facility	4.50	3.00	4.25	5.50	3.00	3.50
Perceived Ability	6.60	3.60	3.20	5.80	3.40	5.00
Work Attitude	6.00	4.57	3.43	4.71	3.00	4.14
Class Work*	93	68	D	C	53	39
Test Mark (%)	88	62	54	79	78	51
% Off-Task Alone	2	5	21	15	15	19
% Off-Task Social	9	5	18	20	46	44
Nuclear Energy						
Enjoyment	6.75	5.75	3.75	4.25	3.25	1.75
Importance	6.75	4.75	5.25	3.50	4.75	4.00
Facility	1.75	4.75	4.00	5.00	3.00	3.25
Perceived Ability	6.80	3.20	4.00	5.60	3.60	4.40
Work Attitude	6.29	5.57	2.57	4.86	4.00	4.00
Class Work*	99	63	C	C	56	46
Test Mark (%)	94	71	63	90	64	51
% Off-Task Alone	0	4	8	10	15	19
% Off-Task Social	18	8	22	13	41	57

* The class work was scored as a percentage in Sandra's class and a grade, A through E, in Peter's class.

age, except for Perceived Ability, on which her self-rating was well below the class average. She rated Nuclear Energy as less difficult than did most of her peers and, although she perceived it to be of less importance than Vertebrates, her Work Attitude score was higher. At the end of Nuclear Energy, Margaret reported that Mathematics and English were her favourite subjects and she planned to carry on with just one science subject (Human Biology) in grades 11 and 12.

Sally's and Margaret's patterns of classroom behaviour were directed at getting information to complete the work, but they interacted in different ways. Sally was often a participant in whole-class discussion and, during small-group work, she conferred frequently about the material with Janila. She often raised her hand to attract Sandra's attention or left her seat to consult her. Interactions with Sandra were always two-way. Sally always was concerned about mastering the work, and this is illustrated by an incident taken from field notes made during the Nuclear Energy topic. In this six-minute segment of whole-class interaction, Sandra described how Henri Becquerel had been working with phosphorescent substances. She asked if anyone could explain, in his/her own words, Becquerel's experiment involving the detection of radiation with a photographic plate. (This experiment was described in Becquerel's own words in the workbook.) Sally responded with a clear answer. Sandra elaborated about why the experiment worked. Sally asked for further clarification and Sandra obliged, trying to get across to the class how Becquerel controlled for possible chemical or light effects to the photographic plate. Sally then restated the information apparently to check her understanding of it.

Margaret's classroom interactions were less public than Sally's because she didn't volunteer answers or ask questions during whole-class activities. She did participate in a whole-class experiment measuring radiation in a passive and non-threatening way (in the sense that her performance was unlikely to be judged). Margaret sometimes raised her hand to ask Sandra for help, but she didn't leave her seat to go to Sandra. The following excerpt from a transcript of a lesson on energy changes during Nuclear Energy illustrates Margaret's interactions with Sandra and the other students in her group.

Sandra: Now, Margaret, are you okay?

Margaret: No.

Sandra: What kind of energy will this have here (points), Margaret? [Sandra is interrupted by another student for ten seconds.]

Sandra: When it's like this, what is it? What kind?

Andy: Potential.

Sandra: Good. Why?

Andy: It's not moving.

Sandra: It's not moving but it's going to be able to move so it's stored ready to produce ...?

Andy: Stored. It's potential then it's kinetic.

Margaret: What about the battery and the light globe?

Sandra: What's in this one? What type of energy is in the battery to start with?

Narelle: Chemical.

Sandra: Good. Yeah. How do you know Narelle?

Narelle: I dunno!

Sandra: You just thought about it?

Narelle: I just guessed it!

Sandra: Good. A battery's got, you know, your zinc electrodes and your carbon and all the rest of it. So, initially you've got chemical energy stored in there. When you connect your circuit ...?

Narelle: You get light.

Sandra: Your final energy in this one?

Margaret: You get light.

Sandra: What's the energy in the middle to light the light?

Andy: Electricity.

Sandra: Right! So when you do your transformations you've got them. Good kids.

It was Margaret who initiated the interaction in this discussion and who, when the first energy change was sorted out, asked about the next example. But she allowed her classmates to answer all of the questions, with her only response being to echo Narelle's answer 'you get light'.

Both Margaret and Sally seem to be task-involved. Sally's efforts always were directed at obtaining mastery of the content; she did not mind asking questions for clarification, even in public. She perceived herself as able, interested and hardworking, and her behaviour and results were consistent with those perceptions. Her perception that Nuclear Energy was difficult (see Table 6.3) could simply reflect her determination to master the content. Margaret, too, maintained a positive attitude to work and, although she didn't offer ideas publicly, she asked for help when she needed it. However, in direct contrast to Sally, Margaret perceived herself to have low ability in science. Sandra commented several times during interviews that Margaret lacked self-confidence and did not feel capable at science. It is particularly interesting to note that both Sally and Margaret were found to be at the formal operational level when tested on the Separation of Variables Piagetian Task (see Chapter 5) and to ponder how Margaret's self-perception of low ability originated. In a response to a questionnaire item asking students' opinions about copying other students' work and about learning by doing your own work, Margaret responded:

> You won't learn anything by copying someone else's work. If you don't do things for yourself in school, then how are you going to cope in the workforce? You learn things by concentrating, trying hard and devoting yourself.

Margaret's behaviour gave no indication of avoidance of work or effort, but she saw her main interests and future career as not including science. (She answered a question about the importance of science in a career and in every day life with '?') So, she didn't value highly the achievement outcomes. Further, her perceived lack of ability might have led her to believe that she was capable of only moderate marks and thus, like Sally, she was producing the work of which she believed she was capable. Research indicates, however, that students with low perceived ability are more likely to be extrinsically rather than intrinsically motivated (Meece and Blumenfeld, 1987). There is no evidence to suggest that Margaret was intrinsically interested in science as Sally seemed to be. Rather, she worked steadily and cooperatively in class, involving herself sufficiently to obtain passing grades in her class work and tests. It is possible to attribute Margaret's lack of public involvement to a fear of being judged unfavourably: her participation was always in non-threatening low-risk situations and she spoke to Sandra on a one-to-one basis, content to listen to her table-mates discuss the work. Sandra created a classroom atmosphere which was non-threatening, taking care not to embarrass students nor to make public her evaluations of their performance. It is possible that, had she been in another class in which teacher-student interactions and evaluations were much more public, Margaret's self-concept and affect about science could have become even less positive, perhaps to the extent that they would interfere with her learning.

Greg and Jeffrey

Greg and Jeffrey were both in the cluster with the highest levels of off-task behaviour in Peter's class. Table 6.3 displays these high levels of time off-task, together with the affective and achievement scores for these boys. Greg's scores suggest that he didn't enjoy science and considered himself neither to be very able, nor to work very hard. Jeffrey had more positive attitudes, particularly for the Vertebrates topic. Both students had grades for their class work which were below average for the class but, whilst Greg's achievement was well below the average, Jeffrey's achievement marks were above the average and he received one of the highest marks in the class for the test on the Nuclear Energy topic. Because both students were tested to be at the fully formal operational level on the Separation of Variables task and, because the cognitive level of the work was low (see Chapter 5 of this volume), both should have been capable of success. Both Greg and Jeffrey intended to proceed to grade 11, but the only science which Greg planned to do was Human Biology because, as he explained in response to a questionnaire item: 'You have to have a science subject to get into university. I don't like science'. Jeffrey planned to take both Physics ('because I need it to get the job I want') and Chemistry ('because it interests me').

Greg and Jeffrey were two of the most visible students in the class. Both sat in the front row, Greg on the left side between Craig and Joanna with whom he interacted socially. Jenny, who sat on the other side of Joanna, often found this social activity annoying and was heard to complain on several occasions. Jeffrey sat at the far right of the front row, next to Steven. Steven was the quietest boy in the class and, had he not consistently ignored Jeffrey's frequent attempts to engage him in conversation, Jeffrey's level of off-task social behaviour would have been much higher. Jeffrey and Greg also were visible because of their prominence in whole-class interaction. Jeffrey asked and responded to more questions than any other student during the observation period and, on one occasion, Peter refused to take his answer, preferring to give another student a chance to speak. Both students also initiated interactions, by asking questions, volunteering information or making comments.

During class, Jeffrey and Greg usually were cheerful. Neither boy seemed to be perturbed if his answers were wrong or if his comments were not appreciated. Greg sometimes received teasing desists from Peter for moving to chat with Nicola in another part of the room and for coming in late. Despite his teasing, Peter seemed to be fond of Greg, referring to him at various times in interviews as 'bright', 'a delightful kid' and 'just interested in rolling along and having a good time'. When asked if he thought Greg didn't take science seriously, Peter said 'No, not at all ... it was more of a "don't hassle me and I'll get there under my own steam" sort of thing'. Peter's perceptions seemed to be congruent with Greg's own views. In response to a questionnaire item asking what he liked best about his science class, Greg wrote that: 'It's good fun talking to Joanna, abusing Jenny and stuffing around with Craig'.

Greg's motivational orientations in the classroom seemed to be associated with neither task-involvement nor ego-involvement. He did not apply himself to the task and inspection of his class notes revealed some errors, incompleteness and disorganization. His involvement seemed to be extrinsically motivated. He did just enough work to scrape through and thus keep out of serious trouble. This interpretation of his motivational orientation seems consistent with Greg's response to a question asked during a discussion with some of the students in Peter's class at the end of the Nuclear Energy topic. When Greg was asked what made him work when he disliked a topic or thought it unimportant, he responded that 'it means a good mark in the test, thus Mum's happy'.

Jeffrey's motivational orientation was different. He, too, enjoyed classroom life. In response to the questionnaire item asking what he liked best about his science class, he wrote 'the people in it and the teacher'. Peter liked Jeffrey, calling him 'mate' and even on one occasion 'me old mate, me old sparring partner'. This reflected some change in attitude by Peter. Peter said in his final interview that he had regarded Jeffrey as the class clown, who often spoke without thinking, but during the year his feelings towards Jeffrey had changed and he felt that their personal relationship had ended on a high note. Nevertheless, Peter did not consider Jeffrey to be particularly able, naming him among the bottom five students in the class. Jeffrey's marks over the year were not high for written work, but his test marks were below the class average on only one occasion. His class notes were brief but basically complete and, although he didn't work hard in small-group activities, he always was involved in whole-class interactive activities. His answers to Peter's questions were mostly right and his own questions often reflected thought on different aspects of the content under discussion. There is no evidence to suggest that Jeffrey was involved for extrinsic reasons; rather his involvement was intrinsically motivated. Further, his willingness to take risks in his overt classroom interactions indicate that he was not ego-involved. It seems likely that, because Jeffrey found the work to be of low cognitive level and to offer limited challenge, he sought involvement in situations which could be made challenging, such as discussion sessions.

Jeffrey's classroom strategy was different from that of Sally, who also was task-motivated but whose behaviour was much more mastery-oriented. Like Jeffrey, she always was willing to be involved in the whole-class discussion which occurred in Sandra's class and asked many questions of Sandra, but Sally seemed to find the topics more intrinsically interesting than Jeffrey did, and found her challenge in understanding the content of the workbooks as fully as possible. Had she been in Peter's class, Sally's patterns of behaviour would probably have changed only to reflect the different opportunities for whole-class and individual activities, but she would have maintained very high levels of on-task behaviour. Conversely, if Jeffrey had been in Sandra's class, his opportunities for involvement in class discussion, and particularly the opportunities for the tangential discussions that he seemed to find interesting, would have been curtailed. The large amount of time which Sandra allowed for students to complete the workbook activities probably would have left Jeffrey bored and seeking challenge in off-task social activity.

Greg's rather care-free statement about his enjoyment of the social aspects of science lessons suggests that, had he been in Sandra's class, he would have continued to give his attention to social activity rather than to learning. Peter kept Greg's social behaviour in reasonable check and, given that the physical arrangement of desks made management more difficult in Sandra's class, Greg's off-task activities might have been a source of disruption to other students had he been in Sandra's class.

Gavin and Wayne

Gavin and Wayne were two boys in Sandra's class. They had the highest levels of time off-task of all students, with over 50 per cent of off-task time during each topic. About three-quarters of this behaviour was devoted to social activity. Gavin and Wayne had similar patterns of attitudes about science (see Table 6.3), which were among the least positive in the class. Neither thought that the science topics were easy, but Wayne perceived himself to be more able than did Gavin, whose self-perceptions were among the lowest in the class. Wayne's test marks were very low, as were his marks for class work. Gavin's marks were better and his mark on the Vertebrates topic test was above the class average. On the Separation of Variables Test (see Nordland's chapter in this volume), Gavin was rated at the formal level and Wayne was rated as transitional.

Gavin and Wayne did not interact often and Sandra said in interview on several occasions that she kept them separate because they argued when together. She also kept Gavin separate from his friend Steve because they tended to be too noisy when together. Gavin sat with Bronwyn, Leanne and Melissa, and most of his social interactions were with Bronwyn. Leanne and Melissa were also involved, but generally as respondents rather than initiators. Sometimes when Sandra's back was turned, Gavin would visit Steve, but mostly he sat slouched over his table doing little work. Gavin did not work conscientiously for more than a few minutes at a time. One morning, about sixty minutes through a 100-minute lesson, Gavin asked Sandra if they could have a break. 'Not go anywhere', he said, 'just have a break'. Sandra said no and Bronwyn laughed and told him that he didn't need it. Up to that time, his efforts had resulted in the writing of only one sentence. On another occasion, when Bronwyn returned to her seat after taking a test which she had missed through absence, she said to Gavin 'How come you're working today?' Gavin replied that he was bored doing nothing. About half way through the Nuclear Energy topic, Sandra began to check both Gavin's and Wayne's work on a daily basis because they were so far behind in their class work. Gavin decided to move on to the next table to work with Craig and Paul and he stayed there until the end of the topic. Gavin spent more time in active work and often sought help from Sandra and confirmation that he was on the right track. He had several conversations with Sandra about the marks that he might get.

Gavin did not appear to be happy in class. He seemed not to enjoy school and wanted to leave. Sandra said that his parents would not allow Gavin to leave because they wanted him to continue on to grades 11 and 12. Gavin usually expended minimal effort and when he did do some work in science, his motivation was clearly extrinsic. He was not interested in science and did not consider it relevant. To the questionnaire item asking how the science class could be improved, Gavin wrote: 'Do more interesting subjects that will help us; learning about animals and nuclear reactors are not relevant'. Gavin did not plan an academic career. He was interested in the martial arts, and in interview he stated that he would like to be an instructor in martial arts and that he worked out for about one and a half hours a day. He thought that it was more likely that he would be a hairdresser and had applied to enter a course for that. Gavin was an able student who was not interested in science. His only reason for doing the work in science was to gain marks, and it seems likely that these marks were pursued to satisfy the expectations of his parents.

Sandra named both Gavin and Wayne as low achievers in her class, as indeed they were, saying that both tended to underachieve. In Gavin's case, she attributed underachievement to his desire to leave school and his corresponding disinterest in science and other school subjects. In Wayne's case, Sandra thought that his underachievement was because 'his social requirements got the better of him'. In fact, the results of the Separation of Variables Test (see Chapter 5) suggested that Wayne was less able than most of the other students in his class. On his last report card (for the Nuclear Energy topic), Sandra wrote: 'Wayne has yet to mature in his efforts and attitudes and continues to give only a little time to serious work. He must develop a greater responsibility if he is to achieve in grade 11'. The field observations of all of the research team provided continuous evidence of the accuracy of Sandra's remarks on Wayne's report card.

Wayne was always noticeable in the classroom. Although Sandra placed him alone at the bench along the back wall, he always joined Table 7 or 8 when there was a vacant seat. He initiated and engaged in social interchanges with the students at these and other tables nearby or, when Sandra's back was turned, he visited students elsewhere in the room. When other students tried to ignore him, Wayne often did something to gain their attention, such as emptying their pencil cases or drawing on their pages. Wayne borrowed pens and rulers without permission and argued about giving them back, and he disclaimed responsibility when his actions resulted in damage to students' property. Not surprisingly, many students found Wayne's actions annoying and, in a written response to a question asking how they would like their classroom changed, a number of students suggested getting rid of Wayne. Wayne rarely was observed to be doing his own work and, when Sandra began to check his work each day, he borrowed other students' work and copied it, rather than doing his own. When Sandra came near, Wayne pretended to be reading the workbook and covered the work he was copying. These excerpts from field notes for one lesson illustrate Wayne's tendency to copy other students' work. Sue was absent and Wayne was sitting in her seat, next to Jody.

> *1.38pm:* Wayne is surreptitiously copying a page of work. He gives the page back to Digby when Sandra comes to see Jody, and gets it back when Sandra leaves.
>
> *1.52pm:* Sandra visits Jody again. Wayne pretends to read. When she goes, he calls Digby for more work to copy.
>
> *2.11pm:* Class dismisses. Sandra checks some students' work [including Wayne's]. She knows Wayne copied Digby's work, 'yet he looked me straight in the eye', she says to me, 'and said it was his own'.

Despite Wayne's disruptive behaviour (which seemed to be designed to draw attention to himself), surprisingly he became white and looked extremely nervous and self-conscious when he was asked to present himself for interview with one of the researchers (for the Separation of Variables Test). When this was mentioned to Sandra, she was not surprised and said that, for all his bravado, she felt that Wayne had a self-esteem problem. Field observations support this perception. Wayne was not as able as many in the class and he never volunteered to participate in class discussion. He rated himself as more able than his results implied and, when marked work was returned to students, Wayne compared his results to theirs, drawing attention loudly to his own low marks. Wayne's motivational orientations seem to be ego-involved and his classroom behaviour seems best described as work-avoidant. Further, he made sure that everyone knew that he was not giving any effort, presumably in the belief that this meant that his real ability was not in question.

The motivational orientations of both Gavin and Wayne were extrinsic. Their efforts to avoid work were enhanced by the environment in Sandra's classroom, which placed the responsibility for learning on the student. Unlike Sally, whose intrinsic mastery orientation enabled her to work independently and at a high cognitive level, Gavin and Wayne both gave up easily when they had difficulties. When Sandra began daily checking of their work, in an effort to make them accountable for working, both sought ways to minimize the cognitive effort involved. Gavin did do most of his own work, but he referred frequently to his peers or Sandra for guidance.

It is possible that Gavin and Wayne would have spent more time on-task in Peter's class, partly because of his more public and forceful style of management and partly because Peter spent time going through the answers, a technique which lowered the cognitive level of class work and also the effort required to complete the workbooks. Further, Peter's consistent efforts to enhance students' interest and understanding by relating the subject matter to out-of-school situations could have helped both Gavin and Wayne to find more interest and relevance in science. If more time was spent actually thinking about the science content, possibly more would have been learned. However, it is probable that this learning would have remained at a low cognitive level.

Summary

Students' patterns of participation were very different in Peter's and Sandra's classrooms. In general terms, the opportunities for different patterns of behaviour were determined by the teaching preferences and management styles of the teacher. Whole-class exposition, whole-class interaction and individual/group work modes were given roughly the same amount of time in Peter's class. During whole-class sessions, he introduced additional background information from his own experiences, related the work to 'real world' situations and set occasional 'problems' for the students to solve. He believed that this approach helped students to learn and understand the work. Peter paced the students through the work with his emphasis on whole-class teaching and made sure that students kept up by checking their answers in class. Because the students were seated in rows, the physical arrangement of the classroom assisted effective scanning and Peter was able to target potential misbehaviour and use public, verbal desists to keep the class moving along.

In contrast, Sandra allocated three-quarters of class time to individual/group work and used time at the beginning and end of each lesson to provide information about the rate of progress through the work which she considered appropriate. Sandra rarely gave answers to the class as a whole; rather, she collected and marked work on a weekly basis. Students were seated around tables and most used the opportunities for group work to engage in social activity. This physical arrangement of the class hindered effective scanning and Sandra's use of proximity and quiet verbal desists did not enable ripple effects to occur. The result was a higher average level of off-task behaviour in Sandra's class than in Peter's. In both classes, there were limited opportunities for higher-level learning to occur. The low cognitive level of the tasks in the workbooks and the available texts did not offer cognitive challenge to most of the students. Further, because the topic tests were designed to measure mainly lower-level learning outcomes (see Nordland's chapter), students were able to pass the tests without demonstrating any higher-level learning. Thus, these students of above average ability were able to spend considerable time in off-task behaviour without suffering the penalty of failure on the test.

Within each class, different students had different but personally consistent patterns of behaviour. Several quantitative measures were obtained of students' attitudes to science and perceptions about their own ability and work attitude to science. Correlations between the affective and achievement variables and an observational measure of the percentage of time-on-task were generally positive but not consistently strong. Students' attitudes seem to be fallible predictors of engagement in an on-task or off-task sense, and time-on-task is an inconsistent predictor of achievement. A more complete understanding of each student's classroom participation and why time-on-task is not more highly correlated with achievement can be obtained by considering the quantitative data in conjunction with the qualitative data derived from interviews and field notes.

Cluster analysis was used to place students from each class into four groups which had similar patterns of engagement and off-task activities. Field observations had shown that, within each of these clusters, some students with very similar patterns of engagement in a quantitative sense appeared, in a qualitative sense, to have different patterns in the nature of, and reasons for, their participation. To illustrate these differences, the patterns of participation for several students were described as case studies and, using data from both quantitative and qualitative sources, an attempt was made to interpret the nature of their participation in class.

Sally and Margaret were students in Sandra's class who had similarly high levels of on-task behaviour but, whereas Sally had very positive attitudes and high achievement, Margaret had lower perceptions of her ability and achievement. Both students were able, in the sense that they were capable of reasoning at the formal level, and it was suggested that the differences in their participation and performance were attributable to their motivational orientations. Sally and Margaret seemed to be task-involved but, whilst Sally was mastery-oriented and actively involved in whole-class activity, Margaret did not engage in public interactions and seemed not to value mastery outcomes as much as Sally. Sandra's instructional style seemed to suit both Sally and Margaret, as each was able to obtain the kind of assistance they needed from her. In Sally's case, this enabled her to obtain mastery of the work at a high cognitive level, which in fact was higher than was demanded by either the workbooks or the achievement tests. Margaret was able to complete her work in a quiet non-threatening situation, at a level adequate to pass and commensurate with her personal expectations. Her interactions with Sandra assisted her to find answers to the required questions without necessarily achieving complete understanding.

The case study comparisons among Greg, Jeffrey, Gavin and Wayne, four boys with high levels of off-task behaviour, suggest different motivational orientations. With the possible exception of Wayne, all were capable of mastering the work which was of low cognitive level. Jeffrey's attitudes were the most positive and, although he appeared to be task-oriented, he seemed to find little challenge in the class work. Greg, Gavin and Wayne had similar patterns of attitudes and achievement, but quite a different presence in the classroom. Figuratively, Peter kept a firm hand on Greg and Jeffrey, so their tendency for social activity was not widely disruptive. Gavin's and Wayne's social activities were not kept well in check by Sandra, and so they were more disruptive (particularly Wayne's). Both Greg and Gavin seemed to be extrinsically motivated. Neither liked science but, because he planned to go on with his schooling, Greg was happy to do enough work to get by and avoid any trouble caused by failure. Gavin wanted to leave school and needed much more direction to get his work done. He avoided work until he had to do it to be sure of passing the course at a reasonable level. Wayne's work avoidance was more likely to be related to ego-involvement than simple dislike of the subject. He sought attention almost continuously and he actively avoided work and effort by copying the products of other class members.

It is emphasized that the interpretations of the students' behaviour and the inferences made about their motivational orientations are speculative. Nevertheless, the outcomes of this study highlight the role of the student in determining his or her own level of learning. The results help to explain why low and variable correlations are found between student attitudes and achievement, and suggests reasons why attitudes and achievement are not more closely related to time-on-task. The relationships among these variables are complex and are intricately bound up both with students' motivational goals and with the strategies they use to achieve them. Within any one classroom, not all students are suited by the teacher's choice of instructional and managerial techniques (Good and Power, 1976). In individualized classrooms such as those observed in the study, there was scope for the teacher to offer a variety of instructional tasks, yet there were still some students who apparently failed to achieve at the level at which they were capable. Part of the reason for this was the lack of opportunity for the students to engage in higher-level thinking because of the low cognitive level of the resource materials. In the case of some students, it appeared that their motivational goals did not involve learning but were directed towards minimizing effort. It could be that teachers need to become more skilled in recognizing students' patterns of interactions and engagement and react to them in ways which challenge students to learn at higher cognitive levels. The observations in this study suggest that, to do this, teachers must be able to recognize and have the ability to adjust the cognitive level of the learning tasks.

References

AMES, C. (1984) 'Competitive, cooperative and individualistic goal structures: A cognitive-motivational analysis', in AMES, R.E. and AMES, C. (Eds) *Research on Motivation in Education: Student Motivation* (Vol. 1), New York, Academic Press, pp. 177–207.

AMES, R.E. and AMES, C. (Eds) (1984) *Research on Motivation in Education: Student Motivation* (Vol. 1), New York, Academic Press.

BANDURA, A. (1977) 'Self-efficacy: Toward a unifying theory of behavioral change', *Psychological Review*, 84, pp. 191–215.

BERLINER, D.C. (1979) 'Tempus educare', in PETERSON, P.L. and WALBERG, H.J. (Eds) *Research on Teaching: Concepts, Findings and Implications*, Berkeley, Calif., McCutchan, pp. 120–35.

BLOOM, B.S. (1976) *Human Characteristics and School Learning*, New York, McGraw-Hill.

BROPHY, J.E. (1983) 'Conceptualizing student motivation', *Educational Psychologist*, 18, pp. 200–15.

BROPHY, J.E. and GOOD, T.L. (1986) 'Teacher behavior and student achievement', in WITTROCK, M.C. (Ed.), *Handbook of Research on Teaching* (3rd. ed.), New York, Macmillan, pp. 328–75.

CARROLL, J.B. (1963) 'A model of school learning', *Teachers College Record*, 64, pp. 723–33.

CORNO, L. and MANDINACH, E.B. (1983). 'The role of cognitive engagement in classroom learning and motivation', *Educational Psychologist*, 18, pp. 88–108.

DOYLE, W. (1983) 'Academic work', *Review of Educational Research*, 53, pp. 159–99.

DOYLE, W. (1986) 'Classroom organization and management', in WITTROCK, M.C. (Ed.) *Handbook of Research on Teaching* (3rd. ed.), New York, Macmillan, pp. 392–431.

DOYLE, W. (1988) 'Work in mathematics classes: The context of students' thinking during instruction', *Educational Psychologist*, 23, pp. 167–80.

DWECK, C.S. and ELLIOTT, E.S. (1983) 'Achievement motivation', in HETHERINGTON, E.M. (Ed.) *Socialization, Personality, and Social Development*, New York, John Wiley.

FLEMING, M.L. and MALONE, M.R. (1983) 'The relationship of student characteristics and student performance in science as viewed by meta-analysis research', *Journal of Research in Science Teaching*, 20, pp. 481–95.

GOOD, T.L. and POWER, C.N. (1976) 'Designing successful classroom environments for different types of students', *Journal of Curriculum Studies*, 8, pp. 45–60.

HEISE, D.R. (1969) 'Some methodological issues in semantic differential research', *Psychological Bulletin*, 72, pp. 406–22.

MAEHR, M.L. (1983) 'On doing well in science: Why Johnny no longer excels; Why Sarah never did', in PARIS, S.G., OLSEN, G.M. and STEVENSON, H.W. (Eds) *Learning and Motivation in the Classroom*, Hillsdale, N.J., Lawrence Erlbaum Associates.

MAEHR, M.L. (1984) 'Meaning and motivation: Toward a theory of personal investment', in AMES, R. and AMES, C. (Eds) *Research on Motivation in Education: Student Motivation* (Vol 1), New York, Academic Press.

MEECE, J.L. and BLUMENFELD, P.C. (April 1987) 'Elementary school children's motivational orientation and patterns of engagement in classroom activities', paper presented at the annual meeting of American Educational Research Association, Washington, DC.

NICHOLLS, J.G. (1979) 'Quality and equality in intellectual development: The role of motivation in education', *American Psychologist*, 34, pp. 1071–84.

NICHOLLS, J.G. (1983) 'Conceptions of ability and achievement motivation: A theory and its implications for education, in PARIS, S.G., OLSEN, G.M. and STEVENSON, H.W. (Eds) *Learning and Motivation in the Classroom*, Hillsdale, N.J., Lawrence Erlbaum Associates, pp. 211–37.

NICHOLLS, J.G. (1984) 'Conceptions of ability and achievement motivation', in AMES, R.E. and AMES, C. (Eds) *Research on Motivation in Education: Student Motivation* (Vol. 1), New York, Academic Press, pp. 39–73.

NICHOLLS, J.G., PATASHNICK, M. and NOLEN, S.B. (1985) 'Adolescents' theories of education', *Journal of Education Psychology*, 77, pp. 683–92.

PARIS, S.G., OLSEN, G.M. and STEVENSON, H.W. (Eds) (1983) *Learning and Motivation in the Classroom*, Hillsdale, N.J., Lawrence Erlbaum Associates.

POPE, M.L. and KEEN, T.R. (1981) *Personal Construct Psychology and Education*, London, Academic Press.

RENNIE, L.J. (1986) 'The influence of the social context of the classroom on the relationship between subject-related affect and achievement', *Education Research and Perspectives*, 13(2), pp. 75–97.

ROSENSHINE, B. and STEVENS, R. (1986) 'Teaching functions', in WITTROCK, M.C. (Ed.) *Third Handbook of Research on Teaching* (3rd. ed.), New York, Macmillan, pp. 376–91.

SANFORD, J.P. (1987) 'Management of science classroom tasks and effects on students learning opportunities', *Journal of Research in Science Teaching*, 24, pp. 249–65.

SAS INSTITUTE INC. (1985) *SAS User's Guide: Statistics (Version 5 Edition)*, Cary, North Carolina, SAS Institute Inc.

STEINKAMP, M.W. and MAEHR, M.L. (1983) 'Affect, ability, and science achievement: A quantitative synthesis of correlational research', *Review of Educational Research*, 53, pp. 369–96.

STEINKAMP, M.W. and MAEHR, M.L. (1984). 'Gender differences in motivational orientations toward achievement in school science: A quantitative synthesis', *American Educational Research Journal*, 21, pp. 39–59.

Uguroglu, M.E. and Walberg, H.J. (1979) 'Motivation and achievement: A quantitative synthesis', *American Educational Research Journal*, 16, pp. 375–89.

Weiner, B. (1979) 'A theory of motivation for some classroom experiences', *Journal of Educational Psychology*, 71, pp. 3–25.

Weiner, B. (1984) 'Principles for a theory of student maturation and their application within an attributional framework', in Ames, R.E. and Ames, C. (Eds) *Research on Maturation in Education: Student Motivation* (Vol. 1), New York, Academic Press, pp. 15–38.

Willson, V.L. (1983) 'A meta-analysis of the relationship between science achievement and science attitude: Kindergarten through college', *Journal of Research in Science Teaching*, 20, pp. 839–50.

Chapter 7: Students' Perceptions of Their Classroom Environments

Barry J. Fraser

In previous chapters, the curriculum as implemented in Sandra's and Peter's classrooms has been described from the perspectives of four members of the research team. But how do students perceive the learning environment and how do their perceptions compare with those of the research team? Because it is the cognitions of students that influence what and how they learn, we regarded student perceptions of the learning environment as essential in building an understanding of the opportunities for learning provided in each of the classrooms.

It was noted in earlier chapters that this study's primary data base was qualitative, consisting of direct observations of classrooms and interviews with teachers and students, and that an interpretive research methodology was used by the researchers. But, a distinctive feature of the methodology of the research reported in the present chapter is that, in addition to this qualitative information, quantitative data were obtained by administering questionnaires assessing students' perceptions of their classroom learning environments. Not only did the use of classroom environment instruments provide another important source of students' views of their classrooms, but a combination of qualitative and quantitative data led to greater confidence in our findings and to richer insights into classroom life than would have been possible using either data source alone.

The purposes of this chapter are to describe how classroom environment instruments were used in this study, to report some of the findings which emerged, and to illustrate how the quantitative data based on questionnaire responses were integrated with the qualitative data collected via ethnographic techniques to enhance the credibility and richness of our results.

Background and Method

Combining Qualitative and Quantitative Methods

For a number of years now, workers in various areas of educational research, especially the field of educational evaluation, have claimed that there are merits in moving beyond the customary practice of choosing either qualitative or quantitative methods and instead combining qualitative and quantitative methods within the same study (Cook and Reichardt, 1979; Firestone, 1987; Fry, Chantavanich and Chantavanich, 1981; Howe, 1988; Smith and Fraser, 1980). For example, in their article entitled *Beyond Qualitative Versus Quantitative Methods*, Reichardt and Cook (1979) make the following sensible comments:

> We have also seen that a researcher need not adhere blindly to one of the polar-extreme paradigms that have been labelled 'qualitative' and 'quantitative' but can freely choose a mix of attributes from both paradigms so as to best fit the demands of the research problem at hand. There would seem to be, then, no reason to choose *between* qualitative and quantitative *methods* either. Evaluators would be wise to use whatever methods are best suited to their research needs, regardless of the methods' traditional affiliations. If that should call for a combination of qualitative and quantitative methods, then so be it. (p. 19)

Similarly, in a book from the Stanford Evaluation Consortium, Cronbach and his colleagues advocate that the large majority of evaluations should include both quantitative and qualitative methods at appropriate times and in appropriate amounts. 'Those who advocate an evaluation plan devoid of one kind of information or the other carry the burden of justifying such exclusion' (Cronbach *et al.*, 1980, p. 223).

In the relatively new and rapidly growing field of classroom learning environments, studies involving qualitative methods have provided rich insights into classroom life (Rutter *et al.*, 1979; Stake and Easley, 1978) and the use of quantitative methods has generated several widely-applicable questionnaires which have been used to replicate certain lines of research with large samples in a variety of countries (Fraser, 1986a, 1986c, 1989c; Moos and Trickett, 1987). To date, however, classroom environment research involving both qualitative and quantitative methods within the same study has been the exception rather than the rule (Fraser and Tobin, 1989). This chapter illustrates the fruitfulness of a confluence of qualitative and quantitative research traditions in classroom environment research through its reporting of our investigation at Southside High. It is hoped that this chapter will stimulate and guide other researchers to seek a richer understanding of classroom learning environments through complementing quantitative scores on classroom environment scales with a substantial base of qualitative descriptive data obtained using ethno-graphic techniques.

The potential of combining qualitative and quantitative technique was well illustrated recently in a study of exemplary teaching of science and mathematics (Tobin and Fraser, 1987). One of the study's major findings that emerged both from classroom observations and from the administration of classroom environment questionnaires to students was that exemplary teachers created more favourable learning environments than did non-exemplary teachers. These findings were especially note-worthy because they validated the judgements of teaching peers who nominated their colleagues as exemplary; that is, the classes of teachers identified as exemplary by their teaching peers also could be differentiated from non-exemplary teachers' classes in terms of students' perceptions of classroom psychosocial environment.

The Field of Classroom Environment

Approximately two decades ago, Herbert Walberg and Rudolf Moos began seminal independent programs of research which form the starting points for contemporary classroom environment research. Around that time, Walberg began developing earlier versions of the widely used *Learning Environment Inventory (LEI)* as part of the research and evalua-tion activities of Harvard Project Physics (see Anderson and Walberg, 1968; Walberg and Anderson, 1968). Two decades ago also marks the time when Moos began developing the first of his world-renowned social climate scales, including those for use in psychiatric hospitals (Moos and Houts, 1968) and correctional institutions (Moos, 1968), which ultimately resulted in the development of the widely known *Classroom Environment Scale (CES)* (Moos and Trickett, 1974, 1987).

The way that the important pioneering work of Walberg and Moos on perceptions of classroom environment developed into major research programs and spawned a lot of other research is reflected in numerous comprehensive literature overviews. These include books (Fraser, 1986a; Fraser and Walberg, in press; Moos, 1979; van der Sijde and van de Grift, in press; Walberg, 1979); monographs (Fraser, 1981b, 1989b; Fraser and Fisher, 1983a), a guest-edited journal issue (Fraser, 1980), an annotated bibliography (Moos and Spinrad, 1984), several state-of-the-art literature reviews (Anderson and Walberg, 1974; Chavez, 1984; Fraser, 1986b, 1987b, 1989c; Randhawa and Fu, 1973; Walberg, 1976; Walberg and Haertel, 1980), including special purpose reviews with an emphasis on classroom environment work in science education (Fraser and Walberg, 1981), in Australia (Fraser, 1981a), and in Germany (Dreesman, 1982; Wolf, 1983). As well, the American Educational Research Association established a Special Interest Group (SIG) on the Study of Learning

Environments in 1984 and this group sponsors an annual monograph (e.g., Fraser, 1986c, 1987a, 1988).

This classroom environment research builds upon and has been influenced by two areas of earlier work. First, the influence of the momentous theoretical, conceptual and measurement foundations laid half a century ago by pioneers like Lewin (1936) and Murray (1938) and their followers such as Pace and Stern (1958) is recognized. Second, Chavez (1984) observes that research involving assessments of perceptions of classroom environment epitomized in the work of Walberg and Moos also was influenced by prior work involving low inference, direct observational methods of measuring classroom climate. Although recent classroom environment work clearly has some historical antecedents in the work of Lewin, Murray and others, earlier writings neither focus sharply on educational settings nor provide empirical evidence to support linkages between climate and educational outcomes. Moreover, the epic work of Pace and Stern (1958), although involving high inference measures of educational environments, focused on higher education institutions rather than high/elementary schools and assessed the environment of the whole college rather than the environment of specific classrooms.

Research on classroom environment has produced a rich yield in just 20 years. Consistent and strong associations have been established between the nature of the classroom environment and student cognitive and attitudinal outcomes (Fraser and Fisher, 1982; Haertel, Walberg and Haertel, 1981), and these findings have practical implications about how to improve student learning by creating classroom environments which emphasize dimensions found to be empirically linked with learning. Person-environment fit studies (Fraser and Fisher, 1983b, 1983c) have shown that student achievement and satisfaction are greater in classrooms in which there is a closer match between the actual classroom environment and that preferred by students. The use of classroom environment measures as dependent variables in evaluations of educational curricula and innovations has revealed interesting differences between educational alternatives when standard achievement criteria have shown no differences (Fraser, 1981b; Fraser, Williamson and Tobin, 1987; Levin, 1980). Comparisons of students' and teachers' perceptions of actual and preferred environments suggest that teachers commonly hold more favourable views than do their students in the same classrooms, and that the actual environment of most classes falls short of that preferred by students and teachers (Fraser, 1982; Fisher and Fraser, 1983). In addition to these and other research applications, it is important to note that teachers have successfully used student perceptions of actual and preferred classroom environments as a practical basis for improving their classrooms (Fraser, 1981c; Fraser and Fisher, 1986).

Assessment of Classroom Environment

In this study of higher-level cognitive learning, use was made of selected scales from the *Individualised Classroom Environment Questionnaire* (ICEQ) (Fraser, 1989a) and the *Classroom Environment Scale* (CES) (Moos and Trickett, 1987). In fact, an important feature of the design of the present study was that these classroom environment dimensions were selected *after* a certain amount of field work had been done and, consequently, only dimensions considered to be salient for this research were selected for inclusion. The dimensions were chosen after discussion among the researchers during team meetings.

The ICEQ was developed to assess those dimensions which distinguish individualized classrooms from conventional ones. ICEQ scales each contain ten items with the five response alternatives of Almost Never, Seldom, Sometimes, Often and Very Often. The published version of the CES consists of nine scales, each assessed by ten items of True-False response format. As well as having an actual form, both the ICEQ and the CES have a preferred form to assess the environment ideally liked or preferred.

For the purposes of the present study, the four scales selected as salient were *Personalization* and *Participation* from the ICEQ and *Order and Organization* and *Task Orientation* from the CES. Students responded to both the actual and preferred forms of each scale and also answered the questionnaires on two occasions, once during the teaching of Vertebrates and again during the teaching of Nuclear Energy. Also, for the two scales from the CES, the original two-point (True, False) response format was changed to the same five-point response format as the ICEQ (Almost Never, Seldom, Sometimes, Often, Very Often). Although the item wording is almost identical in actual and preferred forms, words such as 'would' are included in the preferred form to remind respondents that they are rating preferred environment. For example, the statement 'This is a well-organized class' in the actual form of the Order and Organization scale would be changed in the preferred form to 'This would be a well-organized class'.

Table 7.1 clarifies the meaning of each of the four scales by providing a scale description and sample item for each scale. Also Table 7.1 provides data on the internal consistency reliability (alpha coefficient) for each scale. Data are based on use of the class mean as the unit of analysis for 150 junior high school classes for the ICEQ and for 116 junior high school classes for the CES (see Fraser, 1986a). Reliability estimates are shown separately for the actual and preferred forms. However, reliability data for the two CES scales were obtained using its original two-point item response format rather than the five-point response format used in the present research.

Table 7.1: *Scale description, sample item and alpha reliability coefficient for four classroom environment scales*

Scale	Scale Description	Sample Item	Actual	Pref.
			Alpha Reliability	
Personalization	Emphasis on opportunities for individual students to interact with the teacher and on concern for the personal welfare and social growth of the individual	The teacher takes a personal interest in each student. (+)	0.90	0.86
Participation	Extent to which students are encouraged to participate rather than be passive listeners	The teacher lectures without students asking or answering questions. (−)	0.80	0.75
Order and Organization	Emphasis on students behaving in an orderly, quiet and polite manner and on the overall organization of classroom activities	This is a well-organized class. (+)	0.90	0.86
Task Orientation	Extent to which it is important to complete activities planned and to stay on the subject matter	This class is more a social hour than a place to learn something. (−)	0.72	0.65

Items designated (+) were scored 1, 2, 3, 4 and 5, respectively, for the responses Almost Never, Seldom, Sometimes, Often and Very Often. Items designated (−) were scored in the reverse manner. Omitted or invalid responses were scored 3.

Class reliability data are based on 150 classes for Personalization and Participation and on 116 classes for Order and Organization and Task Orientation.

Findings

The findings emerging from the use of classroom environment questionnaires are organized as assertions in three sections which deal with (1) differences between student, teacher and researcher perceptions; (2) differences between the two classrooms in terms of average student perceptions; and (3) differences between the perceptions of individual students in the same classroom.

Differences Between Student, Teacher and Researcher Perceptions

Assertion 1: Students, teachers and researchers differed in their perceptions of classroom environment.

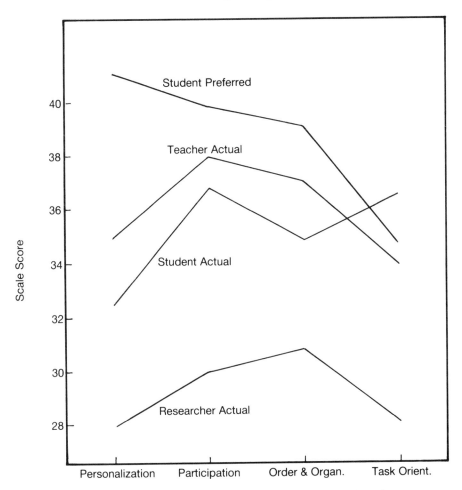

Figure 7.1: *Researchers actual, student actual, teacher actual and student preferred classroom environment profiles for Peter for Vertebrates topic*

Because the two teachers and four of the researchers also responded to the same classroom environment scales, it is possible to compare the perceptions of the same actual classroom environment held by students, teachers and researchers. Figure 7.1 shows for Peter profiles of mean scores for his 31 students, of mean scores for four of the researchers and of the scores obtained by Peter. Similar patterns of findings occurred for Sandra's class, but these are not reported here.

The profiles in Figure 7.1 show two clear patterns. First, with the exception of the Task Orientation scale, the teacher viewed the classroom environment more positively than did the students in the same classroom; this finding replicates past research in science classrooms in which teachers consistently viewed classroom climates more favourably than did students in the same classrooms (Fisher and Fraser, 1983).

Second, the group of researchers perceived the classroom environment much less favourably on all scales than did either the teacher or the students. These marked differences between the responses of the researchers and both teachers and students are interesting and could reflect the researchers' distinctive focus in the classroom during the study. That is, the researchers were present in the classroom expressly for the purpose of observing aspects of teaching, including those assessed with the classroom environment instrument. In contrast, because both teachers and students are busy with many things, they are not attending to and consciously monitoring the classroom environment in the same way in which researchers are able to do. Moreover, group meetings provided researchers with a regular forum for the discussion of classroom environment and enabled them to reach a degree of consensus about what the group as a whole perceived to be the strengths and/or weaknesses in Peter's and Sandra's teaching. In particular, because the researchers chose the dimensions to be included in the classroom environment questionnaire after the study had been in progress for some time, it is not surprising that the group of researchers held some strong views about each teacher's strengths and weaknesses in terms of the dimensions of classroom environment assessed in the study.

Figure 7.1 also depicts the profile of student mean scores for Peter's class on the preferred form of the four classroom environment scales. Clearly, students would prefer somewhat more emphasis on all four dimensions of Personalization, Participation, Order and Organization and Task Orientation than the emphasis perceived to be actually present. Again, this finding that actual classroom environments fell short of those preferred by students replicates results from past research (Fisher and Fraser, 1983).

Differences Between the Two Classrooms in Terms of Average Student Perceptions

Assertion 2: The average learning environment perceived by students in each classroom was related to teachers' knowledge and beliefs.

Figure 7.2 depicts profiles of mean actual classroom environment scores obtained by averaging the individual scale scores of the thirty-one students in Peter's class and the thirty-one students in Sandra's class present at the time when the questionnaires were administered. These profiles have been constructed separately for the responses given by students during the Vertebrates and the Nuclear Energy topics. This figure clearly shows that, despite the existence of some small but systematic changes in

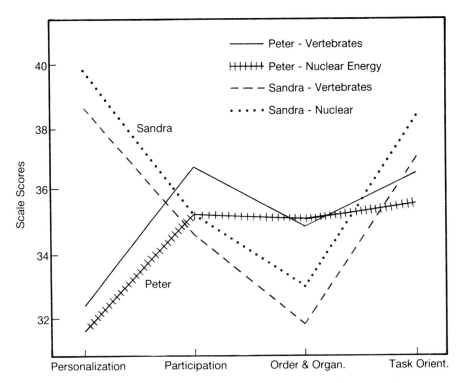

Figure 7.2: Classroom environment profiles for two teachers for two topics

classroom environment between the two topics, overall there is remark-
able consistency between the shapes of each teacher's profile for the two
different topics. The two greatest student-perceived differences between
the teachers for both topics were that, relative to Peter's class, Sandra's
class was characterized by considerably more Personalization and less
Order and Organization. Moreover, two-way analyses of variance with
class and gender as independent variables revealed that differences were
significant at the 0.01 level of confidence for Personalization and Order
and Organization for both topics. All other differences were not significant, with the exception that Sandra's class was seen as having significantly more Task Orientation than Peter's class had for the Nuclear
Energy topic.

Students' perceptions of the learning environment within each class
are consistent with the observers' field records of the patterns of learning
activities and engagement in each classroom. In Chapter 6, Rennie analyses the use of class time and clearly demonstrates important differences
between Sandra's and Peter's classes. Whereas Sandra devoted 75 per cent
of class time to interacting with students involved in individualized or
group activities, Peter used some type of whole-class, teacher-controlled

activities (for example, whole-class demonstrations, question and answer sessions, explanations of concepts using the chalkboard) for half of the class time during both topics. The high level of Personalization perceived in Sandra's classroom (see Figure 7.2) matches the large proportion of time which she spent in small-group activities during which she constantly was moving about the classroom interacting with students. Further, when Sandra offered desists, they were often private and she was never heard to use sarcasm or personal criticism in her interactions with students. It is significant that, of the twenty-seven students of Sandra's class intending to return to school the following year, twenty-four of them expressed the wish to have Sandra as their science teacher again. The lower level of Personalization perceived in Peter's class is associated partly with the larger amount of time spent in the whole-class mode and the generally public nature of Peter's interactions with students. He spent much less time than Sandra did in dealing with students in quiet, small-group situations.

The second significant difference between the learning environments was the lower level of Order and Organization in Sandra's class compared to Peter's class. Sandra's class was observed to be noisier than Peter's was and the high levels of off-task behaviour, most of which was social, are consistent with the students' perceptions of a less orderly class. The physical arrangement of the classroom also contributed to the different levels of off-task behaviour in the two classes. In order to make it easy for them to work together in groups, Sandra's students sat around in tables formed by two desks. Unfortunately, this method of seating not only encouraged social interaction, but also it hindered effective scanning of the class for management purposes. As a result, many students with their backs to Sandra were able to carry on with their social agendas even during her whole-class presentations. In contrast, Peter's classroom had the desks in rows facing the front of the room, where Peter spent about half of the lesson time using the whole-class instructional mode. This seating arrangement facilitated management scanning and Peter quickly targeted potential noise-makers for effective public desists. As a result, Peter's class was managed more effectively than Sandra's in terms of the proportion of student-engaged time.

The differences in the classroom environments created by the two teachers also can be considered in terms of the teaching metaphors adopted. In Chapter 3, it was noted that Peter alternated between the two teaching metaphors of the Entertainer and the Captain of the Ship, whereas Sandra adopted the metaphor of the teacher as Resource. Moreover, our observations and interviews suggested that these metaphors influenced the way in which Peter and Sandra taught.

For Personalization for Peter, for example, some students were confused by being treated in a depersonalized way as crew during whole-class activities (Captain of the Ship role), but treated in a very friendly way during individual activities (Entertainer role). Moreover, only some students liked their personal interactions with Peter during individualized activities because it was not uncommon for him to interact with boys in a 'macho' way and with girls in a sexist way. Consequently, it is not surprising that Peter's class on average perceived a relatively low level of Personalization. Similarly, the very high level of Personalization perceived in Sandra's class is also consistent with her metaphor of the teacher as Resource. Her teaching approach almost exclusively involved individualized work about 75 per cent of the time (see Chapter 6) and she devoted great amounts of energy to moving around the class to give students individual help.

The low Order and Organization perceived in Sandra's class is linked with her commitment not to use whole-class teaching. Although she appreciated that Order and Organization probably would have improved in whole-class situations, her beliefs led her to concentrate on individualized approaches. In particular, Sandra's time was monopolized by a group of disruptive boys whom she tried to control through proximity desists (that is, by moving physically close to these students). Of course, with so much of her time devoted to these two groups, there was a natural tendency for the other students in the class to be off-task and for the average class level of perceived Order and Organization to be low. On the other hand, Peter's management metaphor, especially his role as Captain of the Ship, resulted in higher levels of perceived Order and Organization than in Sandra's class.

The changes in each teacher's classroom environment between the Vertebrates and Nuclear Energy topics, although relatively small, are interesting and consistent (see Figure 7.2). For example, a higher mean for student perceptions of Task Orientation in Sandra's class compared to Peter's class during the Nuclear Energy topic is consistent with the findings based on qualitative data.

It was noted previously in Chapter 3 that both Sandra and Peter could be considered 'in field' during the Vertebrates topic. In contrast, although the Nuclear Energy topic was less well related to the teachers' main area of initial training, Sandra coped better with the content than Peter did. Apparently Sandra's strong science preparation, combined with her knowledge gained through years of careful lesson preparation, enabled her to exhibit a good grasp of the content of the Nuclear Energy topic. In contrast, the researchers noted that Peter's classroom behaviour reflected his relative uncertainty with the content of the Nuclear Energy topic in that he used the workbooks more often and made more content errors than he did for the Vertebrates topic. Moreover, Peter's apparent knowledge limitations for the Nuclear Energy topic were associated with a different approach to implementing the curriculum than the one that he used during the teaching of Vertebrates. Generally, Peter taught in a less confident and less expansive manner during the Nuclear Energy topic.

Students were required to work from the workbook to a greater extent than they did during the Vertebrates topic. Peter did not present information in whole-class activities to the same extent, and he rearranged seating so that students could interact more easily with him and each other. Figure 7.2 shows a decrease in student perceptions of Task Orientation in Peter's class from Vertebrates to Nuclear Energy. In contrast, Sandra arranged the class the same way for both topics, and her knowledge and confidence appeared high in both topics.

Furthermore, Sandra was interested and concerned about the feedback which she received on student perceptions of the learning environment during the Vertebrates topic, and she was determined to change her classroom behaviour in ways which would lead to improvements in the classroom environment. On the other hand, Peter dismissed the classroom environment information for Vertebrates as irrelevant and, in all likelihood, made no attempt to change his classroom behaviour. These observations are clearly reflected in the profiles in Figure 7.2 which show that Peter's classroom environment was less favourable for the second topic than for the first topic on all dimensions except Order and Organization (for which differences were negligible), but that a small improvement occurred between the two testing occasions for all environment dimensions for Sandra's class.

Differences Between the Perceptions of Individual Students in the Same Classroom

Assertion 3: Teacher expectations of and attitudes towards individuals were reflected in individual student perceptions of the learning environment.

Whereas the class means of actual environment scores depicted in Figure 7.2 furnish a useful overall picture of classroom environment, they provide information neither about how an individual student perceives his or her learning environment nor about a student's preferred environment. Consequently, in this section, the learning environment profiles of some individual students are discussed and integrated with other information gathered using participant observation methods.

In Chapter 3, it was noted that Sandra was caring and interested as she moved about the classroom assisting students. With few exceptions, Sandra's projected images did not appear to influence learning in negative ways. An examination of the learning environment data for individual students indicated that only three students had relatively large discrepancies between the preferred and actual environment in the two topics. Gavin preferred greater Personalization in both topics, Jody preferred greater Personalization in Vertebrates and Suzanne preferred greater Per-

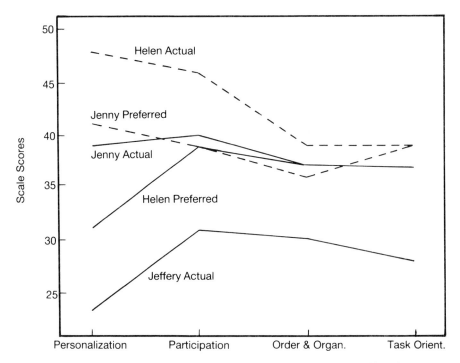

Figure 7.3: Classroom environment profiles for Jenny, Helen and Jeffrey for the Vertebrates topic for Peter's class

sonalization in Nuclear Energy. For the remainder of the students, there was surprisingly little difference between the preferred and actual class-room environment in terms of Personalization.

The nature of Peter's interactions with individuals seemed to reflect his preconceptions of them. From what he said and how he interacted with students, it was evident that Peter favoured the more attractive females in the class. Peter noted that he tended to interact with the females in his class to a greater extent than with the males. He stated that he preferred to interact with 'the most extroverted girls, those who knew how to interact, were beautifully presented, had a beautiful smile, were ready to interact and enjoyed interacting'.

In the case studies of individual students described below, different student's actual environment scores are contrasted with each other and compared with the class mean. Also, for some students, the contrast between students' perceptions of the actual learning environment and how they would prefer the environment to be is discussed in order to provide insight into how comfortable students felt when working in their classroom. When the quantitative scores on learning environment scales are complemented by a substantial base of qualitative description from classroom observation, then a better understanding of students' perceptions of the learning environment can result.

Jenny and Helen

Jenny and Helen were chosen for the first case study because Peter interacted with them so differently, and because they were representative of two clusters formed when a cluster analysis was performed using the actual learning environment scores. Students within a given cluster had relatively similar actual environment scores, but the different clusters varied from each other in terms of the pattern of mean environment scores.* Jenny is representative of a cluster with scores consistent across the scales, whilst the scores of Helen's group were more variable. Their scores on the learning environment actual and preferred scales as measured during the Vertebrates topic are graphed in Figure 7.3.

Jenny and Helen both achieved at a little above the class average and both were involved in frequent interactions with Peter. They also enjoyed their science class and the company of other students. In response to a question about what she liked best about the science class, Jenny said that 'I like this science class because everybody is pleasant. Peter is friendly and I understand what he says'. Helen's response was 'I like the way that the kids get along together and can work and still have fun together'. The last parts of these students' responses give a clue to their classroom behaviour. Jenny was nearly always on task. She paid close attention during whole-class activities, often responding to Peter's questions. Her class notes were complete, well presented and consistently graded 'A' by Peter.

In most respects, Jenny was a model student. She was attractive and personable and she clearly was a diligent student who enjoyed her work. In an interview, Peter described Jenny as 'mature, confident, bright, beautifully presented' and on another occasion as 'pretty close to being one of the brighter kids in that class ... in the top ten if not the top five'. Jenny and Peter seemed to get along well together, and Jenny's enjoyment of her class was reflected in her scores on the learning environment scales. She scored around forty on each scale, and the differences between her perceptions of the actual environment and her preferred environment were negligible.

Helen did not work as well as Jenny in class. She was off-task for

---

* For both the Vertebrates and the Nuclear Energy topic, four clusters emerged for Peter's class and five for Sandra's class. Cluster membership was similar, but not identical for the two topics. The major advantage of having the cluster analysis results was that they provided a non-arbitrary way of selecting for detailed discussion individual students who differed from each other in salient ways in terms of their patterns of classroom environment perceptions.

about 20 per cent of the time, compared to Jenny's 10 per cent, and her classwork was somewhat incomplete, with some parts done well and others not. Her work for Vertebrates was graded 'C' but, for the Nuclear Energy topic, Helen's mark improved to 'B'. When Peter returned students' marked classwork for the Vertebrates topic, he called each student's name, followed by a one-word or two-word comment. An excerpt from field notes reads:

> Louise — excellent. Jeffrey — quite good. Mandy — very good. Gavin no comment. Sally and Rhonda — excellent. Helen — Please don't write with pencil. Jenny — Excellent. Andrea — quite good. Craig — very good.

Peter's comments were heard by all class members and Helen appeared embarrassed by his comments, which were quite different for her compared with other students.

Peter considered Helen to be 'good but lazy' and suggested that he had fallen out of favour with her. As well, Helen was overweight and Peter had told the researchers that his dislike of overweight people had coloured his views about Helen. He also taught Helen's elder sister, who evidently achieved well, and Peter thought that Helen felt that he had the same expectations of her. In Peter's final interview, he remarked that 'she didn't do much in the classroom to impress me ... one of the few students about whom I didn't write a favourable report'. In fact, Helen did seem to be able in that she performed at the fully formal level on the Separation of Variables Piagetian Task administered by one of the researchers, whilst Jenny was rated on the same task at the concrete level (see Nordland's chapter in this volume). Both attained similar test scores for each topic — Jenny scored 76 and 82 on the two topic tests, respectively, and Helen scored 75 on each test.

Helen's perceptions of the classroom levels of Participation, Order and Organization and Task Orientation were similar to Jenny's; it was only on the Personalization scale that there is a marked difference. Comparison of these scores with those for Helen's preferred environment accentuate this contrast with Jenny. Whereas the preferred-actual difference for Jenny was only two points on the Personalization scale, for Helen it was as large as seventeen points. This contrast is especially interesting in view of the fact that, during the observation period, Helen and Jenny had the same number of interactions with Peter. However, about three quarters of Helen's interactions with Peter were in a small-group situation, where Peter also usually interacted with Sue, Mary and Peta, who were Helen's deskmates in the back row. Jenny sat in the front row, at one side of the room, and about three quarters of Jenny's interactions with Peter were in the whole-class mode. The other interactions were with Peter in a one-to-one situation and they always seemed friendly. Peter's interactions with Helen and her friends (particularly Sue) were generally good-humoured, but Helen seemed not to find the same degree of friendship from Peter that Jenny felt.

The contrast between Helen's and Jenny's perceptions of the degree of Personalization in the classroom is best summed up in their own words. To a questionnaire item asking 'How would you like your science class to change?', Helen wrote: 'Peter to be more friendly and help us with our work more.' Jenny's response to this question was: 'In no way. I like my science classes very much. I hope they will be as enjoyable next year.'

Jeffrey

Jeffrey was also in Peter's class, but his classroom environment profile provides a stark contrast to those of Jenny and Helen. Figure 7.3 shows that Jeffrey belonged to a cluster of students whose classroom environment scores were substantially lower than the rest of the class on all of the four scales.

Jeffrey was very visible in class. He asked more questions (18 per cent of the class total) and responded to more questions (13 per cent) than did her classmates. Jeffrey was a 'target' student in that he was someone who dominated verbal interactions during whole-class settings (see Tobin and Gallagher, 1987). He seemed to enjoy arguing with Peter about answers to questions.

In Chapter 6 of this volume, Rennie describes Jeffrey as able but bored. His achievement scores were average for Vertebrates and above average for Nuclear Energy, and the researchers' measures indicated that he was able to use formal operations to solve problems. Yet, Jeffrey was off-task for 35 per cent of the time for the first topic and for 23 per cent of the time during the second topic.

Despite Jeffrey's ability and his high level of participation during question-and-answer sessions, Peter held a negative view of Jeffrey and his ability (although this did improve somewhat towards the end of the year). Peter felt that Jeffrey was overly confident and that he was attempting to impress his peers by being the 'class clown'. Peter's disapproval of Jeffrey and his attempts to quash Jeffrey were evident in the relatively large and harsh verbal desists. These public rebukes were audible to the whole class and could have led to Jeffrey feeling put down.

The most striking feature of Jeffrey's classroom environment profile is the consistently low scores on all scales for both topics. For example, Jeffrey's scores for Vertebrates ranged from 1.0 standard deviations below the class mean for Order and Organization to 2.0 standard deviations below the mean for Task Orientation (see Figure 7.3). Those low scores across the board are consistent with the view that Jeffrey was bored and not liked by Peter. In particular, the especially low Personalization score reflects the absence of a positive relationship between Peter and Jeffrey.

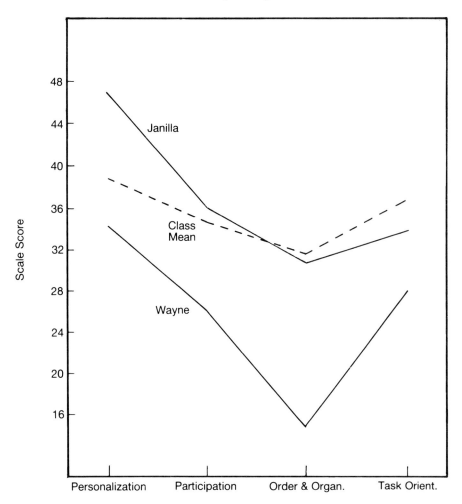

Figure 7.4: Classroom environment profiles for Wayne and Janila for the Vertebrates topic for Sandra's class

Wayne

Figure 7.4 depicts the classroom environment profiles obtained by two students, Wayne and Janila, in Sandra's class for the Vertebrates topic. These two students were chosen for discussion because cluster analysis revealed that they were typical of two clusters of students with very different profiles of classroom climate scores. Like Jeffrey (Peter's student described above), Wayne is noteworthy because he also viewed the classroom environment noticeably less positively than did the class as a whole.

Although Wayne was found to be capable of formal reasoning, both his test marks and class marks were very low. He displayed little interest in science lessons and was off-task for very large amounts of time (63 per cent during Vertebrates and 76 per cent during Nuclear Energy). In particular, Wayne often left his seat for social reasons and engaged in attention-seeking, uncooperative and socially unacceptable behaviour. There often was friction between him and other students (especially Steven and Gavin). Sandra was worried about Wayne, especially because he came from a family where the father often was away. Wayne's behaviour consistently distracted Sandra from helping other students because she frequently moved physically close to Wayne to curb his behaviour.

Wayne's lack of motivation is reflected in his actual classroom environment scores which are shown in Figure 7.4. On all four scales, his scores are consistently low and well below the class mean. For example, his scores ranged from a little less than one standard deviation below the class mean for Personalization to approximately three standard deviations below the mean for Order and Organization.

Interestingly, despite the fact that Wayne's classroom environment scores were well below the class average, his actual-preferred discrepancy scores were comparatively small (between one and three raw scores points) for the three scales of Personalization, Participation and Task Orientation. This finding suggests a certain degree of apathy on Wayne's part in that, despite the fact that he viewed the classroom as having low levels of these three classroom environment dimensions, he preferred the levels to remain low for three of these four dimensions.

Janila

Figure 7.4 also shows the mean score obtained on the actual form of each classroom environment scale for the Vertebrates topic by Janila, another student in Sandra's class. In contrast to Wayne, Janila belonged to a cluster of students whose classroom environment scores were considerably higher than the class mean for Personalization and approximately comparable to the class mean for each of the other three scales.

Janila, again in contrast to Wayne, was very task-oriented in that she asked questions and interacted frequently with Sandra. In fact, Janila was one of the 'target' students in Sandra's class and she occupied Sandra's time by asking probing questions. She was seldom off-task (two per cent during Vertebrates and sixteen per cent during Nuclear Energy) and her marks were high for both tests and class work, although tests of Piagetian tasks revealed that she had not reached the stage of formal reasoning.

Janila's classroom environment scores (see Figure 7.4) reflect her positive attitude to learning science. For each dimension, her scores were higher than Wayne's and either close to or above the class mean. Her

Personalization score was especially high (over one standard deviation above the class mean) and the discrepancy between actual and preferred scores was as low as two raw score points for Personalization. These results for the Personalization scale are consistent with the positive and frequent interactions which she had with Sandra.

Discussion and Conclusions

The combination of the quantitative classroom environment data with the qualitative observational data led to complimentary views of life in the two classrooms studied in this research. The field observations of class-room activities and the student engagement data build the same kind of picture that students reported in their perceptions of their learning environment. For example, Sandra's emphasis on group work, the physical arrangement of the classroom and her personal management techniques resulted in a classroom which students perceived as personalized but disorderly. Sandra's efforts to increase on-task behaviour during the second topic seem to have been reflected in the more positive student views of the environment, but the off-task behaviour increased. It is doubtful that further improvements in the order and organization of her classroom could have occurred unless Sandra changed the seating arrangement to deter social interactions among the students. Because of her belief that students learn best by working by themselves, Sandra was reluctant to make this change to her classroom.

Despite the fact that Peter began the study with the claim that he was open to feedback on his teaching, he did not welcome any interpretations that suggested to him that changes were necessary. In contrast, Sandra requested feedback and acted favourably towards results which suggested a need to make changes. For example, when both teachers received feedback from the researchers based on classroom environment results from the Vertebrates topic, Sandra was determined to change her class-room behaviour in ways which would lead to improvements. On the other hand, Peter dismissed this information as irrelevant and, so, he made no apparent attempt to change his classroom behavior. In particu-lar, Peter disbelieved the feedback suggesting that students perceived a relatively low level of Personalization in his classroom because he felt that his attempts to entertain the students through his singing, quips, etc. would have been associated with high Personalization. Although Peter was keen about covering the content and being entertaining, he did not attempt to enhance classroom Personalization as a way of aiding student understanding of the content. Peter associated his effectiveness with the amount of time that he put into his work and he did not relate what he was doing to whether or not students were achieving the goals set for the course. Accordingly, Peter regarded extra-curricular activities, such as conducting field trips and science fairs, as more important indicators of his probable effectiveness as a teacher than the feedback which he received (for example, student perceptions of the learning environment, gender differences perceived by the research team or researchers' observations of an emphasis on learning facts from the textbook).

From a methodological perspective, the inclusion of classroom environment questionnaires among a range of data-gathering techniques is noteworthy for several reasons. First, the complementarity of qualitative observational data and quantitative classroom environment data added to the richness of the data base. Second, the use of classroom environment questionnaires provided an important source of students' views of their classrooms. Third, through a triangulation of classroom climate and other data, greater credibility could be placed on findings because patterns emerged consistently from data obtained using a range of different data collection methods.

Furthermore, because we selected the scales of the learning environment instrument specifically to be salient in this study, the data were relevant to what was observed in both classes. Statistical analyses were undertaken to provide insights into questions concerning what was happening in the two classes. The results of the analyses of learning environment data were used in conjunction with other data sources to support or refute assertions. The case studies of Jenny and Helen indicated that, when quantitative scores on learning environment scales are complemented by a substantial base of qualitative descriptive information from classroom observation, then a greater understanding of students' perceptions of the learning environment can result. Overall, this study attests to the potential usefulness in science education research of combining qualitative ethnographic information and quantitative classroom environment data within the same study.

Finally, student perceptions of the learning environment data show that student mind frames are influenced by teacher mind frames through classroom practices. The data were important for two reasons. First, the quantitative data enabled us to use statistical analyses to support assertions based on our qualitative data. Second, the findings showed that teachers dealt with students in an inequitable way on the basis of beliefs that were unsubstantiated. Consequently, different students perceived the learning environment differently, not because they erred in their descriptions, but because different learning environments did exist for different students within the same classroom. Researchers need to acknowledge these differences and develop new instruments to provide quantitative insights into the extent and nature of the different learning environments. Qualitative analyses should be used in conjunction with these instruments to provide salient insights into aspects of the environment which are not captured quantitatively.

References

ANDERSON, G.J. and WALBERG, H.J. (1968) 'Classroom climate and group learning', *International Journal of Educational Sciences*, 2, pp. 175–80.

ANDERSON, G.J. and WALBERG, H.J. (1974) 'Learning environments', in WALBERG, H.J. (Ed.), *Evaluating Educational Performance: A Sourcebook of Methods, Instruments, and Examples*, Berkeley, California, McCutchan.

CHAVEZ, R.C. (1984) 'The use of high inference measures to study classroom climates: A review, *Review of Educational Research*, 54, pp. 237–61.

COOK, T.D. and REICHARDT, C.S. (Eds) (1979) *Qualitative and Quantitative Methods in Evaluation Research*, Beverly Hills, California, Sage.

CRONBACH, L.J. *et al.* (1980) *Toward Reform of Program Evaluation: Aims, Methods, and Institutional Arrangements*, San Francisco, Jossey-Bass.

DREESMAN, H. (1982) 'Classroom climate: Contributions from a European country', *Studies in Educational Evaluation*, 8, pp. 53–64.

FIRESTONE, W. (1987) 'Meaning in method: The rhetoric of quantitative and qualitative research', *Educational Researcher*, 16, pp. 16–21.

FISHER, D.L. and FRASER, B.J. (1983) 'A comparison of actual and preferred classroom environment as perceived by science teachers and students', *Journal of Research in Science Teaching*, 20, pp. 55–61.

FRASER, B.J. (1980) 'Guest editor's introduction: Classroom environment research in the 1970s and 1980s', *Studies in Educational Evaluation*, 6, pp. 221–3.

FRASER, B.J. (1981a) 'Australian research on classroom environment: State of the art', *Australian Journal of Education*, 25, pp. 238–68.

FRASER, B.J. (1981b) *Learning Environment in Curriculum Evaluation: A Review*, Evaluation in Education series, Oxford, Pergamon.

FRASER, B.J. (1981c) 'Using environmental assessments to make better classrooms', *Journal of Curriculum Studies*, 13, pp. 131–44.

FRASER, B.J. (1982) 'Differences between student and teacher perceptions of actual and preferred classroom learning environment', *Educational Evaluation and Policy Analysis,* 4, pp. 511–9.

FRASER, B.J. (1986a) *Classroom Environment*, London, Croom Helm.

FRASER, B.J. (1986b) 'Determinants of classroom psychosocial environment: A review', *Journal of Research in Childhood Education*, 1, pp. 5–19.

FRASER, B.J. (Ed.) (1986c) *The Study of Learning Environments* (Vol. 1), Salem, Oregon, Assessment Research.

FRASER, B.J. (Ed.) (1987a) *The Study of Learning Environments, Volume 2*, Perth, Curtin University of Technology.

FRASER, B. (1987b) 'Use of classroom environment assessments in school psychology,' *School Psychology International*, 8, pp. 205–19.

FRASER, B. (Ed.) (1988) *The Study of Learning Environments, Volume 3*. Perth: Curtin University of Technology.

FRASER, B.J. (1989a) *Individualised Classroom Environment Questionnaire*, Melbourne, Australian Council for Educational Research. (in press)

FRASER, B.J. (1989b) *Learning Environment Research in Science Classrooms: Past Progress and Future Prospects*, National Association for Research in Science Teaching.

FRASER, B.J. (1989c) 'Twenty years of classroom environment research: Progress and prospect', *Journal of Curriculum Studies*, 21, pp. 307–27.

FRASER, B.J. and FISHER, D.L. (1982) 'Predicting students' outcomes from their perceptions of classroom psychosocial environment', *American Educational Research Journal*, 19, pp. 498–518.

FRASER, B.J. and FISHER, D.L. (1983a) *Assessment of Classroom Psychosocial Environment: Workshop Manual*, Perth, Western Australian Institute of Technology.

FRASER, B.J. and FISHER, D.L. (1983b) 'Student achievement as a function of person-environment fit: A regression surface analysis', *British Journal of Educational Psychology*, 53, pp. 89–99.

FRASER, B.J. and FISHER, D.L. (1983c) 'Use of actual and preferred classroom environment scales in person-environment fit research', *Journal of Educational Psychology*, 75, pp. 303–13.

FRASER, B.J. and FISHER, D.L. (1986) 'Using short forms of classroom climate instruments to assess and improve classroom psychosocial environment,' *Journal of Research in Science Teaching*, 5, pp. 387–413.

FRASER, B.J. and TOBIN, K. (1989) 'Combining qualitative and quantitative methods in the study of classroom learning environments,' paper presented at Annual Meeting of American Educational Research Association, San Francisco.

FRASER, B.J. and WALBERG, H.J. (1981) 'Psychosocial learning environment in science classrooms: A review of research', *Studies in Science Education*, 8, pp. 67–92.

FRASER, B.J. and WALBERG, H.J. (Eds) (in press) *Classroom and School Learning Environments*, London, Pergamon Press.

FRASER, B.J., WILLIAMSON, J.C. and TOBIN, K. (1987) 'Use of classroom and school climate scales in evaluating alternative high schools', *Teaching and Teacher Education*, 3, pp. 219–31.

FRY, G., CHANTAVANICH, S. and CHANTAVANICH, A. (1981) 'Merging quantitative and qualitative research techniques: Toward a new research paradigm,' *Anthropology and Education Quarterly*, 12, pp. 145–58.

HAERTEL, G.D., WALBERG, H.J. and HAERTEL, E.H. (1981) 'Socio-psychological environments and learning: A quantitative synthesis', *British Educational Research Journal*, 7, pp. 27–36.

HOWE, K.R. (1988) 'Against the quantitative and qualitative incompatibility thesis: Or dogmas die hard', *Educational Researcher*, 17, pp. 10–16.

LEVIN, T. (1980) 'Classroom climate as criterion in evaluating individualized instruction in Israel', *Studies in Educational Evaluation*, 6, pp. 291–2.

LEWIN, K. (1936) *Principles of Topological Psychology*, New York, McGraw.

MOOS, R.H. (1968) 'The assessment of the social climates of correctional institutions', *Journal of Research in Crime and Delinquency*, 5, pp. 174–88.

MOOS, R.H. (1979) *Evaluating Educational Environments: Procedures, Measures, Findings and Policy Implications*, San Francisco, Jossey-Bass.

MOOS, R.H. and HOUTS, P.S. (1968) 'The assessment of the social atmospheres of psychiatric wards', *Journal of Abnormal Psychology*, 73, pp. 595–604.

MOOS, R.H. and SPINRAD, S. (1984) *The Social Climate Scales: Annotated Bibliography 1979–1983*, Palo Alto, California, Consulting Psychologists Press.

MOOS, R.H. and TRICKETT, E.J. (1974) *Classroom Environment Scale Manual* (1st. ed.), Palo Alto, California, Consulting Psychologists Press. .

MOOS, R.H. and TRICKETT, E.J. (1987) *Classroom Environment Scale Manual* (2nd. ed.), Palo Alto, California, Consulting Psychologists Press.

MURRAY, H.A. (1938) *Explorations in Personality*, New York, Oxford University Press.

PACE, C.R. and STERN, G.G. (1958) 'An approach to the measurement of psychological characteristics of college environments', *Journal of Educational Psychology*, 49, pp. 269–77.

RANDHAWA, B.S. and FU, L.L.W. (1973) Assessment and effect of some classroom environment variables, *Review of Educational Research*, 43, pp. 303–21.

REICHARDT, C.S. and COOK, T.D. (1979) 'Beyond qualitative *versus* quantitative methods', in COOK, T.D. and REICHARDT, C.S. (Eds) *Qualitative and Quantitative Methods in Evaluation Research*, Beverly Hills, California, Sage.

RUTTER, M., MAUGHAN, B., MORTIMORE, P., OUSTON, J. and SMITH, A. (1979) *Fifteen Thousand Hours: Secondary Schools and Their Effects on Children*, Cambridge,

Massachussetts, Harvard University Press.

SMITH, D. and FRASER, B.J. (1980) 'Towards a confluence of quantitative and qualitative approaches in curriculum evaluation', *Journal of Curriculum Studies*, 12, pp. 367–70.

STAKE, R.E. and EASLEY, J.A., JR. (1978) *Case Studies in Science Education* (Vols 1 and 2), Urbana Illinois, Center for Instructional Research and Curriculum Evaluation and Committee on Culture and Cognition, University of Illinois at Urbana-Champagne.

TOBIN, K. and FRASER, B.J. (Eds) (1987) *Exemplary Practice in Science and Mathematics Education*, Perth, Curtin University of Technology.

VAN DER SIJDE, P.C. and VAN DE GRIFT, W. (Eds) (in press) *School en Klasklimaat*, Almere, The Netherlands, Versluys.

WALBERG, H.J. (1976) 'The psychology of learning environments: Behavioral, structural, or perceptual?' *Review of Research in Education*, 4, pp. 142–78.

WALBERG, H.J. (Ed.) (1979) *Educational Environments and Effects: Evaluation Policy, and Productivity*, Berkeley, California, McCutchan.

WALBERG, H.J. and ANDERSON, G.J. (1968) 'Classroom climate and individual learning', *Journal of Educational Psychology*, 59, pp. 414–9.

WALBERG, H.J. and HAERTEL, G.D. (1980) 'Validity and use of educational environment assessments', *Studies in Educational Evaluation*, 6, pp. 225–38.

WOLF, B. (1983) 'On the assessment of learning environment', *Studies in Educational Evaluation*, 9, pp. 253–65.

Chapter 8: Conclusion: Barriers to Higher-level Cognitive Learning in Science

Kenneth Tobin, Jane Butler Kahle and Barry J. Fraser

When this study commenced, we held the view that the major problems in high school science education were associated with the extensive use of whole-class activities. This opinion proved to be far from the actual case. Although an over-reliance on whole-class activities certainly was a problem in earlier research (for example, Tobin and Gallagher, 1987), implementing activities with a better balance between small-group and individualized instruction is no guarantee of success. The variety of factors which combine to produce a milieu in which learning occurs include: factors associated with teachers' metaphors for specific roles, associated beliefs and knowledge of what and how to teach; the curriculum that is planned and implemented; characteristics of students; sex-role stereotyping in the classroom and the culture; the physical milieu in which learning is to occur; and expectations associated with tradition of the school and what has been done in the past. The major findings from our investigations of Sandra's and Peter's classes are discussed below in relation to an emerging theory of teaching, teacher change and implications for research in science education.

Teachers Make a Difference

In our study, Peter was able to manage student behaviour in a variety of activity settings (as Captain of the Ship and as Entertainer), but he did not have a sufficient repertoire of discipline-specific pedagogical knowledge to facilitate learning during either the Vertebrates or the Nuclear Energy topic. In contrast, Sandra appeared to have a strong background in science and had developed the specific pedagogical knowledge needed to manage the conceptual aspects of each topic. But, because she did not manage student behaviour effectively, students did not benefit from her knowledge and her effectiveness as a facilitator of learning was questionable. These findings highlight the importance of two aspects of management. If teachers are to be successful facilitators of learning, they must manage both student behaviour and the cues required to initiate and sustain the cognitive processes associated with learning. Discipline-specific pedagogical knowledge and pedagogical knowledge together are seen as crucial ingredients of successful teaching. Neither is sufficient alone, and each is required if students are to attain the elusive goal of higher-level cognitive outcomes in science.

Sandra

Despite the school's advocacy for higher-level cognitive learning, and a preference of Sandra for doing and understanding science, she implemented the curriculum in a manner that emphasized coverage of content and learning of terms and facts about science. Sandra's decision to move about the class, distributing the teacher resource as evenly as possible, placed greater emphasis on the use of print resources and learning from peers in informally constructed small groups. Even though Sandra had the knowledge that would have enabled her to emphasize learning with understanding, as well as strong beliefs that this was what ought to be done, she implemented the curriculum in such a way that students mostly focused on learning facts.

In many respects Sandra was an enigma. Sandra's determination to follow her beliefs about learning were commendable. She believed that students learned best with small-group and individualized activities; she also believed that whole-class activities were ineffective as far as learning was concerned. Although students did not engage in the manner in which she intended, and although the curriculum was not really suited to student aptitudes, Sandra persisted with a learning environment that, from our viewpoint at least, clearly was dysfunctional. We wondered why might Sandra continued to implement the curriculum in that manner? One interpretation could be that she did not have the pedagogical knowledge to do otherwise. Such an explanation is implausible. Sandra was an experienced teacher who had tried many approaches to teaching during her career. She had determined what worked for her and what did not. On that basis, she had formulated a set of beliefs associated with facilitating learning. Her beliefs all were consistent with her metaphor of the teacher as Resource. As her beliefs were formulated, she discarded others that she found inapplicable to her context or which she believed to be no longer true. It seems that this was the case with whole-class activities. Sandra's experience had convinced her that her students did not learn to the desired extent in whole-class activities. We prefer this explanation of Sandra's approach to teaching the observed class to an explanation based on knowledge limitations.

Sandra's reluctance to use whole-class activities to control management problems was understandable. But that was not the only option open to her. Although students were placed in groups of four to six, there was little evidence of cooperative learning. Students had not accepted roles associated with facilitating the learning of others. In groups, most students completed activities independently or copied from one another. This organizational arrangement caused problems of socialization, but it neither led to the benefits of learning from other students nor assisted Sandra in dealing with problems encountered by students as they completed their tasks. However, some students worked collaboratively most of the time. For example, Sally and Janilla had a close working relationship and, although they did socialize as they worked, they appeared to be task oriented most of the time. But the fact of the matter was that most students did not work cooperatively in groups and disruptive behaviour was a major problem. Why did Sandra tolerate so much disruptive behaviour? And why was she prepared to separate constant offenders from their groups and place them with groups that were functioning well? Steven's presence in a group with Natalie, Sally and Janila simply added a source of distraction to a group that was operating well without Steven. Was this the price that students had to pay for being a member of her class?

How did Sandra's beliefs about important concerns such as management and assessment affect her roles and effectiveness? Sandra's beliefs (which she articulated in the repertory grid exercise and subsequent discussions) were closely related to one another. Possibly she had reflected on her beliefs and had modified them to form a set that was internally consistent. The belief set suggested that Sandra assigned greatest value to beliefs about facilitating learning. Consequently, her beliefs about management were consistent with those associated with her role as facilitator of learning.

Why didn't Sandra make changes to her management strategy when it was evident that students were spending a great deal of time being disruptive and dealing with their social agendas? It was apparent to Sandra and to the research team that the manner in which students were organized, and the way in which Sandra chose to interact with them, led to many management difficulties. Yet students were able to complete their activities and achieve reasonably well on the end-of-topic tests. The evidence suggests that the tasks were too easy for most students and that Sandra's expectations might have been too low. The fact of the matter was that students could complete their activities (often at home) and achieve at a satisfactory level, while socializing for more than half of the allocated time.

Sandra's tendency to circulate around the room at a rapid rate, using proximity desists to quieten off-task students and monitoring what students were doing, minimized her effectiveness. The management of learning tended to be left to the workbooks, which focused on learning science facts. Little attention was given to constructing understandings and interrelating new and old knowledge. Students had access to Sandra, but the time usually was not quality time. Usually, there was only sufficient time available for Sandra to answer a question, check the work quickly and move on to the next group of students. In-depth discussions between students or between teacher and students were rare. The implemented curriculum focused on the activities in the workbooks.

Why did Sandra interact with students on an individual basis? Was it possible for Sandra to deal with the needs of so many students? Because of the way in which class was organized, she was unable to ascertain whether or not students were on-task, she couldn't quell disruptive behaviour before it got out of hand, and generally she was unable to monitor the extent to which students understood the concepts on which they were working. Sandra's beliefs about managing student learning led to a situation in which she could not emphasize student learning with understanding. Her beliefs about management appeared to mediate her beliefs about what students should achieve in the course. It might be argued that Sandra's strategy of managing student learning might have worked if smaller class sizes were involved. However, the task of monitoring the understanding of even nineteen learners on an individual basis would be demanding if the responsibility was left entirely to the teacher. On the other hand, if students assumed some of the responsibility for assisting one another to learn and for negotiating meaning through collaboration, Sandra could have assumed a more reflective role and focus on the consensus arrived at in the groups. Further, whole-class discussions could have been used to obtain a consensus of understanding for the class based on the consensus of each of the groups. An alternative approach to managing student learning would recognize students as resources for one another and would transfer responsibility for learning to individuals and groups of individuals.

Sandra's beliefs about the nature of science also were salient in determining how she managed her class. Because, in large part, Sandra viewed science as a process of creating knowledge, she felt that students should experience science at first hand, preferably through elective activities. This view of science did not impact directly on the implemented curriculum because of Sandra's decision to use the workbooks. She grudgingly used the workbooks while maintaining that there should be a greater elective component and more laboratory work. However, her way of grouping students for work did provide students with direct and personal forms of engagement.

Why did Sandra feel that she should use the workbooks? Evidence suggests that the two workbooks were inappropriate in many respects. Gerry, the teacher who had been at the school since the beginning, viewed the workbooks for both topics as below standard and Dennis, the head of science, maintained that he would not use either of them and that the staff should not feel compelled to use all, or any, of the workbooks. Sandra maintained that she would have preferred to use curriculum materials based on cards to communicate activities to students. She had implemented successfully programs using that system before and probably would use it again in the future. However, her beliefs about her role as an administrator gave high priority to giving staff a voice in decisions and abiding by majority decisions. In this case, she used the workbooks because she felt that most staff wanted to use them in order to make it possible for all teachers to use the same end-of-topic tests to assess student learning. Thus, Sandra's views about what a good administrator should do took precedence over her views about the nature of the curriculum. That decision had a direct, and possibly deleterious, effect on the implemented curriculum.

However, Sandra did not always allow conventions or views of colleagues to influence what she did in her classroom. For example, although Sandra accepted the convention of students interacting with her on a first name basis, she did not accept policies associated with restricting homework. In that case, she adopted her own standards, though some of her colleagues such as Gerry were vocal critics of assigning homework. Sandra's actions appeared to be the result of a complex set of interactions between beliefs associated with her roles as a school administrator and as a facilitator of learning.

Peter

In Peter's class, the curriculum emphasized learning of facts mainly because of the manner in which he endeavoured to communicate with students. He represented his science knowledge in verbal form as lectures which often were augmented with terms and sketches on a small chalkboard. Peter perceived science to be a collection of facts and tended to represent it in that manner to his class.

During this study, Peter had to teach five different classes in four different content areas. Consequently, he had four preparations on most days as well as five sets of students to assess. The task of teaching so many different topics at the one time was too great for Peter. Those responsible for assigning teacher workloads should give careful attention to the knowledge required to teach the assigned courses. The assumption that any teacher can teach any part of a general science course was not supported by the results of this study. Peter did not have the background to teach without extensive planning in the Vertebrates and Nuclear Energy topics. However, there was insufficient time available to plan for the two grade 10 general science classes which he taught. In addition, he had three grade 11 and 12 classes for which he had to plan activities and assess students. Because Peter regarded his grade 11 and 12 teaching as more important than teaching his two grade 10 classes, he gave priority to planning for and assessing the grade 11 and 12 curriculum. If financial constraints prevent a reduction in the number of classes taught by a teacher, then it is important to consider reducing the number of different types of courses being taught. For example, Peter might have been better able to prepare for his teaching if he had taught three grade 10 classes and two grade 11 human biology classes. Some provision also should be made for teachers to teach only the components of a general science course for which they are qualified to teach. For example, perhaps Peter should not have had to teach the Nuclear Energy topic without additional education.

Peter's failure to assess student activities for accuracy and completion raised questions about the work undertaken by students in his class. On the one hand, it could be applauded in the sense that students should have some opportunity to practise learning without fear of getting wrong answers. On the other hand, students did not receive feedback about the adequacy of their responses. There was a distinct possibility that any understandings which they had at the time of completing the workbook activities were not retained throughout the topic. At the very least, a greater incidence of cooperative learning or opportunities for students to negotiate a shared meaning would have been beneficial and might have contributed to enhanced learning with understanding.

Learning Resources and the Cognitive Demand of Tasks

The print resources made available for small-group, individualized and self-paced learning in both classes represented science as a set of products or truths about the universe. To know science was to know these facts as unchanging truths. Both teachers used print resources extensively despite the fact they did not have a high regard for the quality of the activities represented in the workbooks and the manner in which the textbooks were written. The teachers commented on the attempt of the textbook authors to incorporate a low reading difficulty level into the texts, but they did not criticize the low cognitive level represented in the science content in the texts or the questions at the end of each chapter.

To be successful in either class, it was necessary to perform well on tests that required recall of science facts or to answer questions from the workbook that required students to locate specific factual information from the textbook. In all cases, these resources were constructed or purchased in previous years. It appears that they were used because of the inconvenience of having to prepare new resources to use in their place. Sandra had alternative materials that could have been used in her classes and, had she been at Southside High for a longer time, she might have taken the initiative to create alternatives to the workbooks and the tests.

Her preference was to try the approach that was in operation at the school for at least a year before making changes. Whereas this decision couldn't be understood readily in terms of being perceived as a fair-minded leader, it was regarded by the research team as deleterious to the learning of many of the students in her class. Peter's decision to use the workbooks, tests and texts probably was based on the inconvenience of having to prepare alternatives. He had to teach a number of different classes, and felt that he already was committing too much of his personal time to school work. However, even if he had prepared alternatives, it is unlikely that the tests would have differed appreciably in cognitive level or that workbooks or substitute resources would have given emphasis to higher-level cognitive learning. What happened in Peter's class was explained readily in terms of his beliefs about the nature of science and what students should learn.

Equity Issues in the Classes

An issue which clearly emerged in the study was the inequitable treatment of boys and girls. Well-known differences in both the achievement levels and retention rates of boys and girls can be understood when one observes and identifies different teacher expectations and different student-teacher interaction patterns for girls and boys. Although they radically differed in their beliefs, both Sandra and Peter used some teaching strategies which disadvantaged girls.

An increasing body of literature addresses equitable teaching behaviours and instructional strategies. Prospective as well as practicing teachers need to be aware of and able to use those techniques. For example, girls prefer a cooperative rather than a competitive classroom environment. Questioning techniques must involve all students, and teachers need to require students to raise their hands before responding. Girls, as well as boys, need to be required to use the equipment of science and to perform scientific experiments. Science must be presented as an acceptable career for both girls and boys, and teacher examples and exemplars must go beyond the world of sport.

Furthermore, because teacher analysis of classroom interactions reveals both subtle and overt sexism in the classroom, both prospective and practising teachers need to be skilled in observational assessment skills. Often, as in the case with Sandra, subtle differences are due to demands of management and are totally unconscious. Other teachers such as Peter might overlook more overt sexism and define it as part of a socially acceptable role, namely, teacher as scientist. In order to alleviate both overt and covert sexism in science classes, teachers need to confront the issue directly and to learn to model and practise teaching behaviours which work well for both girls and boys.

Student Involvement in Science Activities

The efforts of teachers to establish a particular type of learning environment are important, but Rennie's chapter reminds us that the efforts of students are of equal or even greater importance. For example, Sandra placed the onus on students to find answers to questions from the workbooks. In addition, her style of teaching made it difficult for students to eavesdrop on conversations which she had with others. By circulating rapidly around the class, she felt that she could monitor what students were doing and ensure they did the work for themselves. However, some students were determined to minimize their task involvement. Consequently, they wasted time and then produced the required written products by copying from others.

A situation that led to a number of problems in each class was that the activities lacked challenge for students who were able to attend to their social agendas, complete their assigned tasks and succeed on the end-of- topic tests. In both classes, it was possible for students to get reasonably good grades with minimal effort. This was attributable to the relatively low cognitive level of tests and exercises and to the easy pace at which students were required to complete activities. The fact that the tasks did not challenge the more able students diminished the potential interest for them. Lack of challenge and low interest, combined with a tendency to deal with science concepts in a superficial manner, distorted the students' exposure to science. Not only was science presented as facts to be learned by rote, but also students in both classes perceived at least some aspects of science as just a matter of opinion.

The students in both classes demonstrated reasoning patterns that suggested that they were capable of solving challenging science problems. These students could have engaged in activities in which they constructed and explored science knowledge from historical, philosophical and societal perspectives. With few exceptions, the learning activities in which students from both classes engaged were lacking in cognitive demand. The students rarely were challenged to use their thinking skills to analyze and synthesize as part of their learning of science. When students in Peter's class asked questions that demonstrated they were thinking about the content, their questions often were put aside as the teacher pursued his agenda of covering content and completing one topic so that they could begin the next. Sandra answered all questions that were asked of her and she responded positively to students who showed interest in science. Despite these desirable teaching qualities, the students still engaged in low-level cognitive activities provided by the workbooks and texts.

The efforts of students determine whether or not they attain higher-level cognitive understandings of science. The tasks in which students engage are dependent not only on the tasks prescribed by teachers, but also on the motivation of students. Rennie (Chapter 6) demonstrates that students with similar engagement profiles had quite different levels of achievement and different types of motivation to learn. Students with relatively high abilities and mastery-orientations might not have been challenged by the tasks in either of the classes involved in this study. Put simply, the work was too easy for them. Some students such as Sally used her spare time to socialize with others, while other students such as Jeffrey and Jenny endeavoured to increase the challenge by asking Peter questions in whole-class interactive activities. Our study revealed that the type and degree of motivation to learn influenced the tasks in which students engaged and thereby influenced achievement. Learning also was influenced by the disruptions of others. Students such as Gavin and Wayne disrupted the class in a somewhat wilful manner whereas others disrupted peers by engaging them in social discourse. In both instances, the actions of students interacted with the learning opportunities of others.

The distinct types of motivation identified in both classes suggest that teachers should be more aware of these differences. It was apparent that some students were highly motivated to learn with understanding because of an intrinsic drive, whereas others were driven to succeed with the minimum possible effort. These students often were motivated by external factors such as tests and rewards of various types. A third category of student was motivated by a need to sustain his/her ego. These students used the classroom to maintain their self-image and self-esteem. A most interesting case was Gavin, who publicly announced his failing test scores to his class mates, but ensured that they knew that he had not tried on the test. In this way, he could maintain his reputation of not being a good student but, at the same time, not experience a lowering of self-esteem because of his insistence that he had not tried. His poor performance therefore was attributed to lack of effort, not to lack of ability.

On the basis of the findings of this study, other cognitive factors associated with students are identified as potentially powerful. For example, what are the salient roles for students in science classes? How do students conceptualize these roles? What metaphors underlie these conceptualizations and how resilient are the associated belief sets? Although this study did not address these questions directly, the parallels between teacher and student actions are alluring. Is it possible that students come to science classes with specific roles, each defined by metaphors and belief sets? Is this an explanation for why students behave differently in different contexts? Are student metaphors and belief sets context dependent? Is it possible to assist students in changing their approaches to learning by assisting them to acquire new metaphors for given roles in specific contexts? These questions and many more define a research agenda that demands attention. Researchers and practitioners should not ignore the potential of assisting students to forge new learning strategies in science classrooms by reconceptualizing their roles in terms of new metaphors and sets of beliefs.

Towards an Emerging Theory of Teaching

Teachers have many sets of beliefs that are appropriate for a given teaching role (for example, management) in specific contexts. The relevance of beliefs and role conceptualizations are dependent on factors such as the physical milieu in which learning is to occur, the age and ability of students, the time of day, the extent to which the teacher possesses the pedagogical content knowledge needed to implement the curriculum, the other subjects to be taught on a given day, and other within-school and out-of-school factors. Roles are conceptualized in terms of metaphors and are defined by beliefs which influence what teachers endeavour to do during classroom activities. Both the metaphors and beliefs associated with a given role are context dependent and can be 'switched' as the teacher perceives that different courses of action are warranted by the context. It is presumed that experienced teachers conceptualize roles in terms of more than one metaphor and associated sets of beliefs. As a consequence, experienced teachers are able to change their teaching strategies as the contexts of learning change. Whether a teacher is successful in a given context depends on the appropriateness of the strategies selected and the extent to which the teacher succeeds in facilitating learning.

What form must be taken by the metaphors used to define roles take? Must they be verbal? Is it possible for visual metaphors to influence what is done in class? From a constructivist perspective, learning is a mind-body endeavour in which sensory data are interpreted in terms of what is known already. Consider the sensory input of teachers throughout their lives. As teachers sit (as young students) in elementary, middle and then high school classes, they obtain myriads of relevant data by seeing and hearing. Day after day, week after week, month after month and year after year, the images of teaching are engraved in the mind. What comes to mind when a person is first asked about his/her best teacher? Images of the teacher in action enter the mind and words are then sought to describe what it was that made this person so special. In this study, Peter projected images which can be described as visual metaphors. He had made sense of being a science teacher first by presenting himself as a scientist based on a stereotypic image of what a scientist looked like (a laboratory coat and safety glasses). He also felt the need to look like a teacher by wearing a tie. Similarly, Peter projected himself as masculine, macho, trendy and appealing to females.

Is it possible to identify the visual images that have been honed into the mind and now influence what teachers do in the classroom? And, associated with these images, are there non-verbal beliefs that drive actions in the classroom? Is it possible that self-analysis of videotaped segments of teaching could sensitize teachers to the images which they project and to the visual metaphors that underlie what they do in classrooms. Will it lead to verbalization of the beliefs associated with tacit actions and interactions? Was Sandra projecting an image of a concerned mother? Did some students identify with this role and take advantage of Sandra's concerned and gentle manner? Were the misbehaving and often disruptive students following a script that was stimulated by familiar images of the home in a classroom context?

Peter's teaching behaviours provide insights into the complexity of teaching and the evaluation of teaching. He had obvious concerns for out-of-school activities, and he worked hard as a teacher. He wanted to be regarded as a professional and he had a need to be recognized by students and colleagues as competent. Yet, Peter did not welcome feedback that reflected negatively on his worth as a teacher. He was vulnerable, and the science knowledge which he possessed relevant to the two topics studied during this investigation was such that he could not be successful by taking an active role as a facilitator of learning. In the classroom, he had to be reliant on other resources available to assist him. Consequently, he had to use the workbooks and texts to introduce students to science content and to provide them with activities from which they could learn. To maintain his self-esteem, Peter needed to identify other things that would occupy his time and allow him to work hard in his job. Consequently, he organized the science fair and conducted excursions. These visible activities attracted recognition from students, colleagues, school administrators and parents. In the year following our classroom observations, Peter was rewarded for his efforts with administrative responsibilities which involved one less class to teach and a position of authority.

Tradition at Southside High

An important component of the context in which teaching and learning occur is the tradition of a school. The tradition of Southside High was communicated through written documents, through the behaviours and beliefs of teachers and students and through characteristics of the physical plant. The original philosophy of Southside High was enshrined in the original buildings, policy documents and the tools of teaching. As far as Peter and Sandra were concerned, the tradition of Southside High was a strong factor in determining how they implemented the grade 10 science curriculum. The extent to which tradition constrained the teachers was dependent on their beliefs and associated values. For example, Sandra's preference for having students work individually or in groups was consistent with the school's long-standing tradition of emphasizing self-paced learning. Thus, her beliefs about facilitating learning were reinforced by other contextual factors operating within Southside High. The architecture of the rooms was such that student-centred learning was favoured to a greater extent than what might have been the case in most other high schools in Coastal Australia. There were no chalkboards suitable for presenting notes to an entire class, and provision for use of an overhead projector was not entirely satisfactory. Consequently, it was not convenient for either teacher to write extensive notes for students to copy down. This constraint was more of a problem for Peter, who adopted a more conventional style of teaching which was based on whole-class activities and which incorporated the use of the chalkboard.

Although both classes were studying the same topic and had students with similar aptitudes for science, the concertina door which separated the two classrooms was closed throughout the study. Neither teacher appeared to contemplate team teaching seriously, even though instructional strategies based on use of the workbooks would have enabled the convenient implementation of team teaching. In the circumstances described in this book, team teaching would have benefitted both teachers. However, their very different beliefs about management would have required some compromises on the part of both Peter and Sandra. As it was, the concertina door simply transmitted noise between the rooms and, rather than being an advantage, it was a mild inconvenience.

Changing Teacher Behaviour

Sandra's colleagues regarded her as one of the better teachers of science in Coastal Australia. Undoubtedly their view was based on their knowledge of Sandra as a person, on what they had heard from students and on the professional attributes which she possessed. However, none of her colleagues had observed her teaching on a regular basis. What did Sandra's colleagues mean when they said she was a good teacher? Student perceptions of the learning environment indicated that some dimensions were conducive to learning and that others needed to be improved. Those results suggested that, when students say that they like a teacher and would like to have her the following year, as was the case with Sandra's class, they probably were not giving a testimonial to her effectiveness. Among colleagues, students and researchers, there was no dispute concerning her professional attributes. The research team regarded Sandra as knowledgeable about science, innovative in terms of designing activities for her students, well organized and generous in sharing her ideas with colleagues, as well as always being friendly, approachable and interested in what others had to say. All of those attributes made her amenable to suggestions for change, and any of these attributes might be associated with being an effective teacher. Yet, over a period of three months, Sandra was not an effective teacher with the grade 10 class that we observed.

An implication is that conclusions concerning the effectiveness of teachers should be based on intensive and broadly based data which include some observations of teaching and learning processes. Effective teaching is defined commonly as good management and it is related to time on-task. However, Shulman (1987) suggests that issues concerning what the tasks are also affect teacher effectiveness. First, how well does the teacher's understanding of content relate to how well the content is taught? Second, how does teaching vary between situations in which the content to be taught is well understood and those in which the content to be taught is not well understood? Sandra had adequate content knowledge in both topics and she provided examples and exemplars which indicated the adequacy of her content knowledge for teaching both effectively. However, many of the activities prescribed in the workbooks did not lead to higher-level learning. Her effectiveness, therefore, was circumscribed both by the level of the tasks and by her management techniques. Peter, on the other hand, was less effective during the Nuclear Energy topic, compared to the Vertebrates topic, and this situation clearly was related to his limited knowledge of nuclear energy.

Although both Peter and Sandra claimed that they welcomed feedback on their teaching, only Sandra reacted favourably to results which suggested a need to make changes. For instance, when teachers received the classroom environment results, Sandra was determined to change her classroom behaviour in ways which would lead to improvements, whereas Peter dismissed the information as irrelevant and apparently made no attempt to change his classroom behaviour. Peter disbelieved the feedback suggesting that students perceived a relatively low level of Personalization, instead believing that his attempts to entertain the students would have been associated with high Personalization. Also, Peter regarded extra-curricula activities, such as conducting·field trips and science fairs, to be more important indicators of his probable effectiveness as a teacher than was the feedback which he received from the researchers concerning learning environment, gender differences, etc.

Peter was not open to feedback about his teaching. He seemed insecure and would have welcomed good news, but did not want to discuss any shortcomings which he might have had. From the outset, he looked for ways to interpret feedback from the research team in the best possible light. He did not have the mind set that changes could be made to benefit the learning of students. In this respect, his attitude was in marked contrast to that of Sandra. Whereas Sandra questioned the researchers in an endeavour to make sense of the data provided, Peter challenged the validity of the teacher performance assessment measures and of the scales which assessed student perceptions of the learning environment. When he was provided with reports of our observations, he did not comment at all on them. On the other hand, Sandra gave a thoughtful and considered reaction to the initial reports and helped us incorporate her perspectives into the final report.

What was it about Peter that made him so resistant to receiving feedback about his teaching? One interpretation was that he had conceptualized teaching in a very different way than the way in which the research team and many of his colleagues viewed it. He felt isolated from and different from other teachers at Southside High, and that perception might have influenced his conception. It is possible that Peter defined his roles in such a way that he could be successful and feel good about his work. Consequently, he emphasized his work with grade 11 students as well as the planning of science fairs, field trips and alternative topics for which his knowledge was stronger.

In his grade 10 class, he adapted his role to cope with a relatively weak background in science. The work needed for him to overcome his content deficit was too great to enable him to be prepared and do the other things necessary to be both an effective teacher and family member. Consequently, he used the workbooks and textbooks extensively. At times, he adopted the role of assisting students to make sense of parts of the text and, at other times, he elaborated on the information in the text using other text sources to do so. Teaching upper school science was valued by Peter, even though the time costs associated with learning the content to be taught were great. In his opinion, benefit occurred from teaching upper level science because of the importance afforded to it by colleagues and students. From Peter's perspective, he was working hard at his job, probably harder than many of his colleagues. Administrators in the school recognized his hard work by giving him additional administrative responsibilities as the teacher in charge of grade 10 students during the year after the study. What Peter did not acknowledge, however, was that his content preparation for teaching was inadequate. In order to be successful, he needed to plan and learn science content to a greater extent than did some of his colleagues, such as Sandra who could concentrate her efforts on planning for effective implementation. Given his science credentials, it was easy to understand why Peter defined his roles in such a way that he would be regarded as a successful and valued professional.

Sandra was regarded by almost everyone as a first-class person and a first-class teacher. Her colleagues perceived her to be talented, hard working, knowledgeable and conscientious, and her students regarded her in a similar vein. For example, a senior colleague described Sandra as 'almost the ultimate teacher'. Yet, in the classroom, Sandra floundered because she did not manage student behaviour effectively. To be sure, Sandra made conscious decisions to teach in the way in which she did, and she knew that students were off-task frequently during small-group activities. However, she also knew that students became disinterested during whole-class activities. Consequently, she argued that student learning opportunities were at the very least no worse in small-group activities than in whole-class activities. For that situation actually to be the case, Sandra would have needed to develop and implement new strategies and routines. Sandra's challenge was to develop knowledge which actually affected the way in which she taught.

Sandra might have known how to manage the students in her class, but she had not developed routinized procedures for effective classroom management. Is it possible that Sandra's emphasis on facilitating learning and her use of the metaphor of teacher as Resource contributed to her problems in managing the class? Is it possible that a change of metaphor for facilitating learning would have resulted in changes in what happened in her classroom? The findings from Peter's class suggest that such a change might have resulted in a different learning environment.

What was so interesting in Peter's teaching was the quite distinct teaching style associated with each metaphor for managing student behaviour. As Peter switched metaphors, a great many variables changed as well. That finding raised the possibility that teachers might be assisted in acquiring new metaphors for specific teaching roles as a possible means of assisting them to improve the learning environments in their classrooms. The metaphors which Peter and Sandra used as a basis for conceptualizing their teaching roles appeared to be influential in defining the roles which they adopted during instruction. Peter's ability to manage the class in distinctly different ways according to Captain of the Ship and Entertainer metaphors raises the possibility that he might be able to improve his teaching by using different metaphors. For example, if Peter could understand teaching in terms of a gardener nurturing new seedlings, would it be possible for him to attend individually to the learning needs of the students in his class? Would students then perceive the class to be more personalized? Could Peter teach, as Sandra did, according to the metaphor of teacher as a Resource? The answers to those questions have interesting implications for science teacher education. If teachers conceptualize their teaching roles in terms of metaphors, then the process of teacher change might be initiated by introducing a variety of metaphors and reflecting on the efficacy of basing teaching and learning strategies on each of them. By focusing teacher education programs on metaphors underlying teaching and learning science, teachers might be provided with a conceptual base upon which teaching strategies could be built.

Methodological Implications

The students' perceptions of the learning environment were extremely useful data to have in this study. We pushed existing instruments to their limits, but did not realize their full potential in a study of this type. The instruments were not developed for making an assessment of how an individual perceives his/her own environment; rather, items had been designed to tap an individual's perception of the class as a whole. Yet, from a constructivist perspective, the individual's perceptions are precisely what mediate learning. In this study, we selected scales from two different instruments to ensure that environment dimensions were salient for the classes that we were studying. We wanted to know how individuals and small groups of individuals perceived various dimensions of the psychosocial learning environment. Clearly, such information provides invaluable insights into the context in which learning occurred for individuals.

Despite the limitations of existing scales to provide data of the type we needed, the data we obtained still were very useful in providing quantified pictures of life in the two classrooms. These pictures complemented those obtained by observation and interview and encapsulated the differences in the classrooms in a parsimonious way. Not only was it possible to show how the climate in Peter's class differed from that in Sandra's class, it also was possible to compare the students' perceptions of the learning environments in each class for the two topics of Nuclear Energy and Vertebrates. Statistical analyses were undertaken to provide insights into questions concerning what was happening in both classes. The results of the analyses of the learning environment data were used in conjunction with other data sources to support or refute assertions. The case studies of Jenny and Helen indicated that, when quantitative measures on learning environment scales are complemented by a substantial base of qualitative description from classroom observation, a greater understanding of students' perceptions of the learning environment results.

The use of scales to assess students' perceptions of the learning environment is a valuable research tool in studies which probe teaching and learning. However, new instruments are needed to explore the contexts in which learning occur for individuals. Instruments are needed to probe the individual student's perceptions of the social and psychological factors that influence how he/she learns. What we want is a new generation of classroom environment instruments that will provide insights into how individuals construct the context in which learning occurs. Such instruments are likely to facilitate future investigations of the role of the student in classroom learning.

Rennie's quantitative analysis of student engagement (Chapter 6) highlights the difficulty of measuring time on-task using direct observation techniques. The quality of engagement, and hence the tasks in which students engage, cannot easily be inferred by observing students. Because task engagement is a cognitive act, methods of measuring engagement necessarily should involve efforts to monitor the cognitions of learners. It is possible that insights into student engagement can be obtained through the use of projective techniques (for example, scenarios, vignettes, episodes) in which students respond orally or in writing to hypothetical situations, paper-and-pencil instruments to assess student perceptions of the learning environment (of the type described above), and journal entries in which students record what they are thinking throughout the lesson. The use of these techniques offers the potential of obtaining rich data to augment information obtained through the more conventional method of interviewing students.

As was the case in earlier research (Tobin, Espinet, Byrd and Adams, 1988), the current study graphically demonstrates alternative perspectives of effective teaching. Is good teaching in the eye of the beholder? Perhaps it is. We had differences of opinion within the research team, with the participating teachers and with colleagues teaching at Southside school. The most significant of the disagreements concerned Sandra's teaching behaviour. Although most members of the research team agreed that Sandra had a major management problem, one member did not concur and maintained that Sandra elected to focus on the more important role of facilitating independent learning. Therefore, she argued that Sandra *elected* to allow students to engage in the manner observed. Her interpretive framework examined the data from the perspective of the teacher. She argued that Sandra could have changed the classroom climate at any time if she chose to do so. In contrast, the other members of the research team interpreted the data from the perspective of student learning. Constant disruptive behaviour on the part of many students in the class was interpreted as a management problem which Sandra tried to solve through the use of proximity desists. Even though Sandra agreed with the interpretation of the majority of members of the research team, the issue was not resolved within the team. The difference of opinion raised questions concerning the role of teams in educational research. Is it the purpose of a team to obtain consensus on all assertions? Or is it of greater value to retain the multiple perspectives in the written accounts of the study? We favour the latter position and recommend that research teams be formed to include members with alternative interpretive frameworks so that different accounts and theories can be obtained for the environments and cultures under investigation.

Conclusions

Many factors militate against higher-level cognitive learning in secondary science classes. For example, girls were disadvantaged by practices used by Peter, in particular, and by Sandra, to a lesser but nonetheless significant extent. In addition, both teachers indicated that there was too much content to be learned for each topic, and that the tests used to assess student learning emphasized recall of facts. Generally speaking, the teachers, the workbooks and the textbooks underestimated the cognitive aptitude of students. Although most students were able to use formal operations to process data, the teaching methods, the textbooks and the workbooks emphasized low-level cognitive learning. The tradition of Southside High also proved to be an impediment to higher-level cognitive learning. Although the practice of selecting high-calibre staff to suit the school philosophy and approach was no longer adopted, Southside High still adhered to a philosophy of student-centred, self-paced learning. Consequently, teachers with little or no experience in curriculum development, and with differing philosophies concerning what ought to be included in student workbooks, prepared materials which were used in both classes.

The present findings highlight important aspects of teacher mind frames as well as their potential effects on the way in which the science curriculum was conceptualized and implemented. We also linked student perceptions of the learning environment to the metaphors, beliefs, knowledge and practices of teachers. This led to several implications of the research for science educators. We went to Southside High with an expectation that we would find exemplary practices which would illuminate previously obscure teaching and learning strategies associated with higher-level cognitive learning. That our expectations were not fulfilled is yet another reminder of the importance of basing judgements on the quality of teaching and learning on direct experience rather than hearsay.

Perhaps the most important finding of the study related to the question of teacher change. Science educators often seek to change practices associated with teaching and learning science through research and development as well as through courses for prospective and practising teachers. The findings of our study suggest that the knowledge which teachers require to undertake effective science teaching is nested within their teaching roles. Courses should ensure that teachers are given opportunities to construct the knowledge that they need to teach both present and future science courses. Knowledge of the content and how to teach the content are both extremely important. Teachers probably will require specially designed courses of study which address both needs. Furthermore, the findings related to the use of metaphors to conceptualize teaching roles raises the possibility that significant changes in classroom practice are possible if teachers are assisted in understanding the roles of science teachers in terms of new metaphors.

Finally, data describing student perceptions of the learning environment showed that the ways in which students framed the context in which learning occurred were influenced by the ways in which teachers conceptualized their roles, by their associated belief sets and knowledge, and by the manner in which the curriculum was implemented. The combination of quantitative and qualitative data was important for two reasons. First, the quantitative data enabled us to use statistical analyses to support assertions based on qualitative observation. Second, the findings showed that teachers dealt with students in an inequitable way on the basis of their own unsubstantiated beliefs about the classroom environment. Different students perceived the learning environment differently, not because they erred in their descriptions, but because there are different learning environments within any classroom. Researchers need to acknowledge such differences and develop new instruments to provide quantitative insights into the extent and nature of the different learning environments. Qualitative analyses should be used in conjunction with such instruments to provide salient insights into aspects of the environment which are not captured quantitatively.

Our study was intensive and rewarding; firm friendships were developed among the researchers and with the teachers. Each of us, perhaps in different ways, learned more about the teaching/learning process. Those of us who had been out of high school teaching (although not away from secondary school and classes) were reminded of the incredible effort and stamina required of teachers. Daily, we watched Sandra and Peter cope with a multitude of demands. Weekly, we discussed with them their dreams and hopes concerning teaching. Over the ten weeks, we came to know each as a dedicated, concerned science teacher.

We also learned much about the constraints of schooling and learning, including the arrangement of rooms and furniture, teacher schedules, teaching in multiple locations and school prescribed (or suggested) curricula. Indeed, we came to realize that Sandra and Peter were not free agents; rather, each worked within the sociology of the school and its community. In addition, we realized that Peter and, to a lesser extent, Sandra were not change agents. They accepted and reproduced some of the mores of the community and school rather than trying to transform them. Both accepted and used a curriculum with shortcomings. Peter also reproduced within his classroom the prevalent sex-role stereotypes of his culture.

As researchers we changed too. Some of our biases were exposed as we developed and rejected assertions. Previously accepted procedures were shown to be superfluous and were rejected. For example, we now think that only sustained observations clarify and identify teacher effectiveness. Therefore, previously-accepted short-term observations are questionable at best. That knowledge might enable us to improve future evaluation procedures for both student teachers and practising teachers.

All of us became aware of the effect of inadequate curriculum materials on student learning. Bright students learned by rote and demonstrated their knowledge on tests designed to measure rote-learned facts of science. Students did not have the experience to appreciate the differences between cookbook activities and scientific experiments. They did not have to sharpen their minds to analyze complex problems. Largely, they were unchallenged, and they did not know that they were being short changed. As science teachers, we were all frustrated at our inability to warn the students that there was more to science than the information in the texts and workbooks. We could not disturb their complacency; we could not challenge their knowledge. As researchers, our roles were to describe and construct an explanatory framework for what we observed. Hopefully, our explanations, questions and concerns will stimulate further inquiry from researchers, lead to changes in the practices of teacher educators, and challenge concerned science teachers to establish and maintain classroom environments which stimulate learning for all of their students.

References

SHULMAN, L.S. (1987) 'Knowledge and teaching: Foundations of the new reform', *Harvard Educational Review*, 57(1), pp. 1–27.

TOBIN, K., ESPINET, M., BYRD, S.E. and ADAMS, D. (1988) 'Alternative perspectives on effective science teaching', *Science Education*, 72, pp. 433–51.

TOBIN, K. and GALLAGHER, J.J. (1987) 'What happens in high school science classrooms?', *Journal of Curriculum Studies*, 19, pp. 549–60.

Index

S